Stone House Lands

Stone House Lands

The San Rafael Reef

by

Joseph M. Bauman, Jr.

Foreword by Stewart L. Udall

Illustrations by Conrad Bert

Bonneville Books
University of Utah Press
Salt Lake City
1987

Library of Congress Cataloging-in-Publication Data

Bauman, Joseph M., 1946—
Stone house lands.

(Bonneville books)
Bibliography: p.
Includes index.
1. Natural history—Utah—San Rafael Reef.
2. Nature conservation—Utah—San Rafael Reef.
3. San Rafael Reef (Utah)—Description and travel.
I. Title.   QH105.U8B35   1987   508.792'57   87-15975
ISBN 0-87480-275-X

To my son, Sky Bauman. As I write this
you have just gone to bed, to rise
tomorrow morning for your first
kindergarten class.
When you're my age, may the Reef offer
you its wonders undiminished, my dear
Sky.

CONTENTS

FOREWORD

Anyone who has fallen under the spell of the Colorado Plateau will be enchanted by this splendid book about Utah's magnificent San Rafael country. This is not an ordinary work about the out-of-doors. What makes Joe Bauman's work special is that it is the story of a lingering, fifteen-year love affair with a little-known, mystic stretch of the American earth.

The author calls the San Rafael's landscape "a magic country outside of time," and his description of its hidden canyons and vistas and ramparts amply supports his thesis that this once-remote, unprotected expanse of Utah wilderness should be the Beehive State's next national park.

The author has taken the time to explore and to ponder this region's legacy of natural and historic wonders. He begins by taking us on walking tours through sections of the half-million acres that form the heartland of his Stone House Lands. And, for our delight, he records the artifacts left by Indians who once made this their homeland, the facts about the Old Spanish Trail established by the first Europeans to penetrate into this region, the accomplishments of the explorers and settlers who came in the nineteenth century, and the folklore of the rugged ranchers and outlaws who staked out permanent footholds in this stark ground.

A provocative, thorough journalist, Joe Bauman tells us the truth about the ORV invasion that is relentlessly marring the ecological and scenic integrity of this unusually fragile desert environment. And we learn, too, how Utah's BLM administrators stand aside and watch these motorized vandals skin the land strip by strip. The San Rafael Swell and Reef is literally up for grabs—and Bauman is probably correct in his assessment that the race now underway between preservation and permanent impairment will be decided in the next decade.

It is a sad truth, but if Joe Bauman's Stone House Lands were located in any other state, local pride and national public opinion would have given it national park status long ago. I consider Utah the most scenic of the lower forty-eight states. By creating five national parks in Utah and in effect five in California, Congress has expressed its own current opinion on this issue.

In the 1960s, former Senator Frank Moss provided unflinching leadership and the Canyonlands, Arches, and Capitol Reef areas became ornaments of our system of national parks. Is it, in 1987, too much to hope that Joe Bauman's eloquent book might galvanize Utahns to cooperate and get Congress to convert the San Rafael into the tiebreaker park that would restore Utah to the scenic national pinnacle where it belongs?

—Stewart L. Udall
February 1987

PREFACE

Ranchers, a construction company owner, an ambulance driver, retired miners—people from Hanksville, Green River, Castle Dale—thanks for talking to me. Thank you for picking me up and giving me rides when my Jeep was broken down beside the highway. Ken and Lana Kofford, I appreciate your taking the time to tell stories out in the desert while you were busy saddling up.

I deeply appreciate the attention and help of the University of Utah Marriott Library, Special Collections, which made priceless nineteenth-century books, reports, and maps available; and Charles Butler Hunt, whose sharp recollections and zesty life made for a spellbinding interview, and whose advice helped me sharpen my focus.

Thank you, Cory, for understanding I had to go to the desert. Most wives would not have put up with that for so long.

Special thanks to Bill Smart and the *Deseret News*. They nurtured and protected me all the years of my Reef explorations, gave me a platform where I could tell of my love for the desert, and let me use in this book some information I originally unearthed for the paper.

Thank you, Peggy Lee of University of Utah Press, who encouraged me for years when I was out of sorts with myself and the book; without your kind words I never would have completed this. Thanks too to Sharon Arnold and David Catron of the Press, who carried it forward.

Conrad Bert, who did the drawings and map for this book, my best friend and hiking partner: how can I thank you? What words can convey our friendship, hardships, art, talk, speculations?

Stone House Lands

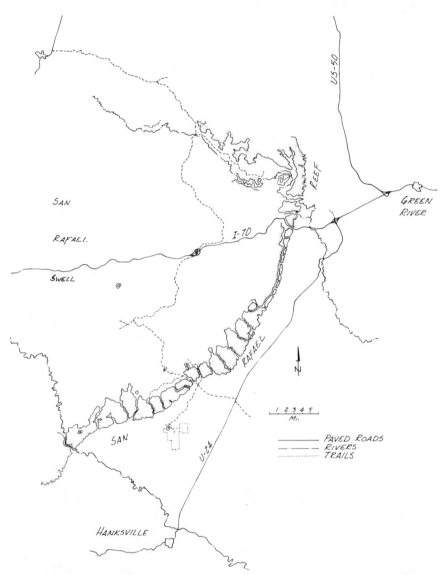

The San Rafael Reef forms the southern and eastern edge of the San Rafael Swell. This chart is based on several federal government maps, and first-hand experience.

1

The End

It is a land timelessly dreaming. At night the wind rushes across the Reef. You can hear it flowing through the canyons and shaking the tops of cottonwood trees. It has always been like this.

This is the San Rafael Reef, a rugged sandstone ridge curving like a sickle blade for fifty-six miles through the southern Utah desert. It once formed the steep eastern edge of a vast domelike structure, the San Rafael Swell.

In the millions of years since the Swell lifted, erosion cut it into mesas, hills, sudden deep canyons, sandstone fins, mountainous plugs, isolated smaller knobs. The hills are naked shale and clay, or covered with pinyon and juniper trees; the canyons are rock-walled gorges. It is a wonderland of dry mountains, a Little Grand Canyon, prehistoric pictographs, painted badlands, grassy natural parks.

This is an uninsulated desert, where the average high temperature in July is just under one hundred, the average minimum in January around ten. Only about five and a half inches of precipitation falls in a year. Half of that slams through in great thunderstorms during the summer and early fall, although spring rains can be heavy too.

The Swell's steepest edge, the Reef, is along the eastern side. It has resisted weathering better than the soft center. Most of it is intact, but channels carrying flood water off the Swell penetrated it, gouging out canyons.

The Reef has nearly two dozen major canyons and many side draws and box canyons. The canyons are usually wide at the mouth and about a quarter of a mile across, but they can be tight all the way through. Some are four miles long. The sides may be broken sets of ridges and slopes or single sheer walls. In either case, cliffs soar from the floor, generally 300 to 600 feet tall, and some are much higher.

The Reef's crests rise between 800 and 1,500 feet above the nearby desert flats. This ridge varies from four miles wide at the Moroni Slopes and Old Woman Wash in the south, and Black Dragon Wash in the north, to only about half a mile across for a short stretch in the center.

Far above the floor of slickrock, sand, and juniper, delicate ocher rock paintings in caves trace the beliefs of people who came before. They hunted, gathered pine nuts, and sought water holes more than six thousand years ago.

Thousand-foot cliffs line the Lower Black Box, where the San Rafael River corkscrews through the Reef. North of Black Dragon Wash, hikers can easily stroll up the Reef slope to the rim of an undercut cliff to peer down past the streaked lip to the wash floor.

The edge of the Reef that faces the Swell is always sheared off as a vertical cliff line. In the central portion, the Reef's front is nearly vertical too. Elsewhere, it's gentle enough to hike. Imagine an ant walking up a piece of cake that's lying on its side. The ant starts off the plate and struggles higher and higher, over bumps and crevices, until it reaches the edge—that is what it's like to walk up one of the easier slopes to the drop-off overlooking the Swell.

The Swell is an uninhabited, broken country of nine hundred square miles. Parts of it are as spectacular as the Reef, and it's something like seven times as large. Desolate ridges are studded with sage and glittering with gypsum. Cattle graze on juniper-pinyon scrub. Two rivers wind through it and slice through the Reef on their way to the Green River. From the Wedge Overlook in the northern part of the Swell, you can see a Little Grand Canyon that is more scenic, to my eyes, than the actual Grand Canyon.

I know little about the Swell. I set out to learn the Reef, and that is all I've managed in more than a dozen years.

In 1973 a group of friends invited me along on a trip to a new camping area. Few went there, they said; nature was not spoiled, and you could do as you pleased.

We were among the first of the great influx of people discovering the tremendous recreation opportunities of the San Rafael country after Interstate 70 opened it. Ironically, largely because of this invasion, these may be the last years that the San Rafael desert country remains as it has been since the time of the hunter-gatherers.

From the start, I was dazzled by this incredible, unknown country. I kept returning, sometimes with friends and my wife and son, sometimes alone. The Reef was stunningly alien. It was beautiful and challenging, dry and lush, close enough to Salt Lake City that I could explore it on weekends. Best of all, most of it was untouched.

In 1981 I bought an elderly Jeep so I could get into more rugged places. I was aware of the desert soil's fragility. I kept my Jeep on the dirt roads, except for these instances: a few times I had to turn around by going off the road to get out of bad ruts; two or three times I drove a short way on the sand into Wild Horse Canyon, staying in the wash bottom where the next storm would wipe out my tracks; in the same canyon, I parked on a sandbar once and on a sandy hillside another time.

At first, I was excited by the desert's physical treasures. I picked up a couple of arrowheads, took petrified wood and fossils, and once dug up a claret cup cactus. I justified this by the thought that the arrowheads were in canyons churned with new motorcycle tracks, the Bureau of Land Management allows collecting twenty-five pounds of petrified wood a year, and the cactus was growing in a dirt road.

Those were my ecological sins. In a few years, the desert taught me better.

Unlike the East, where settlers and trails, towns and commerce wore down the wilderness gradually over the centuries, man's scars are new here. The San Rafael country was so recently opened to exploitation that we can name the date—November 5, 1970.

> GREEN RIVER—One of the scenic wonders of the United States, the jagged San Rafael Reef, was opened today by a newly completed section of I-70. In the years ahead it will attract millions of visitors.
>
> As well as opening the gate to what is acclaimed to be the most scenic 70 miles of Interstate Highway in the country, the I-70 section opens a new and vital shortcut between the Midwest, Denver and Los Angeles.

The report on that date, written by Clarence S. Barker in the *Deseret News,* a Salt Lake City newspaper, marked the opening of the longest stretch of virgin highway completed in a century. The ribbons of concrete sliced through the rugged and beautiful Swell, cutting right across the Reef.

An earlier proposal was for a highway alignment along the route of the Old Spanish Trail, which skirted just north of the Reef. It was last used a century and a half ago, but its traces remain in the desert. That would have been a relatively easy and inexpensive route. But this was during the ecologically backward time before the first Earth Day, and the notion was abandoned. Instead, to amaze motorists and perhaps develop new tourist destinations, the freeway was blasted through the Reef at Spotted Wolf Canyon. As Barker explained in another 1970 article, the Spanish Trail route "would have covered 'run-of-the-mill' scenery, avoiding the rugged defiles and scenic vistas obtained by a frontal assault upon the San Rafael Reef. . . ."

In some places, the canyon was only ten feet wide. It was drilled, dynamited, and filled with concrete, complete with view area turnouts. Now folks speeding from Salina to Green River can glance out the side window and catch a breathtaking vista. The tourist facilities were never built.

I-70 did open the San Rafael country to recreationists, however. They included me. I was fascinated from the start. I wanted to know the Reef. I did not search for beauty alone, though I found it along the way. I also discovered something deeper—nature in timeless balance. Finally, I grew to appreciate the integrity of landscapes that were untouched, places not beautiful to human senses.

To find the heart of the desert, I thought, I'd have to walk every canyon and read every book. To my astonishment, I discovered that no books had been written about it. Most references were in dry mining journals or century-old reports of government expeditions. I hunted up all of these I could, grinding through microfilms and searching along dusty stacks in libraries for old government publications. Books and interviews with geologists taught me about millions of years of sediment, upthrusts, weathering.

Man's prehistory was barely known, but remains in the region reach back toward the time of mammoth hunters. The Reef turned out to have an impressive history of cowboys and bandits, explorers, and traders along the Spanish Trail. Then there was the uranium mining boom of the 1950s and 1960s that damaged some areas.

To take one wash as an example, at both ends of Chute Canyon are relics of historic use. Close to the mouth, toward the Swell, a corrugated tin mine shack shimmered in the sun. It stood away from the cliff in the midst of brown sagebrush, near a huge boulder painted with "Morgan's Cabin 1952." The roof was off in places, exposing gray boards, and the outhouse had been tipped over. A rusted drum, part of some kind of mining machine, lay near the cabin. Mine names were painted on walls deeper inside the canyon, "Brown Dog #3" and other pups.

Four miles south, at the other end of Chute, graffiti were scratched into a sandstone wall: "Warren Allred '99," "Diamond Ruff 1888," other notations more difficult to read. The antique flourishes were so high on the wall they must have been carved by horsemen, either cowpunchers or the bandits who rode through the Reef. The famous outlaw Butch Cassidy and his desperadoes went through these canyons on their raids.

I flew over the Reef and walked on its top. But most of my time was spent walking through the canyons. Of the major washes, I have yet to hike Cistern, Muddy Creek, and Ernie canyons.

Almost never seeing another group, my friends and I admired cliff swallows singing through the air, sandstone walls covered with Swiss cheese holes, lizards ducking under ephedra bushes, cottonwoods offering pools of shade.

Some canyons are plain, short, and dusty. You can get heat stroke or blackfly bites that take months to clear up. Scenes beautiful to my eyes on one trip would appear boring and sullen on others. I came to realize both viewpoints are mere prejudice, false perceptions caused by conditioning. We tend to judge places as good if comfortable, bad if not. We like a wash with a fine play of sunlight and shade and a comfortable temperature. There's much more value to nature than our ideas of prettiness or usefulness. When I matured, I understood that any undamaged landscape is precious, however harsh.

Still, to me the Reef is a strange and lovely wilderness. Within its canyons, cliffs and boulders are predominantly a light tan, although the colors can range from orange, coppery, or gray-white to pink, with great drip marks and swaths of purple desert varnish. Overhangs streaked with varnish show where the pouroff has been thundering off the Reef after every cloudburst for half a million years. Those lines and patches on the buttery wall are stains from minerals dissolved in the water. Iron and manganese dried on the rock, and a dark film has been building up, a little more from each storm.

I found I could learn without words.

What is that? It's slipping into a more natural mental gear. Call it a state of natural grace, a time of spiritual growth and renewal. It must be a kind of meditation—an unexpected disappearance of self when feelings and surroundings are exactly right. A reverie is triggered by hiking on the sandstone hills, or by seeing humble plants and animals make a living in a hard, barren region. Whatever it is, I don't try to think deep thoughts. I don't try. I don't think—when it happens, I have absolutely no thought. Time stops.

I call it going into the rock.

This feeling of harmony with nature may build through a day of tough hiking, and climax in the minutes when I lean, sweating, against a hot boulder. Or it can come suddenly with a glance over my shoulder.

Near the end of Bell Canyon my camera jammed. My friends Conrad and Karen walked through and I stayed to work on it with a set of screwdrivers I carry in my camera bag. Alone, I hunkered in the shade on a slickrock shelf.

The wash has undercut the sandstone. I am floating over the gravel. The lumpy brown ledge cradles an elongated puddle with a silvery rim of reflected sunshine—distinct round pebbles in dry hollows of the shelf—white impurities on the shelf, like growths of rock—the gravel floor a few feet below.

That night, we camped immediately in front of the Reef in a remote area near the mouth of Bell Canyon. During the still evening, we took short walks through the hills. Again, I spaced.

Thousands of clumps of Indian ricegrass shine in the sunset. Among them, an occasional bright red glow: bladderstems, weeds with red seed tubers swelling their center stems. The swellings are glossy, actually dull brown with red vertical stripes. There is no breeze. The ricegrass hang their heads attentively. I stride among them, sur-rounded by these clumps, looking at the gullies, hills, and shining grass on the opposite side of the wash.

A gigantic cumulus cloud towers behind the Reef's rugged escarp-ment, piles of snowy white blossoms. Karen stands reading, a paperback in her hand, looking off from time to time as pink clouds fade into soft pastel gray. Peace without thought.

The bladderstems could have been undersea creatures, with their twigs sprouting like feelers. By winter they will be dry and brown. The ricegrass clusters grew spaced evenly apart, un-doubtedly an adaptation that lets them share the scanty rainfall and soil nutrients. They thrive in a moonscape of pounding heat. That night, bats squeaked across the sky.

It's a magic country, outside of time. The challenges are the same faced by Indians eight thousand years ago: heat and cold, getting enough water, finding shade in the hottest part of the afternoon, when the sun is high in the brazen heavens and no cliff or bush throws a shadow and you wonder why you're there.

It can be dangerous and uncomfortable.

Once my Jeep's water pump failed just beyond North Temple Wash. Four of us had headed for Doorway Wash by way of North Temple; we'd left the pair of five-gallon water jugs in camp at South Temple Wash because there was so little room in my Jeep. I drove along the front of the Reef, past the ruined ranch, then into North Temple. The temperature gauge needle inched to the right. Before we got through, it was pointing off the dial. When I opened the hood, steam and green liquid gushed from the water pump. A puddle spread under the engine, and the coolant kept running into it.

The sun was directly overhead. We had our canteens; they'd keep us alive if we hiked back to camp. Then we could use the other car to get out of the Reef. But what about the Jeep? If I left it, I'd face the expense of having it towed out. We decided to chance it, adding our canteen water to the radiator. If we could drive out, I'd refill the radiator in camp. But if it didn't work, we faced a long, thirsty hike.

We waited for the machine to cool. When it was safe, I poured in nearly all the water from our canteens—a little over two quarts, bringing the level above the radiator's metal grid. And it worked.

Conrad and I were stupid enough to camp in South Temple Wash around the middle of November. We arrived at sunset and I put up my tent. The temperature seemed tolerable to me. In the blackest part of the night, I awoke to piercing cold, shivering violently. Climbing from my sleeping bag, I fumbled into my long johns and sweater, then struggled back into the bag. It was still bitter, so I pulled my heavy coat in too. I lay with my bag pulled up over my head and wondered why Conrad wasn't asking to come into the tent. Must be sleeping happily. I regretted that I had forgotten my Army blanket. For hours, cold seared every inch of skin not tightly bundled. My shins stung. I barely slept. Trying to get a drink from my canteen, I found the stopper was frozen so tightly to the spout I couldn't open it. Later, in the predawn dimness, I saw the clear plastic canteen was half filled with ice spars.

About then, Conrad heard me stirring, walked to the tent and said he had not slept at all. He had had to get up in the night; once outside his bag he shook uncontrollably and began to panic, verging on hypothermia. He thought the tent wouldn't be any better. I burned with guilt for not insisting that he get in. We learned later that the low had been only five degrees Fahrenheit.

But those times were part of the challenge, the testing of physical nature and my soul. Sometimes I passed the tests, sometimes I failed.

Usually, the rewards came easier than on those two occasions. In the evening, we sit drinking red wine, talking and laughing by the fire in the cool air. When the night's fine, nobody wants to bother with a tent. So as the desiccated juniper and sage send up sparks, we lie in our sleeping bags, glasses on, staring at glittering star fields and the filmy highway of the Milky Way. Maybe Sky Arch gives us a realistic perspective of our own importance. We call out shooting stars and satellites, watch the wavering points of light rise above dark cliffs. On clear moonless nights, the stars alone light up the canyon. When the moon is out, it's like a searchlight, and we hike at midnight. Or I can pitch a tent then, seeing every rock and cactus. The sandstone collects and amplifies the beams. Or maybe the human eye can adjust to nighttime better without electricity scorching holes in the blackness.

Eventually, I became so relaxed in the desert that I enjoyed it best while alone. Like a coyote catching winks during the day's heat, I've crawled into a cleft in a giant boulder to nap while the sunlight toasted my pant legs. That was literally going into the rock.

Thirteen years after I started tramping through the Reef, I found the place where the wind is born.

The U.S. Bureau of Land Management is the landlord of nearly all the San Rafael Swell. Agency planners tried to juggle newer environmental laws and old directives to facilitate grazing, encourage oil and gas exploration, boost uranium mining. It's a built-in conflict: laws demand a new ethic, but the BLM has a houseful of old clients. Unfortunately, preservation is not the BLM's strong suit.

An official wilderness designation would offer limited protection for most of the Reef. Under wilderness, which can be established only by act of Congress, scarring activities are supposed to be banned. But this has many loopholes. Chief among them is that the BLM is not obliged to preserve wilderness values on land not in its wilderness study areas. In fact, laws give developers the right to mine, drill, and build roads there. While most of the Reef is in three study areas—and in 1986 the Utah BLM made a preliminary recommendation to protect them —the Moroni Slopes, Temple Mountain, and most of the Swell are not even under study. Altogether, the agency does not support wilderness for three-quarters of the San Rafael country. Because the Reef doesn't exist in a vacuum, damage to the Swell would harm it too. And if Congress should designate wilderness, that is still a weak shield; other loopholes allow mining and road construction across wilderness areas.

Disasters loom on the near horizon like some monstrous impending thunderstorm. The first drops have begun smacking onto the sandstone:

—Motorized recreationists drawn by the opening of I-70 keep coming. Today, they are the greatest immediate threat to the San Rafael ecosystem. Their whining motorcycles and three- and four-wheel drive rigs destroy the solitude. Every year, more trails are crashed through the sagebrush in once-silent canyons. All of the San Rafael country is under savage attack.

Off-road vehicle drivers launched a national letter-writing campaign to prevent the BLM from ''locking up'' this region with wilderness recommendations. For some reason, motorcyclists have tremendous influence with the agency. BLM officials have been catering to them. They not only acquiesced in the ORV destruction, but actually encouraged it. Agency officials signed an agreement allowing a motorcycle club to mark and maintain a trail system in the Swell immediately adjacent to the Reef's Crack Canyon Wilderness Study Area. The routes go close to mouths of canyons in the study area, where ORVs are officially banned.

Motorcyclists roar through many canyons in study areas regularly, and the great holiday weekends of Labor Day and Memorial Day draw hordes of bikers. Thin shelves of sandstone are scraped and broken by motorcycle frames. Tires leave indelible black lines across pale rock. They crush desert plants that grew over many decades.

The desert heals slowly. Breaking the thin soil cover causes erosion. The motorcycle tracks wash deeper with each cloudburst. They are reinforced with more ORV abuse. Eventually, a gully wears into the surface. Everywhere in the Swell, hills are being carved by off-road vehicle tracks. The BLM has made vast portions into ORV sacrifice areas, such as Buckhorn Draw with its heavily vandalized pictographs. This is permanent damage. But the BLM has never kicked them out.

—Several played-out uranium mines are occasionally worked for the trickle of money they might bring should the nuclear industry someday resurrect. Federal rules require that in order to keep claims current, one hundred dollars' worth of assessment work must be performed every year. Sometimes this is done at the mine itself. Just as often, it's "road work," blading new stretches of dirt roads to improve access. Bulldozers and graders open the landscape to further damage.

—The Moroni Slopes are the southern terminus of both the Reef and the Swell. A great channel that is dry most of the year, Salt Wash half-circles the Slopes. Salt Wash is the site for a proposed federal salinity control project. To keep project pumps chugging, a power line would be built along the scenic dirt road that runs from Utah Highway 24, past Factory Butte, and to the edge of the wash. The road would be "improved," drawing in more folks on motorcycles. An eleven-acre evaporation pond would be constructed, along with an equalization pond of more than an acre and a half. Pipeheads would stud the desert. Wildlife "guzzlers" would be put in to offset the loss of water that animals and birds need. These things would be a jarring blight in a harsh, colorful, and rugged natural area beloved by hikers. But Bureau of Reclamation officials filed a formal "Finding of No Significant Impact," which allows the project to roll ahead without further environmental studies. (Editor's note: As this volume went to press, May 1987, Bureau of Reclamation officials said the salinity control unit was being dropped for now, but Harl Noble of the agency's Salt Lake regional office said it could be revived.)

—A gigantic tar sands development, proposed to extract synthetic fuel from gummy petroleum deposits, was okayed by the BLM for tracts of land in the center of the Swell, country as deserving of preservation as the Reef itself. Leases were converted to allow the industrialization, and BLM planners ruled that this would have no impact on the wilderness quality of the nearby Reef. Actually, it would destroy any remaining tranquility in the region.

—The state of Utah is even worse in terms of preservation than the federal government. That's a potent danger to the area's naturalness, because when it achieved statehood, Utah was given four square-mile sections of every federal township of thirty-six square miles. That amounts to around one hundred state parcels scattered throughout all of the Swell and Reef.

The Division of State Lands and Forestry, which manages Utah property, unabashedly boosts all kinds of development. State officials allowed an exploration company to level a drill pad immediately in front of a pictograph panel thousands of years old in South Temple Wash. Coal mine developers were permitted to burrow into state land close to the Moroni Slopes and Factory Butte, but the mine was abandoned.

When I-70 opened, the BLM launched a program of studies on how to deal with the onslaught of visitors. The intention was to protect the Swell while encouraging and controlling limited tourist development. Study teams produced imaginative and sweeping recommendations. Almost nobody knew about the study. No national groups fought for the Swell. Neither the BLM nor Congress followed up on the recommendations. Because of this inaction, the destruction of the San Rafael country seems assured. The natural balance may be utterly overthrown within ten years.

That would be a tragedy. The San Rafael Swell is largely as it has been since the Creation. We don't have many places like it—a stunning section of the Colorado Plateau that is still largely intact. It is an amazing, natural country that belongs to all Americans, literally the birthright of us all.

The San Rafael Swell should be preserved as a great ecological desert park; not developed for mass tourism, but set aside for its own quiet merits. There should be a bare minimum of trailheads, a few access roads, some campgrounds. Traditional nondamaging uses, like ranching, could continue as a living part of the West. The rest should be preserved in a natural state. That is surely the San Rafael country's last chance. And if it does not happen? For a few more years, the San Rafael region will remain a refuge where you can get in touch with your deepest feelings. For a while, you can go into the rock—let the mysterious, blank depths of nature move inside.

Dream, desert. There's not long for the hunting coyote. Not long for the mating swallows.

2

The Environment, Then and Now

Two hundred million years ago the San Rafael Swell was a tropical island partly above a shallow sea whose currents cut deep troughs in it. Fern forests stood above swamps. Flat-headed reptiles slogged across shimmering mud flats.

That's just one of the Swell's incarnations that researchers have pieced together from the geological record. They discovered some kind of ancestral hump is detectable in the rocks dating as far back as 100 million years before that tropical island. Since then, the bulge has undergone half a dozen periods of lifting or severe erosion. This strange slow heartbeat is due to the movement of the earth's crustal plates, which continues today.

For many millions of years, oceans laid down layers of silt and sand on the region. The minerals eventually hardened into sandstone, limestone, dolomite, and shale between 1,000 and 1,600 feet deep.

Sandstone, the main rock of the Reef, is simply sand cemented together by a film of clay and minerals. Its color depends more on the cementing material than the color of the original sand grains. Pink sandstone, for example, is glued together by minerals high in iron oxide.

When the bumps that were the ancestors of the Rocky Mountains began forming around 300 million years ago—a time of vast regional upheavals—the Swell was part of a greater

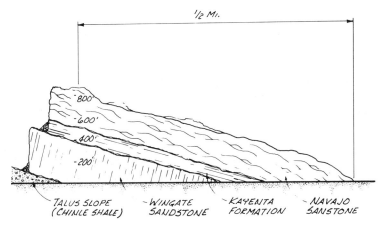

Geologic strata of the San Rafael Reef. Rubble piles up at the bottom of cliffs, and the San Rafael Swell rises to the left.

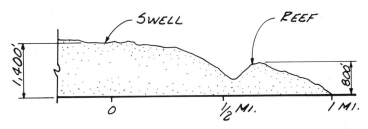

Cross section where the San Rafael Reef is narrow and steep, with the San Rafael Swell rising just beyond (left), around Greasewood Draw.

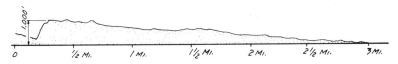

Cross section where the San Rafael Reef is wide and gradual, as near Doorway Wash.

uplift. This is known as the Emery Uplift, of which only traces remain. It extended in from the west and ended about where the Reef is today. The Swell stood partly above the water line. Later, it was nearly drowned again as the seas rose. Sediments drizzled onto it through water in which great plesiosaurs chased fish during the middle Jurassic times, say 150–140 million years ago. Mudstone and gypsum beds were forming. Waves played across mud flats, leaving fine, rippled imprints in bays, stream-beds, and beaches. Some of the Reef's shales and sandstones carry clear impressions of the waves. Dinosaur tracks show up in it sometimes too. For most of the time that the incipient Swell was ocean property, the sea was shallow, said Wallace R. Hansen of the U.S. Geological Survey, Denver, a specialist in western geology. The Swell was "hardly below wave base."

Another gradual lifting brought up the eastern section. By 135 million years ago, the region may have become semiarid. Shifting rivers cut through the formations, while volcanoes to the west and southwest rained down ash and clay. Fields of sand dunes crept across parts of the Swell. Shrewlike mammals rooted in the higher areas, which were covered with dense forests of an early conifer called Auracarioxylon.

Finally, its south and southwest lifted gradually with re-gional uplifts during the early Tertiary epoch, about 60 million years ago. And from the first through this moment, erosion has been at work.

The ancient dome shows up as an uneven, kidney-shaped upthrust that extends about fifty-three by twenty-four miles, the longest measurement being on a northeast axis. The San Rafael Swell rose between other massive bulges in the earth's crust: Capitol Reef and the Henry Mountains in the south, the Book Cliffs to the north.

As the Swell's interior eroded away, it left mesas and flat irons—or thin cliffs—throughout. Since the Reef was the nearly vertical edge of the immense dome, it resisted weathering.

For most of its length, the Reef is a free-standing wall at the edge of rugged badlands. But a dark, lumpy remnant of the Swell's dome remains fused with it for a few miles starting just north of Straight Wash, where the Reef is narrowest.

Another resistant chunk was the San Rafael country's high-est point, the San Rafael Knob, on the west slope of the Swell.

Its peak is 7,921 feet above sea level—3,000 feet higher than the desert to the east of the Reef, and 2,400 feet above South Salt Wash, the valley west of the Swell.

The different conditions under which sediments or dunes were deposited are recorded as varying types of sandstone, shale, and other rocks. Hansen ticked off some of the ways in which soil and sand accumulated: "beach sands and offshore bars; delta sands; eolian, windblown, sand like the Navajo Sandstone Formation, a fossil dune field."

As a result, the immense cliffs of the Reef and Swell are composed of sandstones and shales of varying texture, thickness, and color. Reading from top, or youngest, to the bottom, oldest, the Reef's four main formations are Navajo Sandstone, the Kayenta formation, Wingate sandstone, and Chinle shale.

—Navajo sandstone, the upper formation throughout the Reef, is the field of petrified dunes formed millions of years ago by windblown sand. It can be 400 to 700 feet thick, with massive cliffs and slopes. The highest part of the Navajo sandstone is usually white, light gray, or yellowish gray. The lower and middle parts are pinker. Its cross-bedding resulted from wind blowing sand around, sorting dune surfaces by grain size. Sand heaped up in ridges, the finer stuff sifting to the lee of a dune—so if you know how to read the rocks, you can tell the direction of the prevailing winds millions of years ago.

—The Kayenta formation, a somewhat crumbly combination of red-brown sandstone, green and red shales, and conglomerates, can be from 50 to 300 feet thick. It was deposited by streams. Harder portions form ledges and ridges within the formation.

—Wingate sandstone is a hard rock usually buff to tan or dark gray, often coppery. It includes some layers of limestone. The lowest portion of the canyons through the Reef are usually Wingate, which forms the sheer cliffs. Lower cliff walls are sometimes full of cavities and hung with sandstone "stalactites." The layer can be 350 to 400 feet high. The Wingate is thought to be material piled up during a dry period: lake sediments and desert dunes.

—Chinle Shale is found on the inner curve of the Reef, particularly around Temple Mountain, South Temple Wash, and toward the high land of the Swell. The Chinle beds are layered, dark red and green, from 800 to 1,000 feet thick. Chinle consists mostly of flood-plain or stream deposits, such as beach sand, silt, and ash mixed with limestone. This, the uranium-bearing layer, is the earliest of the Reef's exposed deposits, perhaps 200 million years old.

West of the Reef, much of the Swell is covered with Chinle and the older Moenkopi formation, a reddish fine-grained mudstone. Dating to the early Triassic Era, as long as 230 million years ago, the Moenkopi retains mud cracks and the ripples of prehistoric seas.

Chunks of ripple rock, sandstone imprinted with wave marks, show up here and there on the western slopes of the Reef. But they're abundant in the Swell. The red or green slabs are covered with grooves and ridges from water washing across shallow bays. They are usually flaking, and it's strange to see a line of chunks sticking at an angle from a desolate hill, the wave action showing up plainly on them.

The Reef edge toward the Swell terminates with a sheer drop. High above, vast knobs and flying saucers of pale Navajo sandstone line the crest. The cliff breaks themselves must be one or two million years old. Sometimes new walls, where sections spalled off and exposed lighter, less-weathered sandstone, are painted with pictographs known to be thousands of years old.

Scientists believe rock varnish flowed over the cliffs during a wet period that began about 10,000 years ago. Another great splash of it dripped in a humid period from 3,000 B.C. to the start of the modern era. Where water seeps over the rocks, it is forming today.

Along much of the Reef, Temple Mountain dominates the vista. The mountain is a monstrous rock connected to the Reef and reaching into the San Rafael Swell. It's three-quarters of a mile long and shaped like a figure 8, with a peak at each lobe. It rises to 6,773 feet, some 600 feet higher than the Reef's crest in this area.

The mountain puzzled geologists for decades. Their fascination had a practical purpose: millions of years ago, pockets in the sandstone and shale filled with rock strata that somehow trapped radioactive minerals. The result is the mountain's numerous uranium mines.

For many years, geologists had no idea what Temple Mountain was, speculating it might be a "cryptovolcano." A cryptovolcano, they postulated, was a rock mass pushed up by deeper volcanism. That would explain the apparent upthrust, even though it has no trace of igneous rock.

Now scientists think it is really a plug of sandstone and shale from higher on the Swell's dome, which collapsed into a vertical tube long ago. "It turns out there are hundreds of these collapse structures that are exposed on the north and south rim of the Grand Canyon. . . . I think Temple Mountain is one of those. It looks exactly like that," said the USGS's Eugene M. Shoemaker, a researcher at Flagstaff, Arizona, and Mount Palomar, California.

A cavity formed deep underground when some inland sea dissolved sections of sandstone. The cavity collapsed and formations crashed down into it, through a "pipe" 500 to 2,000 feet across. Some of the Swell's strata dropped as far as 300 feet. This material was compressed. Like the Reef, the plug's harder mass resisted weathering. When the Swell weathered down around it, the plug was left standing. The dome's higher formations are still there, in the form of Temple Mountain. It was a downcrash, not an upthrust.

Rich uranium oxides dissolved in groundwater percolated into some of the mountain's strata. The oxides reacted with pockets of vegetation when wood and other debris rotted. These layers eventually solidified. Since about the turn of the century, they have been mined for vanadium, then uranium.

Uranium, oil and gas, and tar sands claims blanket the San Rafael Swell. The Chinle formation uranium ores were discovered here in 1904, and serious mining began in the early 1920s. For the next forty years mines were worked, particularly around Temple Mountain. During the uranium boom of the 1950s, camps of hundreds of miners, wives, and kids sprang up. By the time the boom went bust in the early 1960s, nearly 600,000 tons of uranium ore had been ripped from the San Rafael country. The camps died, leaving a litter of abandoned cars, open mine shafts, and disintegrating shacks. And the Reef is still riddled with uranium claims.

At the mouth of Bell Canyon, a tilted board is propped up with rocks. Tacked onto it is a printed form, dated July 19, 1982, claiming a potential uranium mine for Energy Fuels Ltd., Denver. Nearby a second claim notice leans against a juniper's trunk, the paper tattered beyond legibility. They are typical of mining claims fronting most of the washes.

Prospectors have always searched out petrified trees, at first because they had higher radiation "counts" than most rocks. Later, mining geologists realized that when the trees were swept in ancient floods, the roots would have remained pointing upstream as the logs swung with the current. They recorded the logs' locations and drew charts that helped them trace the flow patterns of ancient uranium-rich streams, leading to uranium discoveries.

Hikers cannot fail to notice petrified wood and other fossil evidence of remote times. "Sometimes in the Chinle you'll see tracks, and these were animals that were walking across that muddy water or that beach sand," Wallace Hansen said. Other fossils include sandstone slabs with root casts, footprints, brachiopods, corals, even fish impressions. In the Swell just outside Chute Canyon a big sandstone slab had a pair of ten-inch impressions of coelacanths, the lungfish from which land life evolved. They had snouts, ridges across their bodies, diamond patterns suggesting scales, and a couple of well-preserved fins.

Along the vast broken wall of the Reef are many seeps and intermittent streams. Also, natural pockets in the sandstone, called tanks, hold water long into the most severe droughts.

Two important waterways wind through the Reef, although one of them dries up in the summer. They are the San Rafael River in the north and Muddy Creek at the far south.

The San Rafael roams through the deserts of Emery County for ninety or one hundred miles before it joins the Green River. It is formed at the very edge of the Swell by the union of three streams plunging off the high, wooded Wasatch Plateau—Ferron, Cottonwood, and Huntington creeks.

Within the Swell, it twists through rugged country called the Little Grand Canyon. Soon it's enveloped in the narrow, six-mile limestone gorge of the Upper Black Box, exposing the oldest bedrocks of the Swell. It trickles around rock piles, which during high water form a ten- or fifteen-foot waterfall, then flows out of the Upper Box and onto flat, open country for a few miles.

At Mexican Bend, just before the Reef, the river swings clockwise. It circles in a vast oval of perhaps three hundred degrees in five river miles, going nearly all the way around Mexican Mountain. The 6,393-foot mountain is a ragged, pink sandstone butte of four escarpments. The top is formed in two peaks, one of them sharp, the other a wedge. At the base the brown river goes by tamarisk, cottonwoods, an eroded bank, driftwood, flats of rock-stubbled mud. Then in a region of high, purplish buttes and brown cliff walls, the San Rafael cuts into the Reef. For three miles it loops through another deep trench, the Lower Black Box.

The river shines placidly where it leaves the Reef three miles northeast of Interstate 70. Emerging onto flat land, it turns sharply south into Tidwell Draw, which parallels the northern ten miles of the Reef. The draw looks as if it were left by some ancient river, a dry gulch waiting to capture the San Rafael whenever it burst out through the Reef.

A gauging station near the Reef shows record flows for the river are about 12,000 cubic feet per second at flood stages, and nothing in droughts.

The San Rafael's junction with the Green River is fifty miles southeast of its beginning, where the three streams unite. Throughout its entire route, the San Rafael wanders within Emery County.

Muddy Creek winds through the other end of the Reef, seventeen miles northwest of Hanksville. Its high water has been 3,000 cubic feet per second. It too rises in the Wasatch Plateau, and it has been flowing long enough to carve out an impressive canyon. But for many days of the year, no water runs.

If you were to drive along the dirt road on the Reef's inside curve and look out across the Swell, from this angle you'd see badlands of brown mesas flanked with white debris, rank after rank of broken canyons—burnt sienna, pale green, pinks, a distant dark gray mass.

What you can't see is that on top of this steep slope is Sinbad, a high country at the heart of the Swell—rolling, grassy rangeland around forty miles long by fifteen miles wide. Its steep eastern slopes are badlands cut by huge drainage canyons.

The wild landscape of the San Rafael Swell includes ridges, flats, knobs, lengthy canyons, cliffs, and mountains. Gigantic domes like the one called Copper Globe loom above forests of pinyon pine and juniper. Grazing land covers some of the high, rolling hills.

The life of the Reef is based on recycled sand. Sandstone weathers out, and spring floods carry gravel, sand, and rich loam. This builds up beyond reach of floods, where the cliffs bend, in side canyons above the main channels, and around potholes on the Reef. Plants hold the soil in place. Life here performs a delicate minuet, balanced between drying up and washing away.

With sparse rainfall, plants grow slowly. Still, they manage to dig in. They even force roots into cracks on cliff ledges. When a thin piece of the vertical wall fell off in Wild Horse Canyon, it exposed a network of roots. Tough weeds, brush, and stunted pinyons hang on amid the rubble of talus slopes. A canyon widens: a hill of sand and gravel is gray-green with sparse grasses, sagebrush, cacti, juniper bushes, baby cottonwoods.

Often the higher plants have help. Their roots are nourished and the ground is stabilized by a remarkable natural carpet called cryptogamic soil. This thin dark crust grows where the power of flash floods is not so great—in high side canyons and alcoves, interspersed with slickrock and junipers and stretches of sand.

Cryptogamic soil is made up of microscopic and nearly microscopic plants: blue-green algae, lichens, fungi, and mosses in hundreds of one- or two-inch-high lumps, dark brown to black. Patches of it stretch down slopes and over hills protected from the heaviest runoffs, growing in ridges and hummocks. The crust is fragmented by gullies where small streams broke through. Grasses, cacti, junipers, and Mormon tea grow in the soil it protects. Close up, the mantle is a spectacular miniature landscape spangled with white and orange clumps of lichens.

Among the most ancient variety of plants, cryptogams do not produce seeds or flowers, and they are nonvascular. Having no plumbing of roots and veins to move water, they absorb it by osmosis. Reproduction is by spores.

In the Reef, all four kinds of plants make up the cryptogamic soil, with algae predominating. "These organisms produce about as much cover on the desert floor as the seed plants themselves," said Brigham Young University's Dr. Kimball T. Harper, professor of botany and range science and a foremost expert on cryptogams.

Most of those diminutive plants survive in the desert because, when conditions become harsh and the soil begins to dry out, they secrete a protective gelatinous sheath. The membrane traps water so the cells don't become desiccated. The minute a storm wets them, algae and moss will "green up and will be actively photosynthesizing again," Harper said.

The living crust anchors soil and roughens the surface. On a tiny scale, it's a castellated surface, with mounds and valleys and mountains. Instead of running off and roaring away along the wash, rainfall is held in these little cups. It seeps down and nourishes the larger plants. Encouraging the desert's weeds, trees, and brush inhibits erosion. Harper estimates cryptogams double soil stability. Their protective sheaths reduce evaporation of soil moisture—a critical factor for subsurface plant roots, as well as mites and other miniature wildlife. Much to the benefit of big plants, cryptogams also fix free nitrogen and take up phosphorus and potassium. Through them, these three elements are usable by higher forms.

Harper measured the seed and other forage production of desert plots. Land with undisturbed cryptogams had about two and a half times the production of a comparable area with a few millimeters of the crust scraped off. "It becomes questionable whether we can maintain these desert seed plant communities without the little fellows growing on the soil's surface," he said.

Because larger desert plants are more sensitive to exceptionally hot temperatures, their root systems extend deep below the surface, where they are protected. They have few roots in the upper two inches—the region used by cryptogams. Water left in the upper couple of inches would probably evaporate quickly, but can instead be used by the cryptogams. Mosses, lichens, fungi, and algae therefore use water that is not useful to seed plants.

Cryptogams are tough under natural conditions. But the carpet is destroyed by the steps of hikers, hoofs of grazing cattle and sheep, and the ripping wheels of off-road vehicles. "Those things churn them up so much, the next storm that comes washes the soil away," Harper said. Grazing, however, can be managed to reduce damage to the mats, he said. If livestock is pulled off in time to allow the cryptogamic soil to start reestablishing itself before the year's first good storm, the little plants might survive. Otherwise, the remnants are washed away.

Once cryptogamic soil is torn up, it can begin to reestablish itself in five years. That much time must pass before the plants start to recover. To completely restore a disturbed area requires twenty years of growth. But if the area is not protected during that time, "we'll never get them back," Harper said. "They just will not compete with uses of the site that are out of step with their own dormancy cycles."

Although blue-green algae are predominant in the Reef's cryptogamic soil, the mats are thickly studded with another interesting tiny plant, lichens. Actually, lichens are colonies of two plants tied together, a combination of algae and fungi. They require nothing but clean air, occasional moisture and minerals. They can get minerals from naked rock. Their growth is so gradual that that they are among the oldest life.

Some lichen rings are believed to be 5,000 years old. Rings up to half a foot across spangle bare rocks throughout the San Rafael country. Called thalli, these rings can be irregular light green scatterings of buds and crusts. Or the lichens may be bright orange clumps, or powder blue snowflakes in depressions of the red rock.

A careless step will brush a lichen from its boulder.

The most common large plants in the San Rafael country are junipers, pinyons, sagebrush, wavy-leaf oak, and cottonwoods. Walking along in the desert, watching the ground, you can tell what tree you're near by the tangy scent of the juniper, the strong musk of the sagebrush, or the sweet pine odor of pinyon.

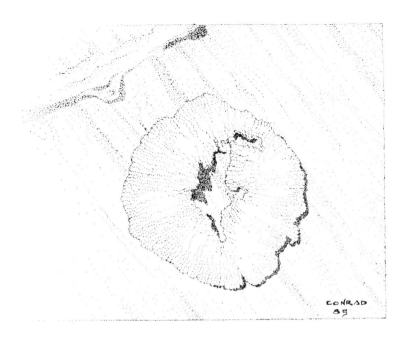

CONRAD
85

Except for lizards, ants, blackflies, and a few birds, animals rarely venture into the harsh sunlight. Yet, with sundown bats emerge, darting after insects. Coyotes prowl the slickrock, kangaroo rats gather seeds, bighorn sheep mosey down to potholes for water. If you knew where to look in the Swell, you'd find mule deer, pronghorn antelope, foxes, bobcats, coyotes, mountain lions, and porcupines as well as lesser mammals.

Birds too abound here, especially in canyons with water. Mourning doves, sparrows, chukar partridges, jays, hawks, and ravens are common. A big prairie falcon, showing its pale underside, lands at the top of a rounded cliff outcrop.

White-throated swifts make the canyons ring with their excited gee-gee-gee-gee-gee, the high notes descending to lower. Soaring near the tops of cliffs, they chitter like canaries. Gracefully they swoop and buzz each other. Sometimes they fly briefly in pairs, sometimes in a formation like the corners of a rectangle.

A few toads live in the streams and potholes, as well as many varieties of lizards. Once in a while a gopher snake slides through the ricegrass.

Blackflies swarm over the Reef and make life miserable for all mammals from early June to early July. They fly around faces in intense, maddening clusters, cover arms, creep into nostrils, stick to hair, bite eyelids. They work their way under shirts. The bites itch and raise welts.

Ants don't find the desert barren, as they clamber through a wilderness of pinyon and sagebrush chaff, harvesting a rich haul of seeds. Their success depends upon cooperation and diversity. The queen lays eggs that develop into different kinds of workers. Bigger workers harvest bigger seeds. Smaller ones scour the brush for little seeds. Group foragers go for heavy material and are active in good times. Individual searchers are more important in times of scarcity.

Should the climate change, prompting a shift in vegetation types, or an offshoot colony expand into a new area where plants grow in a different ratio, the queen adapts. She is able to vary the ratio of her workers. She may change the proportion of small workers to the big brutes, giving the colony more of the specialists it needs to harvest new crops.

Like the more tolerant human societies, ants adapt well to change because they value difference rather than homogeneity.

The three divisions of the Reef are the result of two roads going through—a major dirt route at South Temple Wash and Interstate 70 where Spotted Wolf Canyon used to be. I-70 bisects the entire San Rafael Swell in its cross-continental drive. The route through South Temple is a bit more down-home, being near the end of a seventy-mile dirt road that crosses the Swell diagonally. That road takes off from Utah Highway 10 less than a mile north of the huge Hunter Power Plant at Emery County's seat, Castle Dale. It immediately works its way into the lowlands of the Swell by way of Buckhorn Draw in the north, then cuts across the flats, through the Reef, and connects with Utah 24.

Measuring on a smooth curve along the center of the Reef, to avoid the jags on the highly indented face, we get these distances: the southern section is about twenty-three miles long from the southwestern tip of the Moroni Slopes to South Temple Wash; the midsection is another twenty-three miles, ending at I-70; and the northern section is about ten miles, from the freeway to the end of the Reef.

3

The South

Shadows threw bold patterns on the cliffs as we approached Crack Canyon's first narrows. Here the walls are striped dark gray and white with patches of buff, brown, peach, and a color like rusty cans. Deeper in, a friend stood looking at serene rosy cliffs with slanted sides and vertical potholes. I glanced back and saw the entrance wall alternating glaring brown light and solid shade. We went around a bend, and a great section of the wall looked like mud that had melted, flowed, and coagulated.

That day I was depressed and jittery. I wanted solitude. As they walked ahead, I scrambled into a high alcove among loose rocks.

Cliff swallows swooped past, chirping. They flew in tandem, reminding me of twin dragon flies above a weedy pond. They darted down the canyon, squawking shrilly, then peeled apart.

Without any effort, my brain disconnects. They turn, bank, circle, whiz back again, high as my perch. They are flying through the canyon connected: they are mating. The wilderness rejoices. I watch them with a clear mind. The moment does not end.

I wanted to know the San Rafael Reef. I worked to learn its shapes, the feeling of being in and on it, its history from the most remote ages of shallow oceans to the modern freeway construction. But I couldn't tell exactly where the Reef starts.

Federal and state maps are ambiguous about whether the Moroni Slopes are part of it. If separate, the Reef's southern-

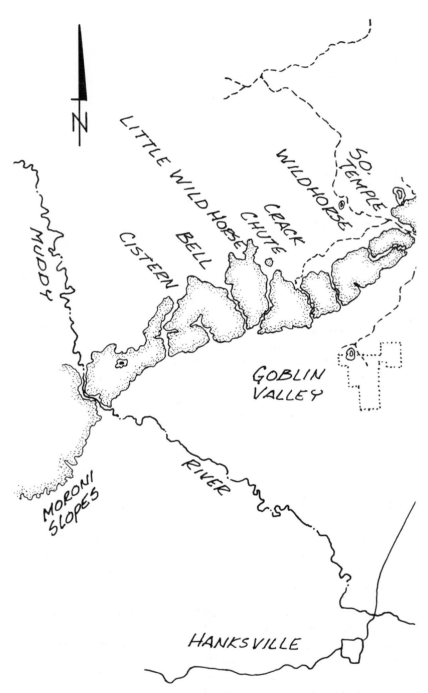

Moroni Slopes to South Temple Wash.

most cliffs would be at Muddy Creek, a canyon that forms the Slopes' northern boundary. If they are the same formation, then the Slopes are the beginning of a mighty ridge that soars northeast for fifty-six miles, measuring along the crest.

Utah state highway maps label as San Rafael Reef only that portion from South Temple to Interstate 70, with the rest shown as strange gray creases. On the state's multipurpose map, "Southeastern Central Utah," the label San Rafael Reef starts at Muddy Creek, and the Moroni Slopes are drawn as if they were separate.

The Bureau of Land Management's old map series, called "Recreation and Wildlife on BLM Lands," shows the Slopes on the "Central Utah" map, without any mention of the Reef; the Reef appears on another chart. The BLM's more recent map for Muddy Creek Wilderness Study Area has a peculiar notation: "Moroni Slope" is printed above "San Rafael." Detailed U.S. Geological Survey quadrangles that outline only part of the Slopes—"Factory Butte, Utah" and "Fruita, Utah"—do not mention the words San Rafael Reef.

Yet, I wondered, how could the Reef suddenly spring from a canyon? And if the Slopes are part of the Reef, what are they like?

THE MORONI SLOPES

Roasting winds at noon, late in May: I climbed out of my Jeep on high land beyond the abandoned town of the Factory Butte Coal Mine, where the road starts down to cross part of the drainage of Muddy Creek. As I stared across, I could see that the Slopes are the tail end of the Reef. They are part of the same rock chain, and Muddy Creek Canyon is like a dozen others cutting through the Reef.

Fan-shaped, eight miles long on the northeast-southwest axis, four miles across, the Slopes are a dark brown sandstone shelf tilted on edge. They lift abruptly to 1,200 feet above Utah's Middle Desert, a vast, eerie, sunbaked wasteland with names like Last Chance Canyon, Wood Bench, and Black Mountain. This is a country of brown-gray bentonite hills, bleak gullies, and purplish rock slabs, only eight miles east of Capitol Reef National Park.

Below, the drainage was mostly gray, banded with wide white stretches that looked like quicksand. Maroon, pink, purple, and greenish-striped hills of the Morrison formation edged the outcrop where I was parked. The side of this ridge was dark gravel.

In the rare seasons when water flows through Muddy Creek, the drainage really is a field of quicksand. It's been known to swallow pickups. But this day, the broad wash was mostly dry, creased with the tracks of half a dozen trucks and motorcycles. Some cyclist had etched rings in the dirt. Hilly islands were speckled with brush.

Across the gulch, the Moroni Slopes wore a crust of Entrada sandstone, the color of an elephant's hide—ridged, wrinkled, layered. Here and there the older Navajo sandstone showed through. The Slopes were broken by channels that looked like they might turn out to be deep chasms.

Stretching away from the Slopes, the San Rafael Reef was steep waves of light sandstone. An orange cliff showed below one of the Reef's dark gray ridges.

Staring into the last big cut in the Slopes before Muddy Creek Canyon, I saw strata of dark lines above white rock. The stone crest was glossy, shining in the sun's glare. The canyon was a gash 1,200 feet deep. It briefly widened into a huge bowl with two cliff lines, one bulging above the other, and sheer sides that were dark with desert varnish.

I started up and drove into the wash, nervously recalling what Reo Hunt, the Hanksville sage, told me—at Muddy Creek he wrenches out the vehicles of many guys that don't know what they're doin'. A dozen seldom-traveled miles back from the highway, that was a creepy thought.

The trail turned south, paralleling Salt Wash along the bottom of bright white ridges that are the end of the North Caineville Reef. I parked there and started hiking toward the Slopes. Three or four hot, colorless clay rills separated me from my goal. My feet sank in the loose soil.

At the base of the hills I found shoals of fossilized oysters. These shells are like modern oysters', but date to the Jurassic, 135 to 195 million years ago. They were everywhere, thousands of them, in lines along the hillsides. Silica casts with a scaly crystalline surface, their tops were burnt sepia. Inside, each was chalky, shining with a startling remnant of ancient mother-of-pearl.

The endless hills were often too steep to climb down. Even if I didn't fall, the crumbly sides would avalanche. I walked along the top of one, slowly drawing closer to Muddy Creek Canyon.

At the end of this one, the sides dropped off all around and the front stuck out like a ship's prow. Then I had to backtrack, searching for a gentler slope. I kept within sight of the high white hills bordering the drainage valley, but I had to angle away from it. On a couple of long mounds were planks or poles stuck in as markers. When I walked, they disappeared behind higher ground.

On the ridge tops, the wind made hiking bearable. But the ravines were a brain-numbing, roaring, heat sink. I swigged from my canteen frequently. Going down the side of an escarpment, I leaned into a steady wind so strong it actually propped me up as I crab-walked down.

Farther along the gully bottom, I found my way blocked. A huge section of the wall had collapsed into the next ravine, leaving a deep, jagged gash. It was a pour-off point for flood waters. Again, I backtracked and found a way around. Now the dips and mounds were becoming gentler.

I walked through a gap between crests and reached the last drop-off before Salt Wash, a gulch that swings all the way around the eastern and southern ends of the Slopes. To my dazzled eyes, the wash seemed a bewildering jumble of Morrison formation hills, scattered areas of dense brush, bentonite mounds, sand, gravel bowls. To cross, I'd have to drop out of sight of the North Caineville ridge.

I worried about wandering around lost in the hot alkaline wind, an irrational fear, because Salt Wash isn't more than a mile across. But experience had taught me anyone can quickly become disoriented in an unfamiliar desert. Still, the Slopes were tantalizingly close, and I was so eager to reach them I broke the first commandment of desert survival: *take plenty of water*. I left my canteen at the top of a rise as a marker and set out across the wash. I glanced back often, watching it recede above me. Wanting tracks I could follow back, I scraped my boots on hard soil. I looked around to memorize landmarks in this maze of hills and crests, but found they all looked the same. My canteen was now the size of a small flat rock.

The Moroni Slopes rose above me, dark against the sky, just across a huge bowl that was filled with sand, rocks and hard dirt. Sagebrush and blooming sunflowers grew in the bowl. As soon as I dropped into it, my canteen would be lost from sight.

In a conspicuous saddle between hills, I left my hat as the final marker. I weighted it with two or three gastroliths, supposedly dinosaur gizzard stones. Then I took off on a last dash to the Slopes.

Sand blew in waves as I scraped through the hollow, nervous about the gusts obliterating my tracks. I believed I knew where the Jeep was, but this was still a spooky feeling—the fear I'd have to find it without water or any shade on my bald pate. I was bothered by blowing dust, heat, dryness, and memories of getting lost in the desert near Canyonlands National Park years before. At last I reached the Slopes. I sat on a flat stretch, gazing up.

They were solid rock broken by deep ravines, steep when seen from the base. Above were light rock formations, cactus and brush, weeds, cryptogamic soil, twisted junipers growing from pockets of sand, boulders looming on the crest. Throughout the ridge, layered gray rock cascaded. It poured downhill like melting wax. The layers formed low, fat bands of sandstone. Streaked shelves jutted out, blazing in the sunlight.

Clearly, the Slopes were part of the Reef. Without the Muddy River's cutting through, there would be no break between the Slopes and the rest of the Reef.

Northeast from Muddy Creek, the Reef's huge hogbacks and sandstone layers were pink, lumpy sandstone, pale folds with blocks and turrets on top. It was light, jagged sandstone, exposed and rough. If the Slopes are an elephant's hide, the rest of the Reef is the ragged meat with the hide stripped off.

Too exhausted, overheated, and worried to scramble up the Slopes, I walked back into Salt Wash. The direct sunlight washed out small features, and I couldn't find my hat. Hurrying, I ran across my footprints again. I pictured myself panicking, running around without hat or canteen, losing myself in the maze of pastel hills and dry gullies. Stay calm. The gravel was too hard to take a deep indentation. I followed my tracks over a sand hill and lost them again.

Another mark. I had to make another mark to be able to get back at least to this point. Anxiously, I shuffled a giant X in the gravel and then trotted ahead. I glanced over my shoulder and watched the X evaporate. I could not see any tracks, not even those just made, when I knew exactly where to look.

Maybe I'd wander around a long time in this desiccating wind. Should I wrap my shirt around my head to ward off the beating rays? And burn my torso?

I decided to walk off blindly in the direction I supposed the Jeep to be, marker or none. Taking a last desperate scan, my eyes stopped at an abnormally straight line twinkling atop a little hill. It was left of where I had intended to go. My hat, must be my hat. Walking toward it, I made out the canteen. If I'd hiked a few paces to the right before looking, I would have missed it. Just as I'd somehow bypassed the hat.

I gulped deeply—blessed water. There was the white, high ridge of the North Caineville Reef. As I walked to it, my Jeep appeared, a tiny box on the horizon beside a line of brown bentonite.

This was one of those times when minutes seem like hours. I staggered into the wind, which blew hard enough to make the air dense. It slowed me while the sun drew out sweat. I kept glancing at my watch. Incredible. It was only a minute from the last time I checked, hours back. Fighting the heat, I tried dumping water on my head. It blew onto my shoulders and camera knapsack instead. I brushed it from the green denim, glad to have something to do with my hands.

Shells crunched on a spooky beach, the shoreline of an ocean dead 150 million years. The Jeep was slowly getting larger. Crunch, crunch. The side mirrors materialized, sticking out. I was baked. My shirt was glued to my chest.

BELL AND LITTLE WILD HORSE CANYONS

These two form a Y within the Reef. The stem is on the side toward Goblin Valley State Park, which is about six square miles of chocolate-colored mudstone and boulders in a flat, desolate bowl. The Y's arms open on the painted desert of the San Rafael Swell, a mile and a half apart. Among the loveliest and least abused of the Reef canyons, Little Wild Horse and Bell offer challenging hiking because of tight squeezes and places that must be climbed over or crawled under.

Starting from the stem, my friend Conrad, his half-sister Karen, and I hiked into the Reef, soon reaching a set of broad natural steps in the bedrock. At a junction, we angled to the left, entering Bell. We walked between purple sandstone ledges and cliffs covered with the potholes and stalactite formations we call Swiss cheese. We had to scrabble upward through tight places with water in the bottom. Sometimes we'd try to chimney across the wet spots, butts on one curvy wall, feet on the other, pushing with our muddy hands.

Long gullets of slickrock were worn into smooth curves, and the walls were traced with white lines. In the lower part of the canyon we passed cottonwood trees. Brush and grass grew wherever the walls did not close in. High overhead in sunny places, bushes sprouted from breaks in the cliffs.

In narrow spots we jumped onto moist sand from the walls above. We climbed to bypass a bad crack, but the ledge petered out and we had to go back and then work our way through the gully below.

The next day, returning after a hike through Little Wild Horse, we found Bell was easier when we headed downhill from the Swell side. We swung and jumped over tight spots that required climbing before. A hairlike worm, eight inches long, thrashed in a puddle. All the pools were drying, and that helped too. The pink-brown Navajo sandstone was smooth here; there, ribbed like a lava flow. Grass bristled from its cracks. Sculptured cliffs wrapped around a bowl-like opening. The walls were rounded, gray, with black streaks and panels.

Little Wild Horse Canyon is rougher and longer than Bell, winding leisurely through the Reef. For a while it's nearly parallel to the Reef's face, but it generally climbs to the northeast.

Tall sides bound us most of the way. We had to jimmy ourselves through sometimes, depending on our arms. Devoid of life, the narrows had walls as dark as limestone. Their slanting strata were worn into curve after indentation after swerve. Arms outstretched, we could let our fingers glide along both sides as we walked in the shade on round stones and gravel. The walls were clean, smooth, deeply scored for the first five feet. Higher, where the floods didn't polish them, they were gnarled. In the sunlight, the gullies were pink at the bottom, fading into gray above.

Suddenly the canyon opened into a great room with the main canyon and a few dead-end passages leading out. This was a sunny brown and white bowl with sloping sides, a cottonwood in a crevice, grass, earth banks covered with trees and brush.

We pushed into a narrows again. The rock curved magically around us, widest at our shoulders. It was close for half a mile of careful hiking, in and out of shadows, walls around us like a whale's intestines. We had to duck under rocks wedged between the cliffs. We came to another park in a wide bowl, this one shaded. A bush flowered over its pocket of sand. Among rugged lumps of pockmarked buff stones, ancient junipers spread their limbs close to the red ground. This room was surrounded by high walls and crevices. A light pink cliff was dotted with pockets, each having a drift of white sand in the bottom.

Cottonwoods grew in Little Wild Horse's deep valleys. We cut across hills and sandbars, through brush, over rock slopes to pick up the main channel again. Whenever we thought we were nearly to the Swell, we saw more ridges and walls, more formations. We climbed out of a big valley, snaking up onto a smooth shelf about chest high. Clear water trickled down the sandstone groove where we crawled.

Finding a fire ring, we rejoiced. Somebody had walked through from the other end for a picnic, we thought. Couldn't be far to go now. Wrong. We were an hour from the exit.

We tried to take a shortcut along a ledge, which kept going up until we were far off the floor. Conrad and Karen turned back. They walked to the canyon's floor and wound among boulders. I stayed on the ledge, thinking sooner or later I'd find a good way down. I was probably eighty feet up before I discovered a way to reach the floor. I climbed down a cleft. Once, I held onto a big rock with my right hand as I went, and it broke off. Weighing twenty or thirty pounds, it glanced off my right forearm, then smashed apart on the cliff wall as it fell. A chunk grazed my left ankle. Pieces crashed along the ledges.

We were close to the end now. Conrad was recognizing formations on the Reef's top—that hump he had seen from camp, which he'd named "the Warthog," had to be near the crest. Just beyond it, the Reef falls off at the edge of the Swell. Soon, through a gap we could see Sinbad Country, dotted with clumps of junipers and green because of the spring rains. We veered to the left and broke out of the Reef.

Walking on the graded road up to Bell Canyon, gazing back along the Reef's noble slabs, fingers, and walls, we saw the formation's base was a tilted purple shelf. This is where a road comes up from Chute Canyon on the inner curve of the Reef. Out in the sunlight beside the Swell, the heat was unbearable.

CHUTE CANYON

January: Chips of ice lay stacked on the wash floor, where puddles froze and expanded. This time of the year, the sun's warm rays are absorbed in their long journey through the atmosphere, allowing the blue tints to penetrate and predominate. Thus, the slickrock, boulders, shadows, dry grass, and streaked cliffs all had a cold stateliness. Chewed orange sides rose high above the floor, making part of the canyon seem like a drafty cathedral. In the late afternoon, the sunset cast shadows from the pinnacles on top of one cliff onto the Swiss cheese and flat planes of the opposite wall.

Mid-April: The bushes were bare. Gusts blew wildly at night. Conrad and I hiked through Chute with Cal Grondahl, our cartoonist friend. We climbed the hills above the canyon's washout toward Goblin Valley and looked across the desert at the red cliffs of Wild Horse Mesa.

Toward the end of April: Only the topmost leaves were out on the cottonwoods at Chute Canyon's mouth. But deeper in, where cliffs protect the trees from wind and where more mois-

ture runs off the high formations, the trees had put out sparkling pea green leaves. Spring advances faster where the cold
gusts don't reach.

A bunch of us camped under the dead-looking trees at the
entrance—my wife, Cory; our boy, Sky; Conrad; reporter Mary
Finch and her son, Curtis Lubbin, who is nine months older
than Sky. The days were balmy and still. The little guys tore
around on the sand, kicking up dust volcanoes, hunting for
dragons, throwing a boomerang. The bunny hid his eggs in the
desert that Easter Sunday.

We walked beside tawny walls in an open wash that was
scarred by pickup and motorcycle tracks. A soft-petaled desert
sprig pushed up from the hard ground. In places the light gray
cliffs were so far apart that we could have been walking across
open country with mesas in the distance. But they were actually
sections of the cliff face, great piled masses.

We stopped to study a vertical wall covered with deep scal-
loped depressions. Below, prickly pear cactus leaves were
swollen, telling of wet spring weather. The canyon bed was flat
rocks and gravel.

Cliff walls began with gentle angles, then suddenly soared.
Some were smooth at the lower levels, while decorated with stalactites higher up. The designs on one flaking vertical cliff made
me think of thousands of sandbars seen from the air, alternating
white and dark gray.

Emerging into the sunshine at an open stretch, I was over-
whelmed with the beauty of that hazy afternoon. The vista was
softened by dust in the air. A field of crested wheat grass waved
golden stalks, the color highlighted against a dark formation.
The stalks' heads hung full of grain. We walked through brush
on a trail above the floor, the boys parading with wheat grass
stalks.

May: Camping alone, I thought this must be one of the
Reef's most beautiful canyons. I put up my tent on a high sand
hill beside a rotted wall. At dinner, I thought I noticed faint
pictographs high on the cliff, a design like a pair of triangles.
After a glass of wine, I searched for a way to reach them. The
holes leading up were too tenuous for footholds. But a long rock

ledge sloped down from higher levels, reaching the canyon floor half a mile beyond my camp.

I started along it, finding it tougher going than I expected. I had to climb past one place, and the ledge continued to climb. More than a hundred feet above the floor, I walked on a slanted surface peppered with loose rocks and soil. Pits in the sandstone looked like petrified antelope footprints. At the slope's top, my way was blocked by a huge boulder. I could not decide if the ledge continued to the pictographs' level or was above them. Twilight was advancing and I saw my Jeep far below.

My stomach hurt when I turned back. Whether this was from fear, apple-pear juice, or wine, I don't know. My face was clammy and I was shaking. I was relieved to get down.

Early October: After sundown, we lay on a sandbar in the middle of the wash. The ground held the day's warmth. The Milky Way draped its mysterious, filmy arms overhead. Stars glittered, we tracked satellites, several meteors trailed across the black heavens. As night deepened, the air grew uncomfortably cold, and we went to bed early. The cottonwoods were losing leaves all over camp.

CRACK CANYON

A couple of days after a flash flood, signs of swift currents were everywhere. Streaks in sand banks showed the water was a foot deep outside the canyon. Farther in, exposed roots and marks on the cliff showed that four inches to a foot of soil had washed from the gravel ridges. Plants were beaten down. Grass clumps lay matted with dirt and leaves.

Conrad, Karen, and I walked between impressive battlements where the canyon's mouth puckers, turrets in the distance, pink rocks rising on the left, the right cliff in shade. Juniper trees stood at the base of the high eastern wall and more grew on ledges. We climbed down a dangerous drop. We had to wade through some pools, jump across others. Cliff tops, sandstone fingers, and the blue-beige sky reflected in the water. Past a shadowed wall the sandstone was a white-pink glare.

Deep inside, after the way narrowed and widened again, we reached the crack that gives the canyon its name. Tan walls three hundred feet high seemed nearly to crash together. They were only a couple of feet apart—slick dark brown cliffs with their broken facets and light streaks. Hiking between the smooth, waterworn cliffs over a sandy floor, we looked up along flights of rock toward an intense sky. The crack soon ended and the canyon opened again.

WILD HORSE CANYON

I hiked through Wild Horse on a late afternoon in spring. A tall, gnarled cottonwood near the entrance was covered with tiny white cinquefoil. In a grassy lawn other trees arched against the dull buff face, a little pine and towering cottonwoods whose light green leaves twinkled in the breeze.

Close to the mouth a uranium claim was marked out by four corner stakes with faded orange plastic strips tied to their tops. Two stakes had fallen over. The strips on the others flapped.

A squat toadstool formation, ten feet high, lifted a black cap above the wash. Dark gray cliff walls were rotted with holes. Long seams ran through the walls, like the lines in driftwood. A high sandstone knob caught the light. A hawk was perched on top. That hard, flat cap keeps the knob from weathering away as the wall erodes around it. It's been going on for thousands of years, weathering and protection.

Wild Horse has a delightful oasis where life thrives, thanks to a combination of greater moisture, shade, and protection from floods. This is a shelf of soil against a tall overhang. A pour point in the wall above funnels the run-off here. The wall slants, so that for most of the day the garden is protected from the sun. Curves in the cliff pass flood water around it. Covered with rank grasses, pines, tall cottonwoods with light green leaves, oak brush, and junipers, the shelf is a natural park within the semicircle of the cliff.

"The Catacombs," Conrad named another pour point where water eroded a ten-foot-deep trench in the slickrock. I was taking a picture of the rounded walls when my glasses slipped off and went flying toward the abyss. By lucky reflex, my hand jerked down and I caught them against my leg.

A couple of miles farther in, the canyon was picking its teeth. A heavy log stuck from a pile of boulders, two or three feet above the floor. At first it looked like a rock as big as a house must have fallen from a cliff, crushing the tree. But a closer look revealed that the tree was crammed into the boulders. Splintered wood, hammered into the rock's fissures, proved the destructive power of the floods.

At sundown I sat on small sand dunes. Junipers stretched shadows across ribbed brown sand and scattered pebbles. The air was still. I admired the sand ripples a long time, looking from them to the glow of the sun on far-off curves of the cliff line.

On another trip, my dad and I hiked Wild Horse after a stormy night. A wispy waterfall flew from the rim of a side canyon. Plants stuck from moist sand where the current had washed depressions around them. Streams that were now only damp patterns on the slickrock had left lines of puffy red foam.

4

The Midsection

Conrad and I climbed onto the Reef beyond South Temple Wash,
where its flanks lift gently from the sand. On the way up I looked
toward Wild Horse Butte. It was six or seven miles away, pink under
ranks of mottled clouds; just a rise in a long pink formation.

Cloud shadows lie along the flat green desert. I admire an outcrop
of yellow and white rock. Closer to us, a juniper tree, partly dead, casts
its finger shadows on flaking beige sandstone. Dark green junipers and
brighter sprays of Mormon tea grow below us along a sand-filled de-
pression in the Reef, reaching down to the desert. A big fly drones
through still air, intent on business.

Garvin's is an abandoned ranch just off the road that goes
into South Temple Wash. A mile and a half west of Utah Highway 24 the five wooden buildings deteriorate.

This was originally a way station, built around the turn of
the century on a trail that once ran beside the Reef. Heavy
freight wagons hauled the necessities along it from Green River
to Hanksville, stopping at Garvin's. Drivers could turn their
sweating mules loose on the grass around a spring, fill up with a
dinner and a beer, and climb between clean sheets for the night.
Around the 1920s the automobile eliminated the need for an
intermediate stop, and Garvin's became a ranch. It was deserted
around 1957 but remained in occasional use for another twenty
years.

In 1973 several of the ranch's sheds were crumbling, and a rock fireplace teetered above the remains of one building. The main bunkhouse was intact, with its plank sides and corrugated tin roof. A metal water tank stood among high weeds inside a corral of leaning boards and a strand of barbed wire. Because of its deep well, this was still a watering spot used during cattle drives. In the bunkhouse torn screens blew stiffly in from the windows. I could read the wallpaper—"She Says 'It's Better Than A Mustard Plaster,' " and "NO JOKE TO BE DEAF"— scraps of magazine and newspaper pages from the 1920s and '30s. Seen through dusty, sun-streaked air, branches seemed to lie about the floor. They turned out to be lizards, as big and nasty-looking as caimans. They crept across sand drifts, ducked under loose planks, hid behind the frames of missing walls. Outside, wooden fences snaked about the property. Mason jars balanced on a shelf in the musty spring house.

The turnoff to Goblin Valley State Park is three miles beyond Garvin's. An antelope stood beside this juncture as I approached at dusk. As most vehicles here are cars and campers of tourists visiting Goblin Valley, the state doesn't bother to maintain the road past the turnoff. A mile beyond, the route penetrates the Reef at South Temple Wash. The pavement has been broken by floods, and it soon ends.

This is the main entry to the Reef, the route opening both middle and southern parts. This badly abused wash is the staging point for exploring our canyons south of Interstate 70. Dirt roads, some of them graded, branch out from here on both sides of the Reef.

SOUTH TEMPLE WASH

Noon: you realize this canyon is wide and boring. Scattered junipers offer shade, and sometimes I lie in the shadow of the huge arm an old one lifts just above the sand at our camp. The branch dangles shreds of bark in my face, and ants crawl across me.

South Temple was badly damaged during the uranium mining boom when ores were dug from here and Temple Mountain, a mile to the northeast. Now these places and most other can-

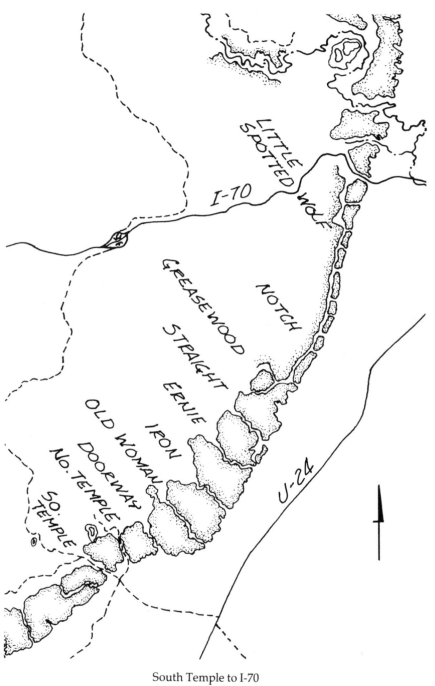

South Temple to I-70

yons are churned by a new onslaught, as the region is a favorite playground for motorcyclists. Big caravans of cyclists, with trailers and campers and volleyball nets, sometimes set up at the Goblin Valley junction. Traffic on the South Temple road is annoying anytime, but most irritating at night. Worse, groups sometimes camp on the opposite side of the canyon, hooting, playing ghetto blasters, flaring their campfires as we try to sleep.

We've arrived to find folks had been using our camp, leaving beer cans and plastic six-pack webs, dumping ashes and coals across the sand. The fireplace was so full of dirt and coal that we had to dig it out. Yet, haggard as it is in the daylight, after sunset on a peaceful evening this wash is magic.

Cory and I once took a long walk above the gullies next to the Swell when we were camping in South Temple one Labor Day weekend a dozen years ago. We discovered gray petrified logs and fragments. It was like finding treasure, searching out fossil trees on naked hills and under the junipers. Not realizing gray wood is worthless and common, I towed out a heavy log, using my belt, and cradled pieces in my other arm. The weight hurt my back.

We reached camp as the sun was setting. Immense cliffs glowed golden red. With the wash bottom in deep shadow, we settled onto the road to watch sunset colors play across the canyon walls and Temple Mountain. The light kept shifting. Huge faces of glossy sandstone blazed and dimmed, then new slabs brightened.

A pair of hawks launched themselves from a cliff rim. Bats chirped across the darkening sky, jerking through the air like hands clenching and unclenching.

The campfire snapped behind us, wafting sparks into the air. Our friends were cracking apart dead limbs for firewood. The dusky scent of burning juniper filled our nostrils. The cliff's light show was fading when we rose to join the others.

"What's THAT?" Cory gasped, pointing down the canyon toward Goblin Valley. It was a sort of UFO breaking above the end of South Temple. I didn't know at first. Then as it lifted, we saw it was the gigantic, blazing, silver rim of the full moon, rising slowly. It lifted directly over the end of the wash. First it was a great silver arc, then it expanded and floated up between the canyon walls.

A decade later, Conrad and I climbed onto the Reef and sat there at sunset. The hunting cries of two big hawks lifted from the opposite wall. They glided over the wash and landed near the end on our side. I realized they probably were the same birds Cory and I saw, or their offspring—they landed on the same lookout rock on the rim.

I sipped my wine. The breeze rustled a sheaf of crested wheat grass that grew from a crack in the gray rock beside me. The grass was like an old woman's hair moving in the breeze. It was beautiful. I thought that almost any natural thing can be beautiful, in context. If these yellow weeds are beautiful, then even stringy hair is beautiful in its own way. I caressed them.

One brilliant September night, Conrad, Karen, and I walked across South Temple to a bowl formation on the opposite wall. Conrad the Namer called this place the Amphitheater. As big as a couple of houses, its ledges and slopes give it two or three levels. Boulders cast shadows in the moonlight and icicles of sandstone hung along the face. We lay talking on the warm rock for an hour. The moon blazed so fiercely on my glasses that I had to lean my head into a shaded pothole.

Later, when I got back in my tent, I heard a sound exactly like someone rushing to me. I thought Conrad wanted to tell me something, and I popped outside. Nobody was there. I called Conrad and Karen. They were many yards away and had heard nothing.

TEMPLE MOUNTAIN

A thunderstorm rumbled above the Swell. Conrad and I ambled on the Reef surface a quarter-mile beyond South Temple, up and down rock slopes, until we were stopped by the chasm of a minor wash. The rain had already swept through, and we sat there in the moist wind staring across at the storm. On the other side of the canyon a seam in the Navajo sandstone leaked broad sheets of water. The gnarled, porous rock must have absorbed water like a sponge. It ran downhill at the surface of a harder strata and trickled out at the wash. Beyond the Reef's chimneys and ridges Temple Mountain was sailing through swift bluish and black clouds, lightning flashing to either side. That breathtaking spectacle counterbalanced my general impression of Temple as a sad, scarred hulk.

Temple Mountain furnished uranium for the Manhattan Project, which developed the first atomic bombs. At the time, this was called the Temple Mountain Mining District. Today, abandoned mines riddle the mountain's sides and base, just below a red layer of the Chinle formation.

The square black entrances are shocking, like gaps between teeth. They slobber lines of green-gray spoils. The lip above them is a thick orange shale bed. Over it, foreshortened, frowns the red and white forehead of Temple Mountain. A rickety chute dangles down the mountain near its junction with the Reef. Uranium ore once thundered down this wooden frame to big trucks. From the hard-packed look of the road and the pyramid of greenish dust not yet blown to the corners of the earth, this continues to happen. We saw two miners working nearby on a weekend.

Among the junipers, dusty levels, and sand hills near Temple are pieces of auto batteries, crushed brown cans, glittering broken glass. A rusted flywheel waits at the rim of one of the Swell's innumerable gullies. And then there are shacks of timber, squat stone buildings at mine entrances, rusted cars with fat fenders. The cars were peppered with bullet holes in the decades since the uranium boom.

From far within the Swell drivers spot the mountain's gray, crumbling spires, which look like eroded limestone. Below the pinnacles, the mountainsides show trails of white or dark gray mine spoils. Each flow has a tumble of boulders at the bottom. If a mountain could bleed, this is it.

Near North Temple Wash, Cal, some of his friends and relatives, and I drove into one of these dead mining camps, really just a couple of shacks. The larger one had lost its front. Long strips of the tarpaper had blown off the exterior, exposing yellow and red pine planks. Amid dry brown weeds lay green shingles, boards, black rags of tarpaper, insulation strips. The second hut was made of sawn logs and had a pipe chimney.

The road was edged with bulldozer tracks. Mining machinery lay everywhere, debris dumped by the nuclear tornado. A coal stove tilted on its side, the door shining with white enamel. Here was a big boiler, there a broken geiger counter, wooden crates, a brake drum, a 1950s car. Afraid of radioactive contamination, I stayed in the Jeep while Cal prowled through a gulch behind the camp. I wanted to get out of there, escape the poisonous dust. Above were the bone-colored peaks of Temple Mountain.

NORTH TEMPLE WASH

In Salt Lake City, North Temple and South Temple streets are main thoroughfares that bracket the Mormon Temple. The ragged steeples of Temple Mountain must have reminded some early prospector of that building, resulting in its name; naturally, the canyons to either side were named North and South Temple.

Where North Temple zigzags, the slanting brown walls are separated by only ten feet. Sagebrush lives on benches just above the gravel streambed, a channel that must fill with dancing waves during rainstorms. The canyon is short enough and level enough that it also serves as a driving route through the Reef.

From the wash, the cliffs seem fifty or sixty feet high with several peaks farther back, but that's an illusion. Hiking higher on the Reef, I realized North Temple is the bottom of a much greater V. It's just that from the floor we can't see beyond the nearest walls.

Near noon one mid-April day, a porcupine was moving around in a downed cottonwood just outside North Temple. The tree had recently been knocked over by a flash flood, and it clung to life. The porcupine, surrounded by cone-shaped flower clusters, flood debris, and branches, browsed on tender spring buds. Then he stopped eating, took a long look at me, and began to pick his way along a branch that was about four feet off the ground. I must have startled him, because he suddenly lost his footing and his butt dropped off the limb. He hung on with long, curving front claws while his thick back legs raked the twigs. Unable to get a foothold, he thumped onto the ground with a loud grunt and lay there a moment. Then he rolled over and waddled to a larger tree, which was still standing. He circled the trunk with his arms and climbed steadily, not stopping until he was twenty feet up. He peered at me through the red flowers, and I saw the bottom of one of his flat bearlike rear paws. His mouth was partly open, showing a ridge of upper teeth. The sun lit up a halo of hair-spines around his head.

DOORWAY WASH

This is a canyon of modern art. The north cliffs are cubist sculptures with roughly chiseled facets, harsh shadows backing each block that pops from the glassy face. To the south, the sensuous wall glows, smooth and slanting, decorated with dimples, seams, scratches. There were potholes in the shaded parts. A chalk white Henry Moore masterpiece of layered swirls is displayed in the runoff channel. It's as big as a coffee table, lounging on brown gravel and chipped stones.

Ripple rock is being formed yet, we could see that. If this flaking mud hardens, we thought, if sand fills in and preserves the water lines, someday it will be indistinguishable from the shelves of Chinle ripples all around us. And if the motorcycle tracks through here are preserved, they'll be the fossils of the future. Maybe they will be the indicators of this era, as trilobites mark the Paleozoic period for geologists. People might think the lines were left by some strange, heavy snake.

High rocks glowed the color of sunburned skin. Massive cliffs shone beyond a hillside of glistening grass and sand, and a dead juniper stood on the hill's crest. The Reef was magnificent, pink spires forming a bowl at the apex of a banded talus slope. The sun's corona blazed around the spires as I glanced at them.

In a side canyon we tracked through grasses and brush. It ended in a tight box with large pinyons and a tangle of brush, limbs, and sand hills. The air was damp from some hidden spring. We rested on slickrock before walking back to the main branch.

A cleft in the wall offered an easy route up, and we clambered onto the Reef, winding higher along the crack until we were on top. We stood among huge sandstone humps. To the east, the La Sal Mountains were covered with snow. Through a gap toward the front we saw Wild Horse Butte, eight miles away, a dark mauve pile on a purple plain. Beyond it rose the hazy blue peaks of the Henry Mountains.

The Reef was miles across. We had trouble distinguishing between its formations and the broken country of the Swell. Both were covered with junipers. Our canyon was hundreds of feet straight down. The opposite wall, which we saw at an angle, was a vertical, streaked line of cliffs. I admired four stone pillars that extended from a sandstone mound. Each pillar had a flat red cap, and they formed a straight line.

Back down in the main canyon, we found Doorway Wash was tightening. For a stretch it was filled with boulders. Then a rock slab twelve feet long tilted in the middle of the wash, with a six-foot chunk of rock wedged at the top between the slab and the canyon's side. This was the doorway that gives the canyon its name.

Sunset lit up a wall with brilliant orange-yellow tints. Another cliff seemed like some giant translucent opal with fire in its heart.

OLD WOMAN WASH

More junipers, pines, and sharp-branched sagebrush were in this canyon bottom than in any other we'd hiked. Elsewhere, the wash was rough and open, and we picked our way over rockfalls. Potholes in the white shelves held water. This was a canyon of shelves. We climbed from level to level, keeping on the lookout for pictographs that were supposed to be here. We explored side gulches, finding a toad that basked beside a natural tank. But we could not locate the rock paintings.

IRON WASH

At the entrance to the canyon a pair of coyotes hiked together. They disappeared before we could get out of the Jeep.

The flanks of Mexican Mountain, right, are shadowed late in the day, while the San Rafael Reef is bathed in light.

A natural ridge leads from one of the canyons in the Midsection.

Stark pink cliffs rise above cottonwoods at Mexican Bend.

Temple Mountain is the backdrop for remains of an old uranium mining camp near North Temple Wash.

The ruins of Smith's Cabin in the northern part of the San Rafael Reef.

A dead cottonwood leans over the San Rafael River near Mexican Mountain.

Little Spotted Wolf Canyon is narrow, short, and lavish with vegetation.

Deep within the Black Box, rare sunlight finds the San Rafael River.

Desert varnish streaks a cliff face in Wild Horse Canyon.

Conrad Bert photographing high on a wall of Crack Canyon.

The walls of Chute Canyon are a sinuous backdrop to a tiny landscape.

Barrier Canyon pictographs, probably thousands of years old, high in
Wild Horse Canyon.

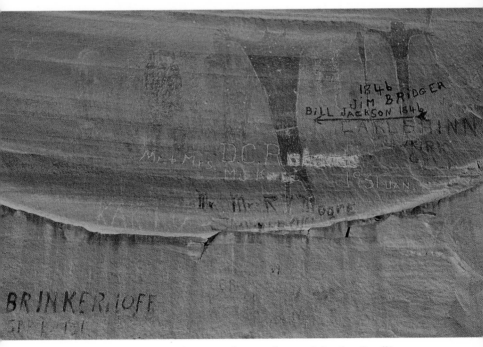

Vandals desecrated Barrier Canyon pictograph panel in the Swell's
Buckhorn Draw.

A landscape in Doorway Wash.

The darker slope of the San Rafael Swell rises from the face of the Reef in the Midsection.

A bird's nest is hidden deep within prickly brush.

A cliff wall catches the day's last light in South Temple Wash.

The rugged face of the Reef just south of Little Spotted Wolf Canyon.

Sunset makes clouds glow above the San Rafael Reef and the San Rafael River.

The moody face of the Reef near Greasewood Draw.

A cottonwood lifts its branches beside colorful walls in Crack Canyon.

Moonrise over Black Dragon Wash.

Stopping for a break in the shadow of a cliff about a mile inside the wash, I thought I heard a waterfall. This turned out to be a tiny stream gurgling over the exposed red slickrock. The canyon looked like a long box here, high walls banded with white and pink layers, the southern face bending in front of us. In the middle of the floor, through a channel in the pink sandstone, the stream splashed down cascades two or three feet high. Pools showed up, a couple of feet deep, a startling discovery in the desert. Their sides were long buckets of glistening, tawny sandstone. Stippled shadows of ripples wavered beneath clear green water.

I brought up the rear as Karen marched across a gravelly hill of cactus and sagebrush. Conrad walked before her, momentarily disappearing in the shade of a cliff face. The wall to our left was bright tan, bruised with faint purple spots of desert varnish. It was a hot day and we needed rest.

Twenty or thirty chukar partridges were inspecting some earth hills. As we approached they flew off in bunches, landing higher on the slopes.

Iron Wash opened onto the Swell. It was a rugged country of buttes and broken cliffs. Puffy white clouds hung just above a twin-peaked butte; sand dunes had collected on the lower sides. Below us, as we stood on the side of the Reef, were short grass, balls of sagebrush, a damp-looking channel, a monarch butterfly.

On the return walk Karen stopped to swim in the faint green pool. She pulled off her running shoes and socks, and plunged in clothed. Then she lounged in the end of the chute, grinning.

When we approached the Reef front, the chukars were scrabbling up a long talus slope together. They were intent on their business, making soft, chuckling calls.

STRAIGHT WASH

On a drizzly April morning, clouds filtering the sunlight, every cliff and rock displayed pastel hues. Cliff walls were like lava flows, rising above rock stairs covered with millions of pebbles. We walked through the short wash between light pink shale ridges that reached up like ramps. Some of the Mormon tea was in winter's suspension, while other bushes were green.

Going up a ridge between the Reef and the Swell, we saw our Reef as an alien land form, a mountain halved. Instead of cliffs and broken formations, it looked like a set of huge talus slopes. They were pink and gray, crowned with a small cliff face. They swept southwest for two or three miles, then appeared to be chopped off where the Reef's inner face abruptly turns south.

The Swell was streaked with lateral ridges that ran toward the Reef, dotted evenly with junipers. We climbed onto the great dome itself, finding a pool of acid green water at the bottom of a pink sandstone chute. We could not climb out of the tank and had to backtrack and work our way up another slope.

Higher, twisted outcrops were studded with rusty iron nodules; the rocks were mottled orange and dark red, and vivid green lichen colonies brightened them. We went directly down through Straight Wash, sighting along the highest outcrops on the walls. My Jeep was a square bump on the landscape.

THE REEF FACE

From Straight Wash to I-70, a little more than ten miles, the Reef becomes much thinner. Some canyon walls are only 200 to 400 feet high. The Reef is more vertical but not as imposing, with crests just 800 feet above the desert. Throughout this region, intermittent triangles of shale and earth line the Reef base, reaching a quarter of the way up.

For most of this central part, the Reef is backed immediately by the tremendous bulge of the San Rafael Swell. Looking west through Straight Wash, the Swell is a dark gray crosshatching of ridges and trees, with a flat, slanted cap. A rock shelf stands in front of the reef, its yucca, sagebrush, and flowering bushes growing in sand.

Walking toward Greasewood Draw, I saw the dark gray Reef stretch northward, shrinking in the distance like a dinosaur's tail with its humps and jagged crests. At a ridge near the draw's mouth, a post was driven into the earth. I unsnapped the cloth container nailed to the top and found a rust-stained uranium mining claim, dated eight years earlier.

Grass sheaves rustled, their shining leaves folded in the wind. Sagebrush dotted the sand hills. This beach was sand that had washed off the Reef through an eon of weathering.

GREASEWOOD DRAW

Greasewood is only a third of a mile long, so narrow I could toss a stone from one side to the other. A gravel bottom gave way to slickrock. Bright, swaying, emerald grass filled much of the draw. A section of butter-colored cliff was potholed. I walked up a slanting wall until it got too steep.

LITTLE SPOTTED WOLF CANYON

Driving south from I-70 on a dirt road, I noticed a lesser nighthawk flying just above the lumpy Reef. It perched on one of a series of brown mushroom rocks. Beyond rose a naked hill and then the Reef's pink, white, and black fins.

Half a mile farther, the entrance to Little Spotted Wolf was hidden behind a large butte. This gave me a feeling of coziness, being out of sight of any traffic that might venture on the road. I was seeking solitude to start my week's vacation in the desert. I hurried on foot toward the canyon, which turned out to be twenty minutes away over hills and escarpments. I scrambled up a ridge on the left, then down a nasty slope to reach the mouth.

Every plant was blooming—pastel prickly pear flowers, both the silky yellow and iridescent pink types; reeking sagebrush with light blue flowers; daisies that had black centers or puffy red middles; orange clusters of cuplike mallows on stems, with one or two open on each stem; a dime-sized flower that looked like a yellow-green cabbage; violet larkspurs; many unfamiliar flowers, some like little trumpets. The blossoms of one type of grass looked like large, shining globes, with many small yellow flowers growing from each globe. Even the tamarisk bore pink flowers.

Little Spotted Wolf is narrow, short, and lavish with vegetation. The opening is a slot that angles down obtusely, say 110 degrees. It carried no obvious imprint of man except the remains of a wire fence that once crossed the entrance to keep cattle out. The fence washed away long ago, all but the wire ends.

The floor is flat and clean in some places where long sections of red rock were washed bare by the floods. In others, islands of sand rise above the slickrock, host to prickly pear, flowering weeds, cottonwood bushes, trees.

Cottonwoods waved clumps of leathery leaves against a red sandstone face. The grass smelled fresh, junipers formed hedges, Mormon tea bloomed with minute gray-green roses at the elbows where the leaf scales grow. Bladderstems remained green, as crooked as sea horses.

In the mud were pronghorn antelope tracks. Water holes were awriggle with tadpoles, while water striders flickered across the surface.

Giant boulders were tumbled about the canyon. The wall stratification was in such high relief that I could have walked right up the Reef, higher and higher on ledges that ran from the floor. Maybe once I was up there past all the loose rubble, I'd walk beside the highest cliff and discover pictographs.

I heard the chattering song of cliff swallows, and the descending jejejejejeje of white-throated swifts rang in the air. I noticed a swallow's nest, a bulging mud jug below a ledge.

Dark rain craters popped into the sand. As I hiked back, a loud thunderclap rolled. At that moment, one of the little gray and white swifts folded its wings and drew magically into a hole in an overhang.

I put up my tent in the driving rain, then lay in it looking out. The rain slowed. At dusk the Reef was brightly lighted but the sky was gloomy. Tremendous peals of thunder echoed over the Swell; gusts shook my canvas walls. Then the air was calm.

In the middle of the night thunder boomed while rain rattled furiously across my roof. With every bolt the same sound was repeated over and over, but with slightly different tones. It had never occurred to me before, but the initial CRACK! must be fragmented as the shock wave travels. Sound waves divide when their spreading rings encounter air masses of different density. They don't arrive together, but because they had the same origin, they are similar. Each boom in this drumroll of thunder is the same as the other peals, only deflected, slowed or speeded. The sound must travel in pods.

A mourning dove woke me at daybreak: ooo-ah! coo, coo . . . coo. . . . A large gray-brown lizard was crawling across a flat rock that jutted near my breakfast fire. It began humping up and down. After a while, a bigger lizard showed up, a greenish skink with a coppery head. They both lifted, squatted, and extended the sacks under their throats. The bigger one moved off and the gray lizard followed it threateningly.

It was a bright, windy day. After breakfast, I hiked south along the Reef's face. A cottonwood leaf shone, a bright silver disk among the boulders in a gully. It was desiccated and burnished by the dry air, wind, and sun. A scattering of antelope dung was wet. I saw the tracks but could not spot the animal.

One of the Reef's hogbacks looked as if it were covered with cobblestones. Thousands of rounded rocks were jammed together over a large hill, then pounded into a tight mosaic. Only a few bunches of wheatgrass bristled from this armor surface. In the sand at the bottom grew high grass and a cottonwood.

The next opening in the ridge didn't go through. Nearby, a bulldozer had been prospecting for uranium, perhaps thirty years ago. It had scraped soil into a ridge, leaving tracks.

All the junipers in this area grew in hollows, because that's where the rain water collects. I walked back to camp and looked to the north. Triangles of dirt against the Reef were covered with grass so that they seemed to be green hills. I gazed at a landscape of rock rills and dead junipers. With its endless pointed slabs, the Reef looked like a row of flickering candle flames.

No canyon worth hiking opened close by in that direction, either. So I went through Little Spotted Wolf again. I sat on the slickrock in the shade just inside the entrance. Sunlight poured through the mouth and onto the stone floor. The light inched closer to my feet. Staring across an island of soil, I noticed an old graffito on the opposite wall. I walked across to it. "O. SHIT," said the faint orange writing. A crude sketch showed a bearded man wearing a bowler hat. The date, in white chalk, was 1900.

Returning to my canteen across the canyon, I lounged in the sunlit curve. Drowsing, dozing, drifting, I felt something tug at me from another time. *I was a cowboy or outlaw. I was in this can-*

yon with someone else. Terrible despair filled me because my child had been taken away. This—what?—ghost or inner fear or echo from another era—lasted only an instant.

At the end of the canyon, I climbed a long shelf, laboring up until I was high against the cliff. On the floor, junipers grew among boulders that looked pebble-sized from this height. A giant white shelf on the left swept down like a scimitar blade, craggy, with a dropoff into the Swell. The highest point of that shelf seemed to hang in the air without support from beneath.

I wondered at the force that had lifted the Reef. The Swell was a badlands of brown slopes and winding dry arroyos, speckled with rocks and junipers. The earth was gashed with runoff channels.

Back at camp, lunch was hamburgers, made from two patties that were cool despite my ice melting. White at the edge, they smelled a little too meaty. I became queasy.

The wind blew in strong intermittent puffs. Cliff swallows sang like canaries, zoomed past, buzzed my tent. They were greenish on the tops of their wings, with dark heads, buff bellies, and light patches just above the tail. Swifts blasted through, darker and larger than the swallows.

As I lay under a cottonwood tree, the giant leaves slapped and rattled and a dove cried in a lonesome voice. I played with Indian ricegrass, running my hands over the elongated seeds, watching them quiver at the ends of their dumbbells. These dumbbells were connected, making larger dumbbells, and all flowed with the motion I'd started. The hair-thin connecting twigs make the same patterns as on a pile of soap bubbles, where the globes intersect. A raven cawed, hovered, caught the currents, soared back toward the Reef.

I spent the afternoon trying to photograph flowers, waiting for the wind to die. As I knelt with camera in hand and close-up lens on, one leg outstretched, the sole of that foot would get uncomfortably hot from sunlight. A white prickly pear bloom showed the faintest tinge of yellow. A beetle with white and black stripes, painted to resemble a bee, rooted among the red stamens. A drab little bird exploded out of a blackbrush too suddenly for me to identify it. Protected far amid the bush's spines and half-opened yellow flowers was a tightly woven nest that held four eggs, shaded by an overhanging branch.

I went back to camp when the light began to weaken and the breeze became stronger. I took a siesta and waited for sunset, miserable with homesickness. The wind knocked down the front of my tent.

I thought of that wind gusting all along the Reef. Not just this cottonwood, but trees from Mexican Mountain to the Moroni Slopes were rustling. But what about that old conundrum, that if a tree falls in the forest and nobody's around to hear it, does it make a sound? Are the trees at Black Dragon Wash rustling? Sound waves are simply a particular kind of disturbance in the air, I thought. They are objective reality. Might as well ask whether the wind blows if nobody is around to feel it. That reminded me of my old ninth grade biology textbook, which reports that man is the supreme form of life. Well, who said so? And was he unbiased? Yet even as I pondered this, the tree seemed the only one in the world whose leaves were rattling.

In the evening, I ached to see another mammal, any variety. Where were the bats? They should have been out by now, I thought. They began showing up about 8:30, and then at 9:00 more came.

Realizing I was lonely and worried about my little boy, I decided to go home. I'd leave next day instead of waiting out the whole week's vacation. Terrible nightmares. I dreamed Sky was kidnapped. Cory and I were frantic, trying to figure out how to locate him. In my desperation I could only suggest that we ask the telephone operators if anyone attempted to dial a number with digits something like those of our own, or Cory's parents' number—maybe someone in another state, someone who didn't know about area codes. Area codes. I had to explain area codes. Or tell Sky he must call the operators if he's ever kidnapped. I awoke in a cold sweat, then slept again.

Next, I thought I heard a tremendous clanging, like a huge cymbal that kept reverberating. I awoke, annoyed by the faint hum of a pump filling a stock pond somewhere. Crickets were chirping and the tent was stuffy because of sunlight beating on it.

I shoved my head outside. The cottonwood's shade was delightfully cool. A breeze floated across my face. I felt I'd returned to my senses. But I went home that day anyhow.

5

The North

Around a pothole high on the Reef at Black Dragon Wash, soil crust cemented together with fungi, algae, and lichens holds moisture in, helping juniper roots find a purchase. The juniper shaded a cottontail that panted through a smothering day. Now, at midnight, a coyote tracks the rabbit. The coyote moves swiftly, yipping along the dark Reef. For the silent man who leans against the Reef, this yipping is life's true ancient song.

Never was the Reef's beauty more stunning and alien than when I flew over the ten miles between Interstate 70 and the northern end. This is a country of gaping canyons, with a river that glitters and winds tortuously. The face of the formation is as jagged as shark's teeth. Here, the Swell collapsed into benches, washes, and plateaus, so the landscape is dominated by the Reef's escarpments.

Most impressive are the Swell's exposed rock strata. The swirled lines, ridge upon naked pink ridge, merge with the Reef, forming a mind-boggling landscape that looks like a mixing bowl miles across. Layers of orange-brown frosting are crushed around the rim. Shining rock slabs and massive fragments of the upper layers are parallel tilted lines around Spotted Wolf Canyon, where I-70 goes through.

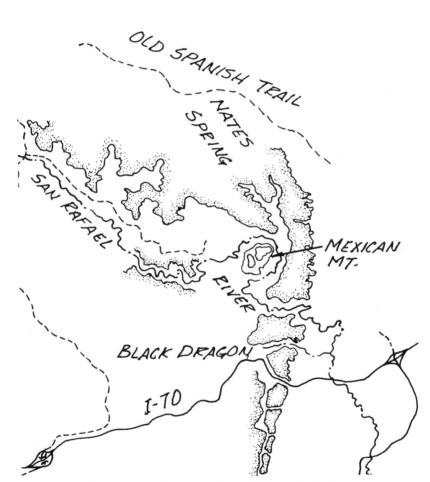

I-70 to Nates Canyon and the Old Spanish Trail.

The Reef extends enormous wedges between Spotted Wolf and Black Dragon canyons, between Black Dragon and the San Rafael River, and in a large zigzag of the river gorge itself. To the east the San Rafael Desert is a placid plain, deceptively green from here with juniper and sagebrush.

From the ground just below the freeway, the view north was amazing too. The Reef was frozen, suede-colored waves, fold after gnarled fold, with dark triangles along the base. Through its openings I could see the dingy Swell.

SPOTTED WOLF CANYON

What a letdown, then, to drive through the remains of Spotted Wolf Canyon on the interstate. The freeway completely fills it. On both sides, chestnut cliffs wear unnatural new faces created when the sandstone was blasted away. It's a new type of ripple rock embossed with the drills' vertical stippling. The polished grooves reflect sunlight.

Once through the Reef going west on I-70, you can look north along the inside of the Reef toward a magnificent panorama of slopes and strata left by ancient convulsions. In the other direction—four miles east, at the juncture of Utah Highway 24 and I-70—a turnout offers another splendid view of the Reef. During a storm, it's a purple snaggletooth ridge under gray-blue clouds. The minarets and chimneys lining the ridge are the most spectacular on the Reef.

BLACK DRAGON WASH

You seem to be going right into the living rock if you drive back on the dirt road here. Streaked, tawny walls immediately enfold the road. The entrance is a curving crack, and both sides overhang the floor. A short distance in, the walls are 500 or 600 feet of shining red-purple rock.

Just after you enter from the east, in a long alcove of the north wall a light rock face is incised with rock drawings. The most recent of these pictographs and petroglyphs were made at least 700 years ago. Others were scratched many centuries before. A few decades ago, some careless and disrespectful researcher chalked in outlines of several pictures, lumping some together. The erroneous outline seemed to form a dragon, giving the canyon its name.

Here are lines that might be counting marks, an ancient tribal census. What are these dots and slashes? Drawn hand prints, hatch marks on a stick, a sun emblem, a maze. And here are the pictographs of the modern Visigoths, initials, dates, "Della Mc."

Calvin and I camped beside the Reef above Black Dragon. That night a coyote yipped as it trotted on the Reef. What a romantic sound! It's the only wild hunting cry most of us ever hear.

Next morning we walked onto the Reef ourselves, finding it an undulating plain with dark, broad expanses of brown rock stretching upward. Chunks of red stone and blocky boulders littered it. The sunlight made the tops of domes glow pink. We peered over a terrifying overlook above Black Dragon. Desert varnish was drawn into it at an angle, dripping hundreds of feet from the smooth rim. Down the wash, a grand canyon of broken layers and ridges unfolded.

We worked our way north, walking on rock slopes and gentle ridges. A red cliff stuck above part of the Reef. Frequently we found big water pockets in the shelf, some in the midst of sand. At these, oases grew, thickets of brush and gnarled logs, junipers studded with sky blue berries, Mormon tea, sheaves of wheatgrass. Paw prints crossed the sand near the sullen brown water, and rabbit droppings were evidence of the coyote's livelihood.

Potholes often form in lines where water drains, the highest excavations of future canyons.

THE UPPER BLACK BOX

The limestone benches on both sides of the San Rafael gave little hint that between ourselves and the pink cliffs was a mighty gorge. Instead, we saw a rough landscape of sandstone castles and lower brown outcrops, junipers, rock slabs. Conrad and I were on Indian Bench, just before the road dips toward the Reef and Mexican Bend. Looking south, we gazed across the Jackass Benches on the other side of the river.

Only when we walked closer did the ground suddenly yawn. At first it was like the side of a little gulch, blending with the beige benchland. But with a few steps, we saw brown and black vertical walls drop hundreds of feet and heard the river's faint roar.

We rambled into a side canyon so we could get closer. To reach the edge, we climbed over rotted limestone ridges and boulders that were rough as popcorn.

The snorting, greenish brown San Rafael filled the bottom of this tremendous gash. The crumbly walls looked almost close enough to jump, maybe only ten feet apart in places. We leaned over and saw mud flats where the river went around bends. Large rock piles cluttered the channel. In most places, the walls were slate black with desert varnish. Their light streaks were the few spots not yet stained. It was a lifeless chasm except for grasses that sprouted from ledges beneath the rim.

The rim of the canyon's opposite wall was a sloping, greenish lip that fell away into black vertical facets. Beyond it, as high as our bench, junipers grew on miles of exposed rock.

Conrad sat crosslegged on a flat-topped pillar at the edge of the chasm. It was undercut sharply. A spray of grass grew from a mound of cryptogamic soil beside him, and tongues of white rock stuck from the pillar's sides. He sat with the sun bright on his silver hair, a contrast to the background of ebony cliff walls.

We threw rocks into the flat water, pitching them carefully toward the opposite wall, delicately because if we threw too hard they'd hit the cliff and fly off in the wrong direction. If we tossed them too gently, they'd sail out of sight under wall projections. Thrown accurately, they hit the water in four seconds —that meant 500 feet. A white peak popped up. Then we heard the echoing splash.

Downstream, we saw a green ridge formation where the river swung to the right. Past this, the cliffs and talus near the Reef were salmon colored. A spire caught the sunlight on the face of the curving wall.

Indian Bench turned out to be one of our most scenic camping spots. Lichens with lavender buds grew on the castellated soil crust.

At sunset a coyote yipped and yodeled over by Black Dragon Wash. It stopped abruptly and did not resume howling. A massive cliff directly ahead, the smaller cone of Mexican Mountain's peak, a slice of the Reef—all were painted reddish orange. Formations in front cast sharp shadows on the larger ones behind. To our left, a cliff was glistening with crimson light.

THE SAN RAFAEL RIVER

"I'm afraid I'll roll."

"If you do, you won't go far," said one of the environmentalists we'd met on this dirt road between the San Rafael campground and Mexican Bend. We were just beyond the Upper Black Box overlook, and the impromptu road tilted crazily here.

"Just pop a beer, shut your eyes, and go for it," offered a second.

Frozen to the wheel, I started down. The environmentalists —young men, wives, and kids—waited by the curve. I thought I saw some looking apprehensively at the Jeep. I backed and got out for a look. I didn't like it.

We were on a trail swinging in a long loop around a place that seemed washed out. I later learned that the main road was graded by Emery County and that the county crews had put in a culvert at a drainage spot. The Bureau of Land Management ordered the county to rip out its improvements because they intruded into a wilderness study area. When the county pulled the culvert, this left a gap. Erosion accelerated and the road washed out. The detour looked impassable by vehicles with more than two wheels. The tracks wound across barren brown hills.

Now came the worst spot: a dip high on a hillside where the road tilted sharply above the desert and started up a ridge. Heading up, the Jeep's left side would be far higher than the right. Fifteen feet off my right shoulder loomed hard earth, the gully, brush and boulders. I kept it in low gear, gunned the engine as I rounded the curve. Conrad cheered. Our new friends looked relieved when I pulled up beside their pickups.

We jimmied past a huge flat boulder and then we were rolling into Mexican Bend. Across the sparkling river loomed the
pyramid called Mexican Mountain. The San Rafael was a muddy
stream maybe 60 feet across, gurgling as it sliced through the
desert. Tamarisk and cottonwoods lined the sides above riffles,
and cows had made heavy deposits on the stream bank. I
stopped within sight of the Reef, got out, and walked to a high
sand hill. I squatted a second, then lay shaking on the hot, fine
sand. The Reef was a solid wall that veered to the left. The
stream sparkled by sand and gravel benches and ranks of bright
green tamarisk. It danced past a field of yellow wildflowers and
a dead cottonwood on a bluff. In the lighting that hour, the Reef
was dark magenta, a wall with huge convex sections and a
jagged top.

I was grateful to be alive.

On another trip, we walked barefooted across the San
Rafael, carrying shoes and cameras. The water was fast and
quickly slid above our knees. Glittering ripples raced away from
a line of rocks. The river was milky blue, and the ragged cliffs
beyond were dark purple above tamarisk. At the other side, I
struggled from a pool and onto a mud flat, searching for a way
onto the bank, quickmud sucking at my feet. I worked my way
up the slick muddy bank. Here were huge cottonwoods, some
gnawed in half by beavers. A dead tree lay on the ground, its
fractured trunk raised upon the pointed stump.

Back in camp that evening, we settled onto a bluff, watching
sunset's shadows move across trees and a natural pastureland.
The side of Mexican Mountain was in shade while the Reef's
angles were red. Mackerel-scale clouds reflected the glow, a
field of pink and silver scallops. Distant sheet lightning
flickered.

Next day, fierce biting blackflies and mosquitoes drove us
out before breakfast.

SPRING CANYON

Spring Canyon opens up parallel to the Reef on its inside
curve, at Mexican Bend. Just before its mouth are room-sized
boulders and slabs that tumbled from the cliffs. A thousand

years ago, Fremont Indians chipped wonderful designs into their dark desert varnish: three kings or gods holding hands, one on the end lifting his left hand in greeting. They have trapezoidal torsos, faces like buckets with little horns on top and slit eyes, loincloths and straps. Another panel shows two hands reaching from the rock's broken edge. There are abstract designs—a circle within a circle with a horizontal line through the smaller disk—a sea slug creature, a lizard with wavy legs.

When we visited on the first day of March, a spring was frozen a short distance within the canyon. The clear water was free of ice at the edges. Sunlight caught on Vs of ice spars radiating out from the frozen part as I walked around it. A broken cattail stalk stuck from the lumpy white crust, its white fuzz heaped on the ice. A stream seemed out of place in this desert. An iron black cliff. Plates of red rock along a spinelike formation.

Bumpy Road Arch, a short way past the spring, is an impressive span shaped like the arm of the Creator in the Sistine Chapel painting, except that the wrist points upward.

An elongated white hillock filled a gully in a shady stretch of the canyon—snow, we thought. But when we walked on it, we found it was compacted by freezing and thawing until it was solid ice. A cow and her calf wandered away from us here, going uphill through the bare trees.

NATES CANYON

In mid-August, on a day the temperature reached 104 in Green River, I walked alone into Nates Canyon. I left our camp above the Upper Black Box at 9:17 a.m. The round trip was twelve miles and took more than nine and a half hours. I carried a heavy canteen, a rolled map, camera gear, a Coke, three bagels, and a small can of tuna.

Nates is the northernmost of the San Rafael Reef canyons. Where Spring Canyon angles off toward the west, Nates continues straight along the Reef. The Reef's sandstone forms its eastern side.

Water holes shimmered in Spring Canyon, alive with tadpoles, water striders, and cattails. Bumpy Road Arch was pale in the bright sky. Beyond it, I crossed a brown trickle on a mat of reeds. Later, reeds caught at my feet as I slogged through a dry streambed.

Dense heat forced me to rest often—sometimes every fifteen or twenty minutes. Lying beneath a rock ledge or cottonwood trees, I'd ration out gulps of hot water and keep an eye on my watch, counting the minutes before I had to hike again. My two pairs of threadbare socks were creasing into the soles of my feet. The right ankle seemed to be slightly injured; it rubbed on the boot. Oppressive, still air floated above white rocks.

Finally in Nates, I scrambled across fields of boulders and admired a rounded pinnacle that reached partly up one wall. A glob of sandstone balanced on top of it. Across the way, the opposite cliff was cubelike chunks, chalky ridges, and layers striped pink and white. The terrain was getting rough. The walls were slowly drawing toward each other but gave no promise of closing together soon.

I ate lunch in a side canyon where white streaks fifteen feet above the floor indicated a tremendous volume of flood water. Every scent was exaggerated—the fine, dry silica of huge boulders, the offensive tuna oils, the green lush smells of plants.

I tried to ignore the soft throbbing in my temples. But I could not pretend away the severe soreness of my right knee, which hurt from bouncing down rock falls. I went over ledges to avoid pour points, and staggered onto hills among prickly pear and thick knots of claret cup cactus. The canyon was a jumble of rocks and brush. A soft ground crust slowed me up. I usually tried to stay off cryptogamic soil and hopped over stretches of it, but in my weariness I did not always bother. I worried about the aching in my buttocks and hips, thinking this might be a symptom of heat exhaustion. It was gone when I took a break, but in twenty minutes the pain would return. I kept replenishing the gooey white sun screen on my nose, cheeks, and forehead. The cream seemed to evaporate in moments. So I walked with head down, keeping the sun off my face. This was turning out much worse than I had imagined, and I considered quitting.

Then I went around a bend and found the end of the canyon, as far as it can be negotiated on foot. At first, I was simply glad this was all. Then I realized it was the most beautiful place I'd ever found.

The back wall formed a semicircle thirty feet high, where runoff wore out the lower canyon from solid sandstone. Everything flowed south from there. Although Nates continued at a higher level for a mile or more—I could see a high butte, looming beyond this pour point, that looked like the side of a huge tanker ship sailing away—this was as far as I could go. Only a helicopter, or a skilled rock climber, could explore beyond.

Ahead, the tall cubical layer that stretched along both sides of the canyon bowed across. This tan rock was cracked, and stained black and purple. A glassy ringlike indentation made part of it look like it had been terrifically compressed. At the pour point, vibrant streaks of desert varnish showed how water streams down during a shower, creating the canyon.

Below this layer a stretch of slickrock folded upward from the wide floor. Where the chute climbed to the blocky layer, it was like the clean, white, scoured end of a bathtub. It widened toward me, walls smooth with little potholes, layered white and pink. In places the texture was fine-grained, while on other knobs it was as brittle as the marrow cells of an old bone.

My heart sang with the clean sweep of the sandstone. I was glad I had found the courage to push on.

Crossing the canyon and working my way around a deep depression where plants grew in a pothole, I climbed boulders, once ducking through a hole under a chunk. The walls drew toward each other. I reached to touch both at the same time, and a big fly landed on my outstretched right index finger. For an instant I felt its legs gently gripping my fingertip and I flung my hand, startled, yelping. It disappeared. Reaching the very end, I stretched my arms up the smooth stone, and my feet slipped in the sand at the bottom. Then I sat in the chute admiring the canyon.

A deeper gully led away across the slickrock floor, and a trickle mark wound through the bottom. This opened on the pothole garden. Vivid green tamarisk filled the pothole's far end, while closer to me, reeds stood just before a crescent of black water.

Without my realizing it, the shadows had moved, filling the narrows. My shirt was plastered to my chest. I took off all my clothes and lay in the tawny rocks, loving the canyon. This was a comfortable place: the Reef was warm against my back, the shade a blessing. A cool breeze suddenly played across my body. It blew around me and down the canyon. Naked, I photographed a pool close to the end. Reflecting from the rim, twin golden humps of sandstone shone in the depths.

THE REEF'S END

Along the outer curve, the last five miles are an unpretentious ridge. Driving northeast on dirt ruts, searching for the final outcrop, we watched the Reef flatten. The crest is only a few hundred feet above the Green River Desert. Heat and dust assailed us. The road wandered across flats, tilted on the edge of a clay embankment, passed a prairie dog colony where a rodent stood guard. It made its way around the sides of shale buttes, then swung by a deserted settlement called Smith's Cabin. We were near a water hole—at least our maps showed one around somewhere. But we couldn't find it.

One hundred and thirty years ago, this was Green River Spring, a major watering stop on the Spanish Trail. Maybe the explorers found it because cottonwoods grew there; maybe the mule trains did not miss it because the desert keeps its tracks for many decades. Now it was an unused ranch of three or four log buildings with tin roofs and torn screens, the wood silvering in the sun's bleaching light. Scattered around were cow flop, stumps, drunken log fences, big cottonwoods, sawn stumps, stacks of squared timber. A dirt road headed toward a corral. Beyond it was a wooden wagon and then the low Reef.

Many stretches of the Reef at this remote northern terminal wear the same brown overcoat as the Moroni Slopes. The crust is broken by light channels that turn out to be box canyons. Where the Reef's white knobs of Navajo sandstone stand above the desert, they look like stone hills.

We lunched on the rim of the last box canyon, musing down at the deep gash in the sandstone. Not much shade at the bottom. The sun was baking a bike trail that snaked among juniper brush, cliffs, and rock walls. The sandstone was white, gray, and light brown. A darker strata near the top caught my eye.

Conrad and I hiked into the last canyon. The sandy floor reflected heat and drew strength from our limbs. In a white, airless hell of sand and scrub brush, we hunched beside boulders for their shade. A few musty-smelling caves in the cliffs were half-filled with rubble, dust and guano.

Then we drove to the end of the Reef, passing a prairie dog. A mile or two north, we discovered what seemed to be traces of the Spanish Trail. Ruts worn into the ground through years of horse and cattle caravans stretched across the desert west of the Reef. Blurred by weathering, the trail was a slender, pink path snaking through the browns and greens of cheat grass, sagebrush, and Mormon tea. Four or five feet wide, unused for more than a century, it was a testimony to the slowness of the desert to heal. It was barren of plants, and still headed purposefully toward the valley where the Reef ends.

We drove on through a region of brush-covered hills and barren red bluffs. To the west, Navajo sandstone domes rose above the treeless crest. Bushes grew from their lower levels. The ridge sometimes lifted into minor buttes.

Finally, we hiked into the edge of a flat valley waving with brown grass—Cottonwood Wash, which passes between the Reef and Cedar Mountain. Large, twin-base power poles marched through it. Across the valley was a cliff of high, purplish Morrison layers below a rubble stratum of sandstone. Pink talus slopes rose against it in waves, sometimes almost as high as those far-off cliffs.

The Reef leading to the valley was a ridge of rolling shelves and buttes, none of them high. It has grassy sides, a white-walled drainage gully in front, and a couple of dark rock layers toward the top. It would be easy to walk up. The northern slope reaches into Cottonwood Wash. This is the last of the Reef.

6

Prehistoric Cultures

In South Temple Wash, a large pictograph panel has been hacked up and carved with initials. A shaman or a god with horns—a being who probably looked like a devil to some devout modern oafs—has been peppered with sixteen bullet holes. The panel overlooks the canyon from a cliff, and once lent a feeling of supernatural dignity to a hilly, sandy spot on state land. A deep cleft before the sandstone wall and some large old junipers made the spot a favorite place for picnickers and campers.

In the summer of 1984 an oil and gas exploration company operating under state lease bulldozed the ground before the panel. Huge piles of dirt and gaping pits were left everywhere. Later that year, the company performed its required rehab work, smoothing the piles. Now the chipped purple shamans and potbellied deer look down on a dead zone of brown, tire-tracked dirt, bare ridges and knolls.

Dry air and the protection of sheltering ledges preserve rock paintings for a long time. That fellow with the horns guarded South Temple Wash for fifteen or twenty centuries before an art critic showed up with a rifle, before metal monsters tore at the earth itself.

Although people have made a living in the Reef since the end of the last Ice Age, they left scant signs of their presence. A broken spear point shines in the gravel of a canyon bottom; pictographs high on alcove walls show up as distant lines glimpsed by hikers.

Jesse E. Warner, a Salt Lake City man who is a noted amateur expert on pictographs, undertook a project to search the Reef canyons for prehistoric rock art. Whenever he came upon an unknown panel, he said, adrenalin pumped through his body.

Ancient paintings and weapons have been found in several of the Reef's canyons. Exactly how old most are, nobody knows. Some Fremont Indian pictographs can be dated by similar art unearthed at Fremont villages. For others we can only guess. But the succession of styles is clear, as a few pictographs were actually painted over earlier works. Many seem to mark some vital resource, like water tanks or pinyon-nut gathering grounds. "Some of the symbols would probably indicate the nearby presence of sacred sites," said Asa S. Nielson, an archaeologist at Brigham Young University, Provo, Utah.

What were these people like? We will never know much about them, but certainly their lives were as tough and as uncertain as those of the cottonwoods that crouch in the canyons, braced against the flash floods that blast through. They were as fully rounded as we—thrifty, stupid, lusty, industrious, lazy, or heroic. They suffered diseases for which they had no remedy. During the spring and early summer, they could not escape the biting insects. When they fell from cliffs, no painkiller eased their agony, no casts helped their bones knit. When a band of hunters walked quickly through Wild Horse Canyon with spears on their shoulders, hoping to find water in potholes near the top of a steep formation, they were not hiking for pleasure. Life must have been desperate and dangerous.

"The problem with San Rafael is it doesn't receive much attention," said Utah's state archaeologist, David Madsen. "There're some sites recorded, a little bit of survey work. . . . From what little we do know, it seems that the area was basically an area where they were hunting and collecting wild plants and animals." Ancient people traveled the Reef's canyons on seasonal migrations to pine nut collecting areas in the Swell or to follow herds of big animals. Madsen thinks trade routes probably wound through Spotted Wolf Canyon, where Interstate 70 has been built. They were there for the same reason I-70 is: "It's the easiest way to get through the canyons."

In November 1984 Abajo Archaeology found evidence of extremely early occupation. Experts working for Abajo, a private consulting archaeology company based in Bluff, southern Utah, were walking through a survey for an oil and gas seismographic company eight miles south of the town of Green River and seventeen miles east of the Reef. Lying on the surface of an open bench that overlooks the Green River was an unmistakable Folsom spearhead: a projectile point ten thousand years old. The classic Folsom point is a finely chipped tool, one to three inches long with an indented base that ends in tiny "ears." It is leaf-shaped and fluted on both sides. The grooves run the length of the point. In addition to the point, the surveyors found worked stone chips, scrapers, and borers on the bench, which measured 500 by 600 feet. That proved the site was a camp, making it more significant than the isolated Folsom points that had been found before in Utah. This was the earliest settlement ever discovered in the state.

The next month, Abajo sent eight or nine volunteers to the sandstone shelf, which is about 350 feet from the Green River. They spent four days collecting all the artifacts. More than a thousand Folsom artifacts were discovered, including two points. Abajo's director, William E. Davis, said the shelf may have been a hunting lookout where several families, perhaps a band, camped repeatedly.

At one time the sandstone may have been covered with small dunes and grasses. Over the millennia the sands drifted or were blown away. Meanwhile, the first towns were settled in the Jericho Valley, Egypt rose to splendor, the Roman empire collapsed. The Folsom artifacts were exposed on the rocks.

These nomads must have splashed across the shallow river on their migrations after mammoths, camels, horses, ground sloths, tapirs—Pleistocene creatures now extinct in North America. The logical crossing, as now, would have been within sight of the Reef. Since this was probably a grassland then, they could have wandered after herds through the Reef's canyons, where streams flowed all year. I can imagine them marveling at the beautiful, sheer walls. Cliff ledges and alcoves offered spots where they could ambush game. Using spears tipped with those elegant stone points, they may have caused America's first environmental disaster. Overhunting was probably the downfall of the long-horned *Bison antiquus* that disappeared about 10,000 years ago.

Not much is known about the Reef's next inhabitants, Barrier Canyon people of the Archaic Culture. But while a Folsom presence can only be surmised, Barrier Canyon paintings are scattered throughout the San Rafael region. If recent speculations are correct, they may be some of the earliest art in the Western Hemisphere. The panels might date back nearly 9,000 years. "Most of the pictographs we've been finding in the Reef are Barrier Canyon," said Jesse Warner, former president of the Utah Rock Art Research Association.

Art of this style also shows up on cliffs in Colorado and Arizona. "The San Rafael Reef is just part of that whole area where those paintings occur. They're part of that whole complex," says Polly Schaafsma, research associate at the Museum of New Mexico, Santa Fe. She is an expert on southwestern pictographs, and her books and scientific articles are standards.

The Barrier Canyon style of rock painting is named after large semiabstract pictographs in Horseshoe Canyon, about twenty-five miles southeast of the Reef, a place that was once called Barrier Canyon. The Great Gallery panel in Horseshoe Canyon is a cliff covered with well-preserved paintings of gods and animals and supplicating people, some eight feet tall. It's intact because a special district of Canyonlands National Park, separate from the rest, was established to protect it.

Barrier Canyon panels in the Reef are at South Temple Wash, Wild Horse Canyon, Straight Wash, Old Woman Wash, and Short Canyon. Many have been vandalized.

The paintings show long, tapering human forms, sometimes with basketlike heads; supplicating snakes with arms; animals, often with bands through their bodies; insect people; rain clouds. By Barrier Canyon times the climate was similar to ours, and rain must have been vital to the desert tribes.

The desecrated panel in South Temple Wash is mainly in the Barrier Canyon style. It is seventy feet across, its color ocher verging on purple. There are animals, footprints, and a larger figure that looks like a sailor with a parrot on one broad shoulder.

Warner said rock art students have dubbed animals that accompany human figures on pictograph panels "companion animals." Similar animal symbols have been used in hunting magic by Indians observed in historic times, he said.

The "parrot" on the big guy's shoulder is actually the head of an elongated Barrier Canyon figure over which the larger design was painted. It's hard to tell the style of the bigger painting, because some of it has broken away, but it is darker and possibly from the later Fremont Culture. Yet another overlay was scratched onto the sailor-with-parrot paintings: "GL 79."

The shot-up "devil" to the left of the other pictures is certainly Fremont.

In 1975 Chase Tessman, then eight years old, found a wonderful spear point on the canyon's north side, the same side as the pictographs. Four inches long, it was made of pigeon-blood agate—a crystal that is milky in some places, clear in others, and spotted throughout with red drops that look like specks of blood within the rock. It had delicate flaking. The point tapered toward the end, which was chipped off. The day he found it, I scoured the same talus slopes without luck.

The snake symbol is found all over the Reef, wherever the Barrier Canyon people went. It is usually shown as causing rain. An elaborate Rain God pictograph in this style is one of several rock paintings in the Swell's Head of Sinbad area, just north of I-70, so close to the freeway that you see traffic whizzing by from the cliff. In this purplish painting, the Rain God stands in air, arms stretched straight out, pointing to either side, where clouds pour rain. Water streaks down, dripping to below his feet. A snake with its tongue flicking crawls toward a symbol just above the god's bug-eyed head. To the left, a doe faces the rain, praying. Her arms and legs are in a human posture, so maybe it's a shaman in doe costume. Nearby, a tall humanoid with moth antennae holds a snake in one hand. Above and below the snake are four circle symbols with lines coming from them—much like Aztec drawings of a sacrificed human heart pumping blood.

Barrier Canyon pictographs were once thought to date from about 500 B.C. to A.D. 500. Today, some scientists suspect they may be far earlier because of excavations at Jim Walters Cave and Cowboy Cave, carried out in 1975 by a team of University of Utah archaeologists led by Jesse D. Jennings.

Shelter caves in the Navajo sandstone, they are on the north fork of a dry, nameless tributary of Spur Fork Canyon, which runs into Horseshoe Canyon's Barrier Creek six miles beyond the caves. Walters and Cowboy caves are about twelve miles from the Great Gallery, measuring along the canyon bottoms. A seep trickles from the sandstone wall 540 yards south of Cowboy Cave, the only permanent water in this side canyon. Twice as far away to the north is a deep pothole, which holds several hundred gallons after every downpour.

The caves apparently served as seasonal seed-gathering stations, rather than permanent homes. Plant remains show the vegetation was similar to that of the present, back 11,000 years ago: pinyon and juniper. Perennial stream flows seem to have occurred as late as 7000 B.C., when the climate was wetter.

Sifting through the undisturbed dust and debris on the cave floor, archaeologists unearthed three levels of human habitation in Cowboy Cave, each separated by many centuries when the cave was not used. Layers of the rubbish of everyday life accumulated from approximately 5625 B.C. to 4400 B.C.; from 1685 B.C. to 1380 B.C.; and from A.D. 60 to 455.

Jennings's crew discovered that people began using Walters Cave a thousand years before anyone found shelter in Cowboy Cave.

Dating was determined by measuring the decay rate of the radioactive carbon that all plants and animals absorb during life. Researchers were able to calculate the age of yucca fiber sandals, twigs shaped into animal effigies, charcoal from fire pits, and a bag of corn dropped in A.D. 395. The earliest dates have a possible error of plus or minus eighty years, while the later ones are more certain.

In Cowboy Cave, they discovered 144 unfired clay objects. Most were cast-off bits used in making figurines, but 29 were shaped into anthropomorphic figures. Most came from the two most recently inhabited layers. The oldest clay objects—which did not look a lot like the paintings—were around 6,500 years old.

But in Walters Cave, archaeologists uncovered what might have been the Rosetta Stone of Barrier Canyon pictographs. Its shape and decorations were exactly the same as many of the pictographs in the Great Gallery. Without much doubt, the people who made the figurine were the same artists who painted the Great Gallery—the very type of the Barrier Canyon pictographs.

Polly Schaafsma said an association possibly exists between the paintings and early clay figures. "The figures typologically are just like the paintings," she said. "The figurines suggest the paintings are older than we previously thought." She is quick to point out that extremely early dates are not proven for the pictographs.

The suggestion of great antiquity comes from what Jennings's report calls a "provenience clouded, but possibly correct": the Walters Cave figurine was discovered next to a sandal 8,875 years old. The sandal's age was determined through radiocarbon dating. Jennings concluded the figurine's association with the sandal may be suspect. Walters Cave was plundered by illegal relic hunters. Remains might have been jumbled from different occupation layers. Even if the sandal and figurine were made by the same people, archaeologists can't prove it. A raider would not dig up a sandal or a figurine and deliberately leave it there—let alone, abandon both. But archaeologists know that during a fast, illegal hunt for pots, shovelfuls of earth and artifacts can be slung around carelessly. Small, overlooked artifacts could be dumped together. So while we may assume that the figure and the sandal were associated and the paintings truly are 8,800 years old, we cannot state it as a certainty.

The greedy pothunters not only looted artifacts. They stole our chance to know the age of paintings throughout the San Rafael country, Horseshoe Canyon, and elsewhere in the Southwest.

Walking through Wild Horse Canyon with Conrad and Karen Bert, a mile or two in from the northern end, I noticed a purple glint among the sand and gravel. In the midst of criss-

CONRAD 84

crossing motorcycle tracks lay a broken spear point. It was a flat piece of agate, covered with slanting purple and gray stripes. Held to the sunlight, it shone with translucent yellows and reddish streaks and bubbles. About a third of the sharp end was missing. Most of one fluke was broken off. The remaining ear, both side notches, and the center were all that remained.

I have it here as I write. It's an inch and a quarter long, just over an inch wide at the shoulders, tapering, never as much as a quarter-inch thick. Sighting along its edges, I estimate it was once almost twice as long.

Who lost the weapon? Maybe a hunter hurled his spear at a rabbit and missed, the point breaking on slickrock. Perhaps he carried a collection of spare dart tips and this one slipped from his pouch as he trotted up a sand dune.

A fine Barrier Canyon panel is hidden in the same canyon, a mile or two upstream from the place where I found the purple spear point. I noticed it while hiking alone on a broiling day while my friends rested in the shade of an overhanging cliff.

Tiny straight lines seemed etched on the rock high above the floor, in an alcove near the top of a cliff.

I climbed up a line of massive boulders that had tumbled from above and stopped on a less inclined part of the cliff. At the top of this, I had to work my way back toward the alcove, around a projecting corner I crept, and up loose rocks at the apex of a smooth, steep sandstone wall that dropped off scores of feet. The cave went back only ten feet or so, and I had to stoop to get inside. Slabs lay on the floor and against the crumbly chinle pillars. A low rock wall seemed to be outlined on the dusty floor.

The lines I saw from the ground were three tall pictographs, the largest of about fifteen ocher and white paintings, all in the Barrier Canyon style. That was a spooky feeling, looking at those ancient paintings high in a lonely canyon.

Many of the paintings have bloody themes. Perhaps sacrifices were made to the Rain God, as this shrine is near several tanks that fill with water after a downpour. Toeholds are carved in the cliff wall above one of them.

The three big pictographs are close together, the longest figure in the center. He sports a pair of antennae, with eight matching balls along each antenna. A set of white dots runs along one of the antennae, possibly an outline painted over later with the ocher that makes up the rest of this figure. To his left, a figure has blood or roots shooting from his feet and one hand. Or he may be holding a bleeding snake. The figure on the right has two strings of white dots extending from his head, a wide body with big spaces between his sides and the swath of color that defines the center of his torso. Another looks like a mosquito man with a long tail. Crossing the tail is a snake that kinks near a man with either a loincloth or blood flying from both hips.

Nearby looms a large ocher and white figure with a round head. The body is defined in four streaks. Dots to his left shower down rain. A horned snake with arms supplicates before the larger figure. Venom or tears spray from the snake's face and six little people dance below the snake. Two, who wear a lot of decorative white dots on their chests, hold hands. Two others seem to be women with scraggly hair and white breasts.

Another snake figure, its head dripping, stands in an upright position. He not only has arms but tiny feet to prop him up. Yet another figure holds a clublike object. It could be a stick, a thick snake, or a bow.

Deep scratches were gouged through some of the pictographs. The lines were ancient, as faded as the walls. Perhaps the Rain God failed and the Barrier Canyon people defaced him. Or maybe the artist scoured the wall to make it smooth for his figures, and the pigment later flaked away from his scratches.

One of the six dancing figures is a man with a feather or pigtail in his hair. It had been attacked by an imbecile with a saw. The defacer gave up before he could pry it off.

In Black Dragon Wash, an alcove of light rock at the bottom of hundreds of feet of vertical sandstone shelters the pictograph "dragon" that gives the canyon its name. Jesse Warner and his wife, Judith, discovered that an earlier researcher had chalked in the outlines of what he thought was a single rock painting. "This site is a prime example of several of the major evils of chalking," the Warners wrote in a paper presented at a 1985 rock art symposium.

The dragon really is a collection of several unrelated Barrier Canyon designs: two quadrupeds, two vertical snakes, two human figures with outstretched arms, and a large horizontal snake with open jaws.

The Basket Maker people apparently left designs in Black Dragon Wash too. These abstractions, painted below the Barrier Canyon panels, probably date from the time of Christ to A.D. 500. They include hundreds of dots and lines arranged in groups, hatch marks, bear paws (or maybe thumbless human hands), concentric circles, a sunlike emblem, a big stalk of grass with grain. Many are outlined with chalk, undoubtedly so they would show up better in photographs.

Remains from the early days used to be more abundant in Black Dragon than most other parts of the Reef. Years ago, a Green River man found many artifacts there, including human bones and pottery. He carried the bones out in a five-pound coffee can and put them on display in a barber shop. A dentist said the teeth showed the people were full grown, and local folks who looked at the bone fragments decided the ancient ones were only two or three feet tall. Maybe they were wrong about the size of the Indians' skeletons—but they have always known uranium. Many prospected during the atomic boom that started in the 1940s. With their geiger counters handy they found that the pots' decoration of yellow paint was radioactive uranium ore.

The Fremont culture is represented by a few paintings and petroglyphs in the Reef. Dating from the end of the Basket Maker phase to around A.D. 1300, the Fremont style is more naturalistic than earlier designs. Some clay figurines uncovered at central and southern Utah sites are distinctly Fremont. Pictographs from these times often represent people as trapezoidal, with headdress and chicken feet. Sometimes they're decorated with dots. Farther north, more detailed Fremont pictures show people wearing jewelry.

The Fremonts—named for the Fremont River hundreds of years after their demise—were geographically and stylistically close to the Anasazi, the sophisticated people whose culture included the cliff dwellers of Mesa Verde. Probably both groups evolved from the Basket Makers; at the boundaries of their ranges, the distinctions blurred.

Fremont people made pottery and built masonry homes, but not as skillfully as their relatives, the Anasazi. But they too lived in towns, and some Fremonts raised corn, squash, and beans. They ranged generally north of the Anasazi, reaching as far as present Salt Lake City. Both Anasazis and Fremonts disappeared from the region around A.D. 1300, probably driven out by a thirty-year drought.

The Fremonts built pit houses, communal dwellings, and granaries. A town of 108 houses, located twenty-five miles southwest of Richfield, Utah, was excavated in 1984 as part of the I-70 construction project. Researchers found thousands of artifacts—arrowheads, jewelry, a fertility statue, bowls, jugs, awls of hard coal, shells from the Pacific Coast, and metates for grinding wild seeds and cultivated vegetables.

"They were amazingly adaptive to the local environment," said Brigham Young University's Asa Nielson, who excavated the site. "Whatever it took to survive, they did. In some places they irrigated, in other places they diverted, and in other places they didn't farm at all. We're finding more and more they were a very diversified people." He said many pictographs and petroglyphs may have been used for hunting magic. "They were also used to tell histories and travels."

Today vandals threaten the San Rafael's ancient works of art. At Buckhorn Draw, in the Swell near the Reef's northernmost extension, a huge Barrier Canyon panel has been savaged. Dozens of names and dates have been scrawled and gouged across this excellent panel: "1846 Jim Bridger Jim Jackson 1846" say modern letters in black paint crossing a small purple batman. Someone wrote his name, then chipped it off. Under that is scratched in the sandstone "1931 Jan." "DCR" is scratched over a faint reddish ghost, next to a batman with little horns whose hands are raised threateningly. Maybe he'll get whoever did this crime.

I hope so.

7

The Spanish Trail

The Utes who fish at the Seedskeedee's crossing could hear the caravan coming a long way off, once it swung around the Reef and approached the river. They are always alert for a chance to beg or intimidate travelers out of food and mirrors, knives, or gunpowder, and now they wait at the crossing.

Dust clouds stirred up by the animals hang in the hot air in front of Stone House Lands, the Reef, a blue-gray wedge with knobs on top. The Utes hear the bawling and trampling of cattle. As the caravan draws closer, they listen to faint yells of vaqueros and a distinct clatter of muskets knocking against stirrups.

Soon the caravan splashes across the broad brown river, a hundred long-horned cattle bellowing, swimming with the whites of their eyes showing and their heads tossing. Herders slash at them with whips from the backs of plunging horses. Nine terrified Indian boys and girls—slaves—go across on mules, hanging onto the heavy wooden pack saddles, swollen hands bound tight together with rawhide. Once over, the children slide off to stand on the sagebrush hills, soaked.

The Utes hesitate to beg from such a large caravan. Better hunch warily on the bank's rock shelves and watch. Mexicans adjust the pack mules' girths, slam bundles upright, gulp from wooden canteens, count the children once again. These are men with mud streaked on their tooled leather jackets and sombreros tilted back on their heads and sweat glistening on their dark faces, men whose curving sabers slap their legs and whose spurs leave scratches in the dirt. The Mexicans remount, whistle, shout, wave their hats. Eastward they herd the cattle. Horses jingle, puffs of dust rise from the hoofs. The slaves stagger forward, coughing.

That's where most of the early history of the San Rafael country took place, where the Spanish Trail swung around the Reef just before the crossing of the Green River. Scenes like this happened from the 1830s through the 1850s.

But a kind of pseudohistory begins many years before with explorers who never saw the San Rafael Swell. The nine members of an expedition led by Spanish priests Francisco Atanasio Dominguez and Silvestre Velez de Escalante crossed a river in west-central Colorado on September 5, 1776. This "abundant" river, which had many stones in its bed, they named the San Rafael. The Ute Indians called it the Reddish River, the priests noted in their journal. Today, the Spanish translation of the Utes' name for that river is the one by which we know it: the Colorado. Somehow, travelers misapplied the Spaniards' name to the river that cuts through the Swell and the Reef.

The Spanish Trail was a 1,200-mile trade route that once reached from Santa Fe to Los Angeles. The trail's ghost remains in the form of tracks etched into the Green River Desert where it headed for the end of the Reef.

The trail did not always terminate in Los Angeles. At first it was used mostly for slave-trading trips from the Mexican settlements to central Utah, particularly the area around Utah Lake. That was the destination in 1813 when authorities caught members of the Mauricio Arze-Lagos Garcia party in their illegal business. They were trying to avoid a dangerous encounter with the Timpanogos Ute Indians as they traveled back to New Mexico from central Utah. Mexico had outlawed the slave trade in 1812. We know of the seven men of the Arze-Garcia trek because slavery charges were lodged against them the following year. They were tried at Rio Arriba, and the trial records show they obtained twelve slaves and 109 pelts on their trip.

However, in this raw frontier of northern Mexico, the law rarely intruded. Trading for Indian women and children continued through the 1850s. Often, worn-out horses, valuable only as food, would be swapped for children.

Fur trappers, slavers, traders, horse thieves, government and private exploring expeditions, Mormon missionaries, columns of soldiers—all detoured around the Reef. Heading west from Santa Fe, travelers crossed the Green River somewhere near the present town of that name. Then they angled northwestward toward the end of the Reef, which is visible from the river. A water hole five miles from the Reef, called Akanaquint Spring or Green River Spring, was the first good resting spot after the crossing.

In the 1820s fur trappers like Etienne Provost and Jedediah Strong Smith pushed into the area from trapping grounds to the north. The earliest record that seems to report reaching the edge of the San Rafael Swell is a copy of a journal kept by Smith. In 1826 he and about eighteen other trappers left a rendezvous at the Bear River in southern Idaho and headed toward the Great Salt Lake, then went to the vicinity of the present city of Provo, Utah. They turned southwest from there. Smith noted, "In taking the charge of our S western Expedition I followed the bent of my strong inclination to visit this unexplored country and unfold those hidden resources of wealth and bring to light those wonders which I readily imagined a country so extensive might contain."

Approaching the San Rafael Swell, he wrote,

> The country extremely rough until ascending a considerable Mt we kept on the top of a ridge running Easterly. The next day I left the indians and proceeding onwards a few miles came to a valley and a Creek about 20 yds wide running north East. At that place were some Beaver, so I remained there trapping 2 or 3 days. At this place I saw some verry old Buffalo sculls and from their appearance I would suppose that it is many years since the Buffalo left this country. they are not found beyond this place. I then moved on South having a high range of Mountains on the West and crossed a good many small streams running East into a large valley the valley of the Colorado. But having learned that the valley was verry barren and Rocky I did not

venture into it. The country is here extremely rough little appearance of Indians and game quite scarce a few Mt Sheep and Antelope. after traveling in this direction 2 days the country looked so unpromising that I determined to strike westward to a low place in the Mountain and cross over.

The report is vague. No matter what route is surmised, directions are mixed up—sometimes the journal says south when Smith meant north.

George R. Brooks, who edited the journal, concludes that Smith found his way out of the Wasatch Mountains, turned south, and discovered the buffalo skulls at the Price River. He continued south through Castle Valley—which forms the west side of the Swell—on September 1 and 2, 1826. Deciding the country was too desolate for beaver, he turned back west and ascended the Wasatch Plateau via Ivie Creek. The barren and rocky valley of the ''Colorado'' is actually that of the Green River, and the many streams running off the plateau eventually form the San Rafael River a short distance within the Swell.

The confusion over directions may be the work of Samuel Parkman, a nineteenth-century transcriber who copied Smith's original field notes, which are missing. Brooks said that occasionally when Parkman was copying a single letter that stood for a direction, he would turn it on its side so it could be read as either an ''n'' or an ''s.'' At any rate, Brooks is certain Smith knew which way he was going.

For twenty years or more, the Spanish Trail's loop around the Swell was popular. During all that time, the Reef was a barrier to east-west travel. It must have added one or two days to the long, weary journeys. Going through the desert to the north meant herds of cattle had to make their way from spring to pothole to stream—at least twenty rugged desert miles farther than a direct crossing of the Swell. In that hilly terrain, landmarks are hard to recognize. Travelers sometimes got lost dangerously far from water.

Water is always available in the canyon of the San Rafael, but the river is filled with rockfalls and quicksand. Often the water reaches from wall to sheer wall. The San Rafael is impassable on horseback; nobody would try to drive herds of livestock up the canyon. So this branch of the Spanish Trail swung around the Reef just past Green River Spring, which was located near the now-deserted settlement of Smith's Cabin. Traces of the trail, really a scattered network of tracks, also show up at Tidwell Draw, Cottonwood Wash, and Spring Canyon.

Next the route angled southwest through the San Rafael Swell, climbed along Ivie Creek onto the Wasatch Plateau, and entered Salina Canyon. The trail reached Utah Lake, then turned south to Santa Clara Springs and Mountain Meadows in extreme southwestern Utah. Caravans recruited at Mountain Meadows before crossing the brutal southern Nevada desert on the way to Las Vegas and Los Angeles.

For several decades, the Spanish Trail was a transcontinental thoroughfare that carried a brawling, restless tide of frontiersmen and bandits. Mule caravans loaded with coffee and woolen cloth plodded west from New Mexico; southeastward went cattle and horses from California, along with slaves captured from the Utes of Utah Lake. Again, donkeys led by fur traders were piled high with beaver pelts to make top hats for dandies. Sometimes Indians joined forces with Mexican bandits, and they stole horses from California ranches, then herded them around the Reef.

The first party to travel the entire route of the Spanish Trail, all the way to Los Angeles, was led out of New Mexico by traders William Wolfskill and George C. Yount in the winter of 1830–31. Yount and Wolfskill settled in California as soon as they arrived and became prominent citizens. Although Yount described the journey many years later, the fragmentary records did not mention the Reef specifically. But the skimpy descriptions indicate that he probably used the cutoff around the Reef. Yount recalled that after crossing the Green River, the party passed over "an extremity of mountainous and barren territory." Then they entered a ravine that ran directly into the Sevier River. This was probably Salina Canyon, the route used for many decades to come.

The legendary guide Kit Carson rode the trail several times. At first, he took a longer route far to the north. He said in an autobiography dictated in the late 1850s that around 1832 or 1833 he followed the Spanish Trail toward California until he reached the White River (now called the Price). Then he went up the White to the Green, to the Wintey (Uinta River), and there found the French trader Antoine Robidoux. In March and June 1848, after the cutoff closer to the Reef was well established, Carson carried naval dispatches east from California along the Spanish Trail—news that changed the course of history. In his saddlebag was the first notice of the gold discovery in California. When this intelligence reached the States, it touched off the California gold rush.

Riding the Spanish Trail was a grueling, dusty ordeal. George D. Brewerton, who accompanied Carson, left a vivid description of a *Jornada del Muerto*—"journey of death"—through the desert before reaching the Swell. Water holes were eighty miles apart, forcing them to travel at night. These scenes must have been much like the crossing of the Swell, which some travelers accomplished at night too.

> Sometimes the trail led us over large basins of deep sand, where the trampling of the mules' feet gave forth no sound; this added to the almost terrible silence, which ever reigns in the solitudes of the desert, rendered our transit more like the passage of some airy spectacle where the actors were shadows instead of men. Nor is this comparison a constrained one, for our way-worn voyagers with their tangled locks and unshorn beards (rendered white as snow by the fine sand with which the air in these regions is often filled), had a weird and ghost-like look, which the gloomy scene around, with its frowning rocks and moonlit sands tended to enhance and brighten.

When Carson's party reached the Green River, they lost much of their equipment in getting across, including Brewerton's notes.

Later that year, Orville C. Pratt, a lawyer and government agent, journeyed from Santa Fe to Los Angeles. His diary, the only known account of the entire route, is sadly vague about the Reef. Pratt says only that after crossing the Green River, his party went west and got lost about twelve miles from the river in a place without water and with little grass, where they camped. They had intended to follow the Spanish Trail around the end of the Reef but somehow got off the track. If they went directly west from the river, they camped nearly in the shadow of the Reef. Picking up the story there:

Wednesday Sept. 20th
Left the dry camp of last night at an early hour this morning and retraced our course back into the California trail & stopped & nooned at the Green riv. Sp. & went on from there to some dry grass on the route about 10 m. from the sp. & camped—Found water in a canion to the left of road about 400 yards—Left a pack saddle today—worn out—

Thursday Sept. 21st 1848—
Made a fine march today of 30 m & camped on the St. Rafael —A fine stream, & the best grass we have found since leaving Santa Fe—The animals came along without any difficulty, & if I can get them all as far as Washach lake, when I intend recruiting, it may be reasonably supposed that every one of them may be got through—The country continues, as almost all the way heretofore, sandy, hilly & utterly barren—Water is also scarce, & if there is no mineral wealth in these mountains I can hardly conceive of what earthly use a large proportion of the country was designed for!

On March 3, 1853, Congress had an idea about what the desert was designed for. It approved a scheme by E. F. Beale, the new superintendent of California Indians, to acquire land in California and parts of Utah and New Mexico territories where Indian tribes could be resettled. The scheme was supposedly designed for the "protection, subsistence, and colonization" of California's natives. Congress, eager to exile the Indians to reservations, ordered Beale to California by the shortest route to begin selecting land.

His twelve-man party left Washington, D.C., on April 20, 1853. It included Beale, author Gwinn Harris Heap, a Delaware Indian named Richard Brown, a Mexican named George Madrid, and George Simmis, "(colored man)." They arrived in Saint Louis on May 2, and in "Kanzas" three days later. Heap kept a journal of the trip and drew on it to write a lively book recounting their adventures, *Central Route to the Pacific, from the Valley of the Mississippi to California*, published in 1854.

The report gives a vivid account of what the trail was like immediately before the Reef, where it crosses the Green River.

According to Heap, the region from the Huerfano River (near the present town of Pueblo, Colorado) to Sevier Lake in central Utah had never been mapped, and nothing about it had been published before. That included the country around the Swell. "All information regarding [it] has therefore been derived exclusively from the reports of trappers and Indian traders."

The bull hides they carried for making a portable boat were soaked when they crossed the Huerfano River. By the time they reached the Green River, the hides were rotting and filled with holes. Beale and his crew patched them with "pieces of India-rubber blankets and sheepskins." They made a frame from wood found beside the Green, then stretched the hides across it to form a primitive bateau. Seams were smeared with a mixture of tallow, flour, soap, and pulverized charcoal to tighten them.

The men crossed on July 25, 1853, bailing constantly to keep their leaky tub afloat. In four trips, all their gear was on the west side of the river. The following day, Heap recalled,

> I went with the first load to guard our packs, as Indians were on the left bank watching our proceedings.
> Mr. Beale made great exertions to hurry the train over this river. He went across at every trip, jumping into the river where it was shallow, and taking the boat in tow until he was beyond his depth. He was thus for many hours in the water, encouraging the men by his example. We had now an excellent party; the men were daring and adroit; they exhibited no fear when we were so hard pressed by the Utahs, and when exposure or toil was required of them, not one flinched from his duty. . . .
> At sunset, the crossing of the Green River was effected, and we gladly gave the boat to the Indians, who ripped it to pieces to make moccasson soles of the hides. We proceeded a mile up the stream, and encamped in the midst of luxuriant grass. A band of twenty-five mounted Utahs accompanied us and passed the night in our camp; we gave them to eat, and they seemed quite friendly. . . . Day's travel, 1 mile; whole distance, 1,106 miles.
> *July 26.* In the morning the Utahs, who, the night before, were apparently so friendly, showed a disposition to be insolent, but our party kept close together, and they did not dare to commence hostilities. Most of them had rifles, and all had bows and quivers full of arrows with obsidian

heads. They accompanied us for some miles, importuning us for presents, and finally left us in a bad humor. Had we been able to conciliate these Indians with a few gifts, such as blankets, beads, tobacco, brass wire, &c., we should not have had the least trouble with them. . . .

Started at five, and at noon encamped at Green River Spring [beside the Reef]. The water here was cool, but not abundant; it is, however, constant, and good grass and some cottonwoods and willows are found around it.

The character of the country and soil continued unchanged, rocky ridges worn into fantastic shapes, and soil loose, dry, and barren. The trail led through rocky ravines of red sandstone. Day's travel, 18 miles; whole distance, 1,124 miles.

The "rocky ridges worn into fantastic shapes" were the Reef. They were camping just beside its northern end, about to head directly west and swing into the San Rafael Swell, following the Spanish Trail.

As late as 1852 the Spanish Trail was used in the Indian slave trade. That November, Pedro Leon and a company of "Spaniards" were arrested in Nephi for selling Indians. They were tried and ordered to leave Utah.

By then, few caravans worked their way along the Spanish Trail. The Mormon Trail became a main funnel for emigrants crossing the country after the Saints colonized Utah. Not until Interstate 70 was built through Spotted Wolf Canyon in the 1970s did the Reef become easily passable. In a way, the interstate is the successor to the Spanish Trail, following its general trend for many miles.

8

Fremont versus Gunnison

In the 1840s Americans were convinced their Manifest Destiny was to conquer and settle the continent from Atlantic to Pacific. The entire Southwest was seized as spoils of the war with Mexico. As soon as gold was discovered in California, setting off a stampede of miners and settlers, the nation became obsessed with building a transcontinental railroad. It would stretch from the Mississippi across this new wilderness, all the way to California.

Two serious roadblocks faced this project. The first was the sectional rivalry, with each region demanding its own terminus on the rail line. This was a small part of the bitter schism that would soon rip the country apart in civil war, delaying completion of the rail project until 1869. The second was that little was known about the interior. It was 1,500 miles of hostile tribes, blinding windstorms, parched deserts, buffalo herds, and tall grass prairies; rivers swept away boats; mountains were unscalable; maps were marked "unexplored territory." So in 1853 Congress sent out four major expeditions to reconnoiter separate swaths westward, covering all likely routes, with two smaller surveys to fill in the details.

The War Department selected Captain John Williams Gunnison to head the exploration of the central route. At forty-one, he was a faithful officer of the Topographic Engineers, the main government exploring and mapping unit. A West Pointer, he was a vigorous and intelligent man who had won the respect of the Mormons when he lived in Utah during a previous exploration with Howard Stansbury. The report of his expedition for the railroad survey contains the first good description of the San Rafael Reef. It refers to the northern end as the Rock Hills.

When his orders arrived, Gunnison lost no time outfitting. They had to get rolling if they were to forge through the Rockies before snowfall. They took off June 16, 1853, from Fort Leavenworth, Kansas, a large expedition of eighteen wagons, an instrument carriage, an ambulance, an eighteen-man military escort, a wagon master, teamsters, an astronomer, a surgeon, an assistant topographer, and several civilian employees.

Three months later, when they were between the Colorado River and the Green, guide Antoine Leroux of Santa Fe went ahead to search out the Spanish Trail. He returned, told the men how to reach the trail, described the country before them, and turned back to Santa Fe.

"The Spanish trail, though but seldom used of late years, is still very distinct where the soil washes but slightly," Gunnison wrote. In some parts, they "counted from fourteen to twenty parallel trails, of the ordinary size of Indian trails or horse paths, on a way of barely fifty feet in width."

They approached the Green River on September 29, 1853, southeast of the present town of that name. Gunnison climbed a bluff and looked around:

> Except for three or four small cotton-wood trees in the ravine near us, there is not a tree to be seen by the unassisted eye on any part of the horizon. The plain lying between us and the Wahsatch range, a hundred miles to the west, is a series of rocky, parallel chasms, and fantastic sandstone ridges. On the north, Roan mountain, ten miles from us, presents bare masses of sandstone, and on the higher ridges, twenty miles back, a few scattering cedars may be distinguished by the glass; Salt mountain, to the east, is covered half down its sides with snow; and to the south, mass after mass of coarse conglomerate is broken in fragments, or piled in turret-shaped heaps, colored by ferruginous cement from a deep black to a brilliant red, whilst in some rocks there are argillaceous layers, varying from

gray to glistening with white. The surface around us is whitened with fields of alkali, precisely resembling fields of snow. . . .

We now know those distant uplands as the Wasatch Plateau. Roan Mountain was the captain's name for the Book Cliffs, which stretch in a huge S from Price into Colorado; the formation we call the Roan Cliffs is about fifteen miles beyond the pagelike strata of the Books' front. Salt Mountain is the old name for the La Sals, near Moab, Utah. The masses of brilliantly colored turrets Gunnison described must have been Canyonlands National Park. His "fantastic sandstone ridges" were the San Rafael Reef and the badlands of the Swell.

Next day, they reached the Green River close to the Spanish Trail's crossing. Gunnison's second-in-command, Lieutenant Edward Griffin Beckwith of the Third Artillery, wrote, "Many Akanaquint or Green river Utahs were on the opposite bank as we encamped, and soon crossed it to beg tobacco, and, if possible, to trade; dressed in deer skins being the only article they offer for this purpose."

They splashed through an excellent ford on October 1, 1853. Taking readings of the sun, astronomer Sheppard Homans fixed the latitude—but longitude could not be determined. "The astronomical instruments taken by us into the field proved so imperfect that the longitudes deduced from observations made with them were very unreliable. . . . The latitudes were deduced from observations made by Mr. Homans."

The latitude they calculated is a few miles south of where Green River, Utah, stands today. Signs of Gunnison's crossing were noticed by men of John Wesley Powell's second expedition in 1871 and remembered by one of them as being half a mile north of the town, that is, six miles from the base of the Beckwith Plateau.

"The river is 300 yards wide, with a pebbly bottom, as we forded it, but with quicksands on either side of our path," wrote Beckwith. They camped in cottonwoods just across the ford. Indians thronged their camp for hours.

Leroux had claimed that the White River (the Price) cut into the Green only three miles to the north of where the Gunnison party crossed. Between the two rivers loomed "Little Mountain," the massive outcrop of the Book Cliffs, since renamed the Beckwith Plateau. Actually, Leroux was mistaken about the plateau's size: the Price River enters the Green twelve miles north of the Gunnison crossing. Three miles below the Price would have been within the walls of Gray Canyon, with the edge of the plateau forming the west side and the Books the east.

Trying to fit the Beckwith Plateau between their position and a river only three miles away, Gunnison decided they must be "but a mile or two from its [the Beckwith Plateau's] base." Expedition members reckoned the plateau was only 300 to 500 feet high. In reality, it rises more than 2,000 feet above the desert floor. The clear air and Leroux's miscalculation deceived them into thinking it was closer and smaller.

On October 1, 1855, Gunnison jotted down feelings shared by later generations of hikers sensitive to the desert: "Desolate as is the country over which we have just passed, and around us, the view is still one of the most beautiful and pleasing I remember to have seen."

The Reef had loomed higher as they worked their way west toward the Green River. Taking time to reflect on October 1, Gunnison remembered the scene.

As we approached the river yesterday, the ridges on either side of its banks to the west appeared broken into a thousand forms—columns, shafts, temples, buildings, and ruined cities could be seen, or imagined, from the high points along our route.

If that was not exclusively the Reef, it was mostly. For many miles, the Reef's ridge (just north of Interstate 70) dominates the horizon, a fantastic collection of flying saucers, domes, and minarets.

They left the Green on October 2 and moved "a little south of west" on the Spanish Trail. Then they swung northwest, making for the end of the Reef. All afternoon, the temperature was a pleasant 75 degrees Fahrenheit.

During the day they passed over crumbly soil, then traveled along a creek where they found a little standing water. They went "over sandstone hills, the upper strata of which were red, and the lower resembling the yellow argillaceous sandstone of the Arkansas river.'' They were within five miles of the Reef's end.

At 16.76 miles from the river, as measured by odometers attached to wagon wheels, they camped at ''a fine spring of cool water, called Akanaquint by the Utahs.'' That was Green River Spring. At 9 p.m., when they checked the temperature, the air had cooled to 50 degrees.

October 3, 1853: toiling up the dry creek bed, sometimes jouncing over the rock hills, they made slow progress. The wagons advanced only four miles in four hours over stony soil as they followed the Spanish Trail. They were close to the Reef's slanting ridge.

Then, as the Reef was ending, the Spanish Trail turned west toward the San Rafael Swell. Rather than continue into what looked like rugged country at Tidwell Draw or Cottonwood Wash, Gunnison decided to swing farther north. He was surveying for a railroad, not a pack-mule path. He wanted to find a flatter grade.

Its [the trail's] course then bore off more strongly to the west, over very rocky, broken hills—and we left it, taking a northwest and a north-northwest course by compass, leaving these rocky hills to the left, and skirting along others to the right, as rocky but perhaps less broken and cut transversely with cañones.

The rocky, broken hills to the left were the Navajo sandstone humps and the ridge formations at the Reef's northern end. The valley formed by the Reef on the left and red sandstone bluffs on the right is not actually rough, but it must have looked bad when the trail neared the Navajo knobs from the southeast. Gunnison went far north around these hills.

A lithograph in the report, made from expedition artist Richard H. Kern's drawing, shows the ''Rock Hills'' between the Green and Price river drainages as seen on October 3, 1853, with the Wasatch Plateau in the distance. The Rock Hills' resemblance to the Reef's final Navajo sandstone domes is striking.

On October 6, they turned west-southwest onto an Indian trail that ran down the far side of the Swell. Four days later, having crossed the San Rafael River, they picked up the Spanish Trail again on the other side of the Swell.

Beckwith had an idea for another route. He wrote, "The San Rafael also deserves an examination; for if it is practicable to ascend it, a better route might possibly be found to Grand river, from the confluence of the former with Green river, than the one we followed."

They ascended the Wasatch Plateau. After reaching the Sevier River, 135 miles west of the Reef, they divided the expedition. Gunnison took eleven men for a two-day reconnaissance along the Sevier's western bank. Beckwith and the main group continued toward Salt Lake City.

Early on the morning of October 26, 1853, on the bank of the Sevier, most of Gunnison's command was massacred by Paiutes. The Indians were enraged at the killing of one or two of their tribe by members of an emigrant wagon train two weeks before.

Only four of the twelve explorers escaped. One, thrown from his horse, lay in a bush for hours as Paiutes walked around him; one swam the Sevier; the remaining two rode horses to Beckwith's detachment and safety, though they were chased for hours.

Another expedition reached the San Rafael Reef three months after Gunnison's, a private party led by the famous explorer John Charles Fremont who had risen quickly through the army's ranks—too quickly for the military establishment. He was the son-in-law of a powerful senator, Thomas Hart Benton of Missouri, and that made his promotions suspect.

Fremont was in California with a heavily armed troop of "surveyors" on the eve of the Mexican War. Before he knew fighting had begun in Texas, Fremont sponsored rebellion among American settlers in California and then used his soldiers to wrest the province from the Mexican government. Ordered back to the States and court-martialed for his conduct in California, he was found guilty in 1848 of mutiny, disobeying orders, and bad conduct. President James K. Polk, recognizing his contributions to the conquest of California, found him innocent of the first charge and upheld the court on the other charges and restored him to active duty. Believing he had done nothing terribly wrong, Fremont resigned his commission.

In the winter of 1848–49 he led a private railroad expedition through the West with the backing of Benton and wealthy Saint Louis businessmen. It was his fourth expedition and the first since the court-martial. He wanted to discover a route so reliable that trains could use it in any season. He foolishly tried to cross Colorado's San Juan Mountains with a worthless guide, and the expedition floundered in deep snow. Ten of the thirty-three men died of cold and starvation, and some turned to cannibalism.

In 1853 Benton maneuvered to have Fremont appointed to one of the government railroad expeditions, but Secretary of War Jefferson Davis chose Gunnison. Benton and Fremont decided to launch their own survey of the Central Route. At age forty, Fremont was a reckless and brave leader with a point to make about mountain passes.

Outfitting the party that summer, he recruited a daguerreotypist, Solomon Nunes Carvalho, to record the territory on polished silver plates. Carvalho was to leave a great record of the journey, but in words, not in pictures. His 1856 book, *The Rocky Mountains And Western Deserts: A Narrative of Perilous Adventures*, is the only extensive account by a participant.

Not until September 22 were the twenty-two men and fifty horses and mules ready to leave their base of Westport, Missouri. Snow was already falling in the Rockies. Then, only six miles out of Westport, Fremont grew ill. He returned to Saint Louis for treatment while the rest waited for more than a month. By October 31, when they finally left, the torn bodies of Gunnison and seven of his men lay frozen to the ground beside the Sevier River.

Again, Fremont led his men through the 10,000-foot passes of the San Juan Mountains, this time in December. Poorly equipped and short on food, they faced more ranges and unexplored wilderness. The temperature was frequently thirty below zero.

Several days after crossing Cochetopa Pass, while they were still in the San Juan Mountains, they had a serious accident. Halfway up a steep, snowy mountainside, one of the front baggage mules slipped, throwing the animal off balance and top-

"Colonel Fremont and the Author taking astronomical observations,"
from *Incidents of Travel and Adventure in the Far West*, by S. N. Carvalho.

pling the whole string. A horse and a mule were killed. Worse,
the men lost a crucial day gathering their equipment; then a raging snowstorm detained them another day. Finally, the tent
poles for their large communal lodge were broken when the
animals banged them against tree trunks on the trail down the

mountain. "The lodge," Carvalho wrote, "afterwards, became useless, and the men, myself among them, had to sleep out upon the open snow, with no covering but our blankets, etc." The expedition's Delaware Indians slaughtered horses as they gave out, dividing each carcass into twenty-two shares.

They ran across Gunnison's months-old trail, easy to see by wagon ruts wherever the ground was not covered with deep snow, and marked by trees felled to make a passage.

Just before the end of 1853 they reached the Green River and crossed it near the mouth of the San Rafael, where the Green starts to go into canyons. It was a biting cold, snowy winter and they were out of food.

The descent into the valley of the Green River was over most dangerous projections and different strata of rock, thrown into its present state by some convulsion of nature.

When we arrived at the river, we saw on the high sand bluffs, on the opposite side, several Indians, whose numbers soon increased. As our party was much exhausted for want of wholesome food, we were buoyed up with hopes that we could obtain supplies from them.

We crossed the river, and were conducted by the Indians to a fertile spot on the western bank of it, where their village was. We found that they lived on nothing else but grass-seed, which they collected in the fall. Their women parch it, and ground it between stones. In this manner it is very palatable, and tastes very much like roasted peanuts. . . .

After crossing, the entire party went on foot. To spare their mounts, they led the remaining horses and mules.

They traced the San Rafael River to the Reef. Then Fremont decided to try pushing along it and out into the Swell. Probing into the Reef through the San Rafael's narrow canyon, the Lower Black Box, they followed the stream around Mexican Mountain. They plunged into the rough and forbidding Upper Black Box, four or five miles from Window Blind Peak. This route was much too rugged for a railroad and they gave up on ascending the river.

They followed the San Rafael back out through the Reef, swimming their mounts in places and scrambling down rock falls. Outside the Reef again, they could go north or south. Instead of driving north around the end of the Reef, as did both the Spanish Trail and Gunnison's route, Fremont headed south. Plainly, he was unwilling to follow in Gunnison's tracks, which must have been fresh. They worked their way along the Reef's face. Somewhere beyond the Moroni Slopes, after they had explored its whole front, they turned disastrously into the mountains.

A Fremont biography by John Bigelow, published in 1856, prints an account of the route along the Reef's front, among "extracts from the journal and letters of S. N. Carvalho." It says, "About the end of January we crossed the Green River, and entered upon a country—barren and sterile to a degree, over which we travelled until we got to the base of the Wahsach mountains." They thought of the high plateaus to the west as part of the same range, the Wasatch Mountains.

By now the hardships were so great that Carvalho's notes had become sporadic, and he never described the Reef in his book.

An unpublished memoir about Fremont, written by his wife Jessie and their son, Lt. Francis Preston Fremont, says,

> There remained now only the bed of the Wah-satch range to cross; the question was, whether the snows would be deeper in it—if so, in the exhausted condition of the men and animals, they would prove unable to break through it. To turn back was impossible, even in the face of this contingency. The expedition entered into the mountains and found the snow gradually increasing in depth. A feeling of disaster impending, was upon all; the memory of the expedition of 1848 was constantly in the men's minds. It took the utmost efforts of Colonel Frémont, [Alexander] Godey, and a few others who had had experience in such dangerous situations, to keep up the spirits and morale of the party, for if united action was to fail them now, the majority of the party must perish. . . .

They were forging westward across the high mountains of the Aquarius Plateau, the Bryce Canyon region, the Markagunt Plateau. Their clothing was tattered, they were malnourished, and blizzards howled around them. Three men usually lagged behind the rest, struggling through the snow: cartographer F. W. Egloffstein, assistant engineer Oliver Fuller, and Carvalho, "our scientific duties requiring us to stop frequently on the road." The three became fast friends.

Fuller's horse was one of the first to give out, so he was afoot longer than the others. But soon all three were in bad shape. "One of my feet became sore, from walking on the flinty mountains with thin moccasins, and I was very lame in consequence," Carvalho wrote. "Mr. Fuller's feet were nearly wholly exposed. The last pair of moccasins I had, I gave him a week before; now his toes were out, and he walked with great difficulty over the snow." Fuller got lost, was found, and then was allowed to ride, half frozen. He soon died in the saddle.

About then, "for the first and only time in his extended travels in inhospitable lands," the Fremont memoir says, the leader suffered a breakdown. He was going up a long mountain slope, breaking his way through snow, slightly ahead of the rest, when his strength suddenly drained away. The memoir quotes him: "All power of motion left me, I could not move a foot; the mountain slope was naked, but it just happened that near by was a good thick grove of aspens, and across a neighboring ravine, the yellow grass showed above the snow on the south hill side. Saying to Godey as he came up, that I would camp there, I sat down in the snow and waited." Fremont believed nobody noticed this momentary weakness.

They went a short distance the next day, rested, and on the following day started the final push toward Parowan. Desperate, they cached everything in the snow and made a dash for civilization. They were lucky enough to be rescued by Utes who led them into a camp at Red Creek Canyon. The twenty-one survivors reached Parowan, near the Little Salt Lake, on February 8, 1854. Carvalho was a wreck—dirty, frostbitten, and "suffering . . . from diarrhea, and symptoms of scurvy. . . ." Egloffstein, who was just as miserable, stayed in Parowan with Carvalho until February 21. Then they abandoned Fremont and hitched a ride with Mormons going to Salt Lake City for a church conference. Fremont and the rest continued the expedition to California. Egloffstein, weak as he was, made geographic notes on the road.

In Salt Lake City, Egloffstein hooked up with the Gunnison survivors. Carvalho declined to join them. He was in a hurry to retrieve the daguerreotype plates, and no doubt he'd had his fill of the wilderness. In the spring Chief Kanosh's Paiutes recovered the equipment, including as many as 300 daguerreotypes. Carvalho took them to California by a southern route and then shipped with them for New York City.

Returning east, Fremont wrote two brief accounts of the expedition for the *National Intelligencer* of Washington, D.C. He referred to the An-ter-ria range, apparently his term for the San Rafael Reef. "The falling snow and destitute conditions of my party again interfered to impede examinations," he wrote. Fremont claimed he had saved "nearly a parallel of latitude" by his new route, shortening the distance from the Green River to central Utah by a hundred miles.

He had Mathew Brady's photographic studio copy the daguerreotype plates onto glass negatives during the winter of 1855–56. Prints were to be used in making lithographs for the book he planned to write about the expedition.

Then in 1856 the Republicans nominated him for president. Charles Wentworth Upham, a campaign biographer, said, "When his full report [of the 1853–54 expedition] is published, it will contain a rigid and thorough discussion of all the obstacles and difficulties in the way of the construction of a railroad connecting the Atlantic States, centrally, with the Pacific coast. It is well known that he is fully convinced that it can be done." Fremont barely lost the election to James Buchanan.

A few years later, he fought in the Civil War—he was a controversial general. President Abraham Lincoln fired him for refusing to retract an emancipation proclamation of his own, issued before Lincoln was prepared to go that far.

With all this turmoil, Fremont never got around to the writing project until three decades had passed. At last, in 1887, the first volume of his memoirs was published. This book, rich in illustrations and scientific detail, included data from hundreds of observations and sextant readings taken during his first four expeditions. According to the table of contents, the fifth expedition—the only survey in the nineteenth century that explored along the Reef—was to be detailed in the second volume. A map in volume 1 shows Fremont crossed the Green River where the "San Raphael" enters, followed the San Rafael into the Reef, then turned south and went along its front. Volume 2 was never published and the daguerreotypes were probably destroyed when a "fireproof" warehouse where the Fremonts stored their treasured belongings burned down. But a copy of the second volume—either printer's galleys corrected by hand or a typewritten manuscript—is preserved in the Bancroft Library, University of California at Berkeley. While the first volume compiled Fremont's writing, drawn from his published reports, the second was written by his wife and their son. For the section covering the last expedition, the authors obviously did not have access to Fremont's field notes. The geography is badly mixed up. The only expedition members named are Fremont, Carvalho, Godey, Captain Wolf of the Delaware Indians, and Fuller.

Were it not for the book by Carvalho and maps by Egloffstein, we'd know little about the journey. Carvalho's exciting narrative brings the men to life, in a way Fremont failed to attempt with a report of his own.

Two of Egloffstein's maps of the region were published in the 1850s. They were based on his own notes and those of the Gunnison party, whose survivors he joined; the Gunnison notes were recovered after the massacre. They were the first charts to show the San Rafael Reef. The more detailed map was printed with the railroad survey reports on a scale of twelve miles to an inch. The northern part of the Reef appears above the map's border. From the northern end, the formation extends at least twenty-five miles southwest of Mexican Mountain, on a diagonal, until the map's border cuts it off. Here is the intricate winding of the San Rafael River through the Reef. Below, Black Dragon Wash can be discerned. Gunnison never got that far south. So the map is good evidence of the way Fremont tried to find a route along the Reef's front.

Both Gunnison's route and the Spanish Trail around the Reef's end are sketched in too far north. The crossing of Ferron ("Garambulla") Creek is shown twelve miles farther to the west than it is. Other inconsistencies resulted from bad estimates of distance. West of Mexican Mountain, the San Rafael River is

EXPLORATIONS AND SURVEYS
FOR A RAIL ROAD ROUTE FROM THE MISSISSIPPI RIVER TO THE PACIFIC OCEAN
WAR DEPARTMENT.

ROUTE NEAR THE 41ST PARALLEL.

MAP Nº 1.

FROM THE VALLEY OF GREEN RIVER TO THE GREAT SALT LAKE ;

from Explorations and Surveys made under the direction of the

HON. JEFFERSON DAVIS, SECRETARY OF WAR.

by Capt. E. G. Beckwith, 3ᵈ Artillery.

F. W. Egloffstein, Topographer for the Route.

1855.

Scale of 12 Miles to one Inch or 1: 760320 .

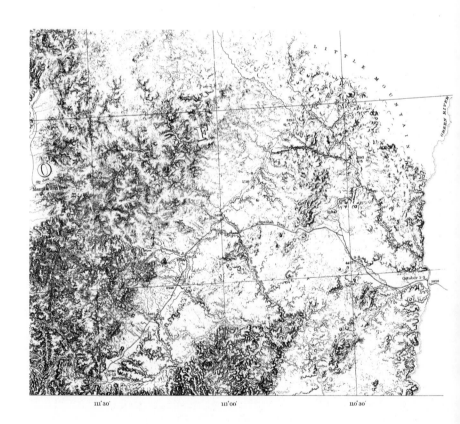

represented as coming down Buckhorn Draw. It actually swings up from the south before it reaches Mexican Mountain. However, Egloffstein was accurate from the mouth of the river to the mountain. His wrong notion about the river beyond Mexican Mountain shows that Fremont traced the San Rafael through the Reef, splashing upstream in the Lower Black Box as far as Mexican Mountain—but no farther.

The map proves they never got through the Upper Black Box. Probably the expedition gave up at the huge rock fall in that chasm, which would be almost impossible to ascend with horses. Doubling back along the San Rafael set the stage for tragedy in the mountains.

9

Exploration and Settlement

My search for the story of the San Rafael Swell brought me
to the airy library of the Mormon Church Historian's Office in
Salt Lake City, where I sat at a research table and leafed through
the diary of a tragedy. The stained paper had the texture of delicate old parchment, making wrinkling sounds when the pages
were turned. Bound ledger-fashion, the pages are covered with
handwriting in brown ink. This was the official journal of the
Elk Mountain Mission, a band of proselytizers sent out by the
Mormon Church in 1855 to the vicinity of the present city of
Moab, Utah, on the Colorado River. The forty-one men, led by
President Alfred N. Billings, were called to preach to the Indians. They were outfitted in Manti and left that Utah town at
noon on May 21, 1855, equipped with fifteen wagons, sixty-five
oxen, sixteen cows, thirteen horses, two bulls, one calf, two
pigs, two dogs, and twelve chickens. Their reports would be
matter-of-fact, saying little about weariness in the bones, sweat
trickling beneath clothing, thirst, and the columns of dust.

Southward they went first, skirting the western edge of the
Wasatch Plateau. Then the wagons rolled up Salina Canyon,
down one of the creeks that pour off the Wasatch Plateau, and
onto the Swell by way of the Spanish Trail.

Two reporters jotted down notes: the official journal was
kept by Oliver Broadman Huntington, a noted frontiersman,

while a personal diary was written by Ethan Pettit. The diaries form a vivid picture of what it was like to push across the San Rafael Swell in the days when it was nearly unknown desert wilderness.

On May 29 Huntington took note of the missionaries' attempts to make the Spanish Trail passable for their wagon train. "As usual the horsemen rode on ahead with spades & shovels to fix all the bad places in the road, which was pretty good & as the day before, through a valley country—traveled North-easterdly 15 miles to Muddy Creek. . . ." That night they camped within a few miles of the place where Gunnison had again picked up the Spanish Trail after swinging too far north. Pettit wrote:

> Wednesday 30th morning Prayer by C. Perkins mail left at 7 OC we left at 8 OC to where we leave muddy 5 m N.E. by N. to Sweet Cotton wood creek 6 m N. Campt at Hunt-ington Creek at 4 OC 3 m N.N.E. good camping place here we found the first Indians that we saw since we left manti except the one that we have with us they advised us to leave the gunison trail and take through straight to green river and they would go with us evening Prayer by E. Petit guard W. Buchanan [Behunin] D. Thomson J Louis R. W. James

The Utes realized Gunnison went unreasonably far to the north. A faster route was the Spanish Trail, cutting through the northern part of the Swell. It was disused and many of the Saints thought they were discovering a new way. But Huntington knew where they were:

> Thursday—31. Took the right spanish trail & traveled over a good country for a road without water until 2 o'clock P.M. when we came to a large gulf in rocks with nearly per-pendicular bank a hundred feet high. We camped at the head of this where there was a little water standing in the rocks. By further search Greg. Metcalf found 2 other pools down about a mile from which we drew water to give all a the stock a few quarts each, & get done about sunset, & at half past 9 we started again & traveled over a good road around until just daybreak when we came to other pools of standing water more convenient; where we watered all our stock with all they wanted & thanked God with all our

hearts. Traveled during the day 15 miles and during the night 15. Just as we were comeing into camp one wagon tongue run in the ground and broke an ox yoke—in a minute or two another wagon run against a cedar tree & broke a reach.

They pushed all night to cross the Swell. Pettit, who seemed unaware this was the Spanish Trail, recorded the marathon effort:

> Thursday 31st morning Prayer by W. Stirrit left at 8 OC turned to the right of gunnisons trail over rough ridge 4 m E.S.E. then Down smooth valley 5 m E.S.E. this valley is a bason and has no outlet up rough and sandy road 3 m. N.E. over ridge 3 m E good road Campt at 4 OC we call this road the Elk Mountain cut off. here is very little water and what there is a man can hardly get down too we watered our Cattle from the bottom of rocky kanyon 150 feet deep and its banks nearly perpiendicular we put laraets together and Drew it up. evening Prayer by W.P. Jones
> left at 9 ½ OC at night campt at a rocky Kanyon at 4 OC 15 m E. over smooth plane the best kind of road

Huntington picks up the story:

> Got our breakfasts while the cattle were serving themselves well, with rich grass.
> Left our morning camp June 1st 1855 about 1 o'clock. Had a crooked & sandy road some of the day traveled 10 miles & camped near the head of a small cottonwood creek on Gunnisons trail. Turned our cattle loose to range for the night without guard, it being sundown when we camped & cattle very tired.

Pettit said,

> Friday June 1st 1855 the only water here is basons in the rock and that is about all drank up therefore we have to leave left at 1 OC very crooked road 1 m N.E. here we strike gunisons trail then very sandy road 1 m E. Campt on a small creek at 7 OC 4 m S.E. here is some Cottonwood Trees evening Prayer by E Wright guard W. Hamblin A. Billings R. Brown and J Clark

At this point, they were close to the open valley where the Reef ends and where Gunnison decided to swing north. Huntington wrote,

> Saturday June 2nd 1855
> Had some delay in finding cattle—Started about 8 o'clock—travelled until 2 P.M without water & then had but poor stuff—the day was excessively hot & roads sandy & stoney; very heavy roads, had traveled but 10 or 12 miles up to 2 o'clock—rested our teams ¾ of an hour & traveled on over good roads 7 or 8 miles & come to Green river with very large bottom covered with cottonwood & most excellent grass,—
> Arrived in camp after dark, making 18 miles that day which very much exhausted our teams. It was plain that God had by his power sustained us and our teams for not one had failed or been lost and all hearts joined in acknowledging the hand of God.
> In the cut off we made we gained or saved 3 days travel and had a better road.

They reached the Green River on June 2, 1855, and rested there the next day, Sunday. Indians who camped nearby were invited to attend the services. Huntington said the Spirit of God was with President Billings and his interpreters, and "fell upon the Indians also, even that we could all see it & feel it, and all with exception of one or 2 got up & bore testimony to it, to the truth of this work & of their good intentions to honor the mission; even wild, vain & foolish boys hitherto, now spoke of the goodness of God & acknowledged his hand in all things."

When they reached the Colorado River, the Elk Mountain Mission seemed to be succeeding. The Mormons built a fort and began winning converts. But a little more than three months later—on September 23, 1855—Indians attacked. James W. Hunt, William Behunin, and Edward Edwards were killed, while President Billings was wounded. The next day, the survivors retreated, heading back to Manti.

During the "Mormon War" of 1857–58, when federal officials were determined to suppress a supposed rebellion in Utah,

Colonel Albert Sidney Johnston's army rolled west. In the spring of 1858 Colonel William Wing Loring marched to northern Utah from Fort Union, New Mexico, with reinforcements. The troubles were peacefully settled, and Loring returned from Camp Floyd, west of Utah Lake, to New Mexico by way of the Spanish Trail. He kept notes of his route, and these provide a glimpse of the San Rafael Swell, seen through a soldier's eyes.

The next year, by authority of the War Department, Captain Randolph B. Marcy published a guide for pioneers. *The Prairie Traveler* had tips on everything from what to do should a rattlesnake strike (put on a ligature, bleed the wound, cauterize with a strong solution of silver nitrate) to how to build a hide boat. For thousands of people creaking across the desert or prairie in wagon trains, the eighty pages of small type in the back were most valuable. They detailed twenty-eight major trails throughout the West, noting miles between water holes. Itinerary XXVII is Colonel Loring's route.

Mileage was shown before each segment, so travelers would know immediately how long the route was on that part of the trail. Each section was named for the suggested camping place where they would arrive at the end of that segment. For example, Loring's first section begins:

Miles.
        Camp Floyd to
23.   Goshen.—The road runs through. . . .

In Loring's depiction of the Spanish Trail through the San Rafael region, we'll start with the section that leads to a camp on "St. Raphael Creek," probably Ivie Creek:

Miles.
19 3/4. St. Raphael Creek.—Road passes a rolling section for 4 miles; then 1 ½ mile to Garamboyer Creek, where there is a good camp; thence, with the exception of a short distance, the road is good to the Knobs, 9 miles, when it is broken for 4 ½ miles. Good camp.
11 3/4. San Matio Creek.—For 3 miles the road is over a rolling section, with steep hills, to a creek, where is

a good camp; thence, for 3 miles along the creek, soft soil and heavy road; thence 5 miles to another creek, some grass, but not plenty; then to camp the road is rough in places. Good camp.

14 1/4. In the Hills.—Road runs over a rolling country 2 ½ miles to San Marcos, or Tanoje Creek, where there is good grass and water, with sage. Two miles farther over a gravelly road, then a good plain road for 9 ¾ miles to camp. Good wood, water, and grass.

23. Spring.—Road for the first ten miles is rocky, when it strikes a spring, where there is a good camp; thence 2 miles to water in a tank, not permanent; thence the road is on a ridge for 6 miles, and is good; thence 3 miles the road is sandy. The spring at camp is large, with plenty of wood, but the grass is scarce. Down the creek it is more abundant.

18. Green River.—For 5 miles the road is sandy; thence the road is good for the remainder of the distance to camp, where there is plenty of wood, water, and grass.

Where the road goes along a ridge for six miles, it's working around the Reef. Then for three miles, it goes through Cottonwood Wash, to wind up at Green River Spring. Gunnison said the distance between the spring and the river was sixteen and three-quarters miles. Heap said it was eighteen. Loring figured it at eighteen miles also.

John Wesley Powell, the great explorer who traversed the Green and Colorado rivers in 1869, was the first scientist to walk specifically to the San Rafael Reef to investigate it. That happened on his second descent of the rivers, the earlier expedition being so rushed that he and his men had little time for geological studies.

In 1870 Powell started organizing the second trip and landed a hefty congressional appropriation. This excursion could take years, if necessary, charting the landscape on both sides of the Green and Colorado and photographing natural features.

The only veteran of the first trip was Major Powell himself, and he sometimes left the men while hunting supplies or appropriations. They had Jack Sumner's diary of the 1869 journey, but its six pages of foolscap were at times terse to the point of use-lessness. Frederick S. Dellenbaugh, the expedition's seventeen-year-old artist, cited "hell of a foam" as a Sumner description of a stretch of rapids.

Leaving Green River, Wyoming, on May 22, 1871, were: in the *Emma Dean*, Major Powell in an armchair strapped to the deck of the cabin, Stephen Vandiver Jones at the steering oar, Jack Hillers at the aft oars, Dellenbaugh at the bow oars; in the *Nellie Powell*, Professor Alvin Harris Thompson (Powell's brother-in-law and second in command) steering, John F. Steward at the aft oars, Captain Francis Marion Bishop forward, Frank Richardson (Steward's assistant) in the middle deck; aboard the *Cañonita*, photographer E. O. Beaman who also acted as steersman, cook Andrew Hattan rowing aft, and assistant photographer Clement Powell (the major's cousin) forward.

While Powell was getting supplies, his boatmen worked their way through Desolation and Gray canyons behind the Beckwith Plateau, reaching the end of the canyons on August 25. Low on food, they waited there for the leader.

They were posed at the edge of the chart's last great blank reaches, ten thousand square miles of unknown country from the San Rafael south to the Paria River and west to the Wasatch Range, Dellenbaugh wrote in his classic account, *A Canyon Journey*.

Meanwhile, in Salt Lake City, Powell learned of the failure of two supply expeditions and organized a third. They went overland along the Spanish Trail. He got a look at the Reef. It must have fascinated him, as he soon afterwards made two hikes back from the Green River to see it.

Powell showed up at the Green River on August 29, 1871. Coming with a pack train by way of Manti, he and guides Lyman and Fred Hamblin were able to bring only 300 pounds of flour, some jerked beef and twenty pounds of sugar. That was barely enough to stave off starvation for the stretch between there and the next supply point, the Crossing of the Fathers, just above the Arizona border.

On September 1 the boatmen shoved off, happy to be run-ning with Major Powell in his accustomed place atop the *Emma Dean*. The following day they ran eighteen miles on a smooth, shallow river "with broken, picturesque low cliffs and isolated buttes everywhere," Dellenbaugh wrote. Walter Clement Powell noted that they were passing Castle Valley, which is actually the draw bordered by the Reef. He said the Indians called the curious formations "Sau-auger-towip" or Stone House Lands. The great spires and domes must have looked like tipis and lodges.

Next day they stayed in Camp Number 53, as the major wanted to see the Reef. Jones's diary of that hike is the first record of a trip to study the San Rafael Reef.

Sunday, September 3rd [1871]. Steward, Clem, the Major and Myself crossed the river about 8 A.M., the former to examine the nearer hills; we, Major and self, to go across the country to examine a long range of hills that stretched from north to south and seemed to be upheaved. Took with us 3 canteens of coffee and bread and meat enough for dinner. Climbed the hills on west side of the river, descended again and followed the winding bed of a dry gulch some 2 miles, then struck across more to the west and travelled over loose, sandy soil with scarce a shrub or blade of grass. I never understood before the full meaning of the term 'bare ground.' Walked until 11 o'clock, the 5 or 6 miles that seemed to intervene between camp and the range, stretching into 10 or 12. . . . [We] sat down and tried to eat but were so warm and tired and the sun shone so hot that we did little except drink our coffee. No shade could be found, nothing but bare rocks and bare ground.

Walked about 2 miles farther, obtained a good view of the vertical range. It consisted of Tertiary (probably) rocks greatly upheaved from the general level at the north, growing more and more steep until it became nearly vertical, then sloping to the south. Composed of mostly of red sandstone. To the south we marked the windings of a stream, either the San Rafael River, or some one of its branches.

They examined the Reef and the San Rafael River from a few miles away, then turned back toward camp. About 5 p.m., after walking another two hours, they drank the last of their coffee. They had to march to the Green River without a drop from that time on, arriving in an hour and a half. Both were worn out.

A fourteen-mile river run the next day brought them to a cottonwood grove just above the mouth of the San Rafael, where they camped. Many pieces of worked flint and broken arrowheads were scattered around, and the men collected them. Jones said the Indians called the country Toom-pin-con-to-weep, which meant Stone House Land. W. C. Powell and Jones disagreed about the pronunciation of the Indian word, but both had the same idea about its meaning.

Major Powell launched another hike toward the Reef. Jones wrote of this second side trip:

> Tuesday, September 5th. . . . climbed the cliff then a hill of bare rocks that rose in terraces to the height of more than 1000 feet. From here we could see the windings of the San Rafael from the mouth far up toward the Wasatch range. Also obtained a good view of the upturned range before visited. The San Rafael runs through low cañon walls in short curves, the cliffs coming to the water on one side, a narrow valley on the other. It was near sunset when we started to return and long after dark when we reached camp.

Dellenbaugh said that on this second trip to the Reef, Powell and Jones walked back along the San Rafael River for twenty-five miles. Powell told them the drainage basin of the San Rafael was woefully barren and desolate.

That October, they arrived in Kanab, a Mormon settlement established the year before. They set up winter headquarters while the major went back to Salt Lake City. The second river expedition was over. From then on, the exploring and laborious mapping were performed by land.

Powell's survey was not the only one operating near the Swell. Congress had funded four great western surveys shortly after the Civil War. Powell organized and promoted his own survey of the Green-Colorado river region, under Interior Department auspices as the U.S. Geographical and Geological Survey of the Rocky Mountain Region. Among others in the field, First Lieutenant George M. Wheeler, Corps of Engineers, headed a survey west of the 100th Meridian.

Wheeler, concentrating on economics and military concerns, sent out a small party from Salt Lake City in 1873 under

Lt. R. L. Hoxie of the Corps of Engineers. Gilbert Thompson was the topographer and Edwin E. Howell the geologist. They went through the western branch of Castle Valley, which at that time was defined as an inverted V, wrapped around the northern part of the San Rafael Swell. (Since then, the term Castle Valley has come to mean only the western branch.) They skirted the Swell.

The Wheeler Survey's published report ignored the Swell except for saying, "This coal horizon in Utah extends far northward in Castle Valley, and just outside the limits of our survey, on the Muddy and San Rafael, are coal beds, reported by the Mormon explorers to be of great thickness."

A century later, an unsuccessful coal mine burrowed into the desert near the Muddy River, close to the Moroni Slopes. But no thick beds of coal have shown up on the banks of the San Rafael.

In 1875–76 Powell sent Grove Karl Gilbert to study the Henry Mountains, which Powell and Jones had spotted when they hiked along the San Rafael River in 1871.

Gilbert's study, *Report on the Geology of the Henry Mountains*, became a scientific classic. He climbed Mount Ellen on August 30, 1875, getting a good view of the Reef, and sketched a dramatic panorama from his Station Number 27 on top of the mountain. The sketch is in one of his notebooks, which were recently edited by Charles B. Hunt. It shows the entire Swell, with the humps along the top of the Reef in the middle ground. He drew in the Dirty Devil River, Factory Butte, and North Caineville Mesa to the left.

From Thousand Lake Mountain, located twenty-five miles southwest of the Moroni Slopes, Gilbert was awed by the beauty of the San Rafael Country.

> To the left is the San Rafael Fold, the rival of the Waterpocket in grandeur; and all about are tables and cliffs. The vivid hues of the naked rocks are obscured only by the desert haze, and the whole structure is pictured forth by form and color.

He also cut through the San Rafael Swell, en route from the Henrys to Castle Valley, November 9–14, 1876.

In 1878 Powell published a revolutionary report that attempted to guide the development of the West, *Report on the Arid Region of the United States, with a More Detailed Account of the Lands of Utah*. In this landmark work, Powell printed a beautifully colored map of Utah compiling findings of several of the surveys. The entire state is shown in fine detail, except the corner east of the Colorado River and south of the La Sal Mountains—today San Juan County. All of the Reef is drawn in, with trails designated. The Spanish Trail is shown crossing "Gunnison Valley" and rounding the northern end of the Reef. What is apparently Gunnison's route arches northward, angling away from the trail about six miles east of the Reef.

Powell wrote:

> Castle Valley is abruptly walled on the west, north, and northeast by towering cliffs. East of its southern portion a region of towers, buttes, crags, and rocklands is found, known as the San Rafael Swell. In this valley there is a large amount of good land, and the numerous streams which run across it can all be used for irrigation.

In a section of the report written by Professor Thompson, the San Rafael River is described in more detail:

> This stream flows in an easterly course, and enters the Green 32 miles above the junction of that stream with the Grand [the former name for the Colorado]. It has three principal branches—Ferron, Cottonwood, and Huntington Creeks—all rising in the Wasatch Plateau at an altitude of about 10,000 feet. These streams have a rapid fall in their upper courses, and leave the plateau through almost impassible cañons cut in its eastern wall overlooking Castle Valley. They flow across that at intervals of a few miles apart, and, then uniting, cut a deep, narrow cañon through the San Rafael Swell.

Powell left Captain Clarence Dutton to carry on the survey in the high plateaus. The result was one of the best early studies of western geology, *Report on the Geology of the High Plateaus of Utah with Atlas*. Dutton studied Utah plateau country in 1875–77, working directly with Powell's survey. The early reconnaissance was by Howell, whose notes Dutton used. He noticed the close kinship of the San Rafael Reef and the Waterpocket Fold, which later became the heart of Capitol Reef National Park.

The third [great displacement] is the San Rafael flexure, beginning as a branch of the Water-pocket flexure, where the latter changes its trend, and running north-northeast along the eastern side of the San Rafael swell, passes off into the northeast and dies out again. These are all monoclinal flexures of imposing dimensions and of perfect form. . . . The San Rafael flexure remains to be studied.

Dutton counted five uplifts on the west and north sides of the Colorado. The greatest is the Grand Canyon; then there were uplifts east of the Kaiparowits Plateau; one about fifty miles south-southeast of the confluence of the Green and the Colorado; and the Henry Mountains. The fifth was the San Rafael Swell, "between the Green River and the Wasatch Plateau."

Of these five centres of maximum erosion, the San Rafael Swell is by far the best suited for study, and may be regarded as the type of them all. If we stand upon the eastern verge of the Wasatch Plateau and look eastward, we shall behold one of those strange spectacles which are seen only in the Plateau Province, and which have a peculiar kind of impressiveness, and even of sublimity. From an altitude of 11,000 feet the eye can sweep in a semi-circle with a radius of more than 70 miles. It is not the wonder inspired by great mountains, for only two or three peaks of the Henry Mountains are well in view; and these, with their noble Alpine forms, seem as strangely out of place as West-minster Abbey would be among the ruins of Thebes. Nor is it the broad expanse of cheerful plains stretching their mottled surfaces beyond the visible horizon. It is a picture of desolation and decay; of a land dead and rotten, with dis-solution apparent all over its face. It consists of a series of terraces, all inclining upward from the east, cut by a laby-rinth of deep narrow gorges, and sprinkled with numberless buttes of strange form and sculpture. . . . There are five of these concentric lines of cliffs. In the centre there is an ellip-tical area about 40 miles long and 12 to 20 broad, its major axis lying north and south, and . . . completely girt about by rocky walls. . . . It has received the name of the San Rafael Swell.

Meanwhile, the country was no longer so remote. As the century was ending settlers spread into the region. Livestock operations ranged through Cottonwood Canyon near the northern end of the Reef. Sheep grazing began in Sinbad's high country around 1875, with Orange Seely one of the main stockmen. Horses were grazed near the San Rafael River. The "Smith Ranch," just east of the Reef at its northern end, was home to Tom Tidwell and his sons Frank, Keep, and Roland. They raised horses and cattle. Cattle grazing in the Swell, begun with Texas longhorns around the 1880s, is still going on. Joe Swasey, a famous rancher and desert rat from Molen, Emery County, traveled extensively through Sinbad and the Reef country. Around the turn of the century, he discovered the uranium at Temple Mountain and shipped ore out by pack train.

The most famous legend of the Reef is Sid Swasey's leap. Sid, one of the Swasey cowboys, supposedly bet his brothers he could jump his horse across the Lower Black Box—where the San Rafael River goes through the Reef, about fifty or sixty feet below. The gap is eleven feet across. Swasey won the bet, and the place is marked on maps as Swasey's Leap.

Later, sheepherders threw a bridge across that spot, using poles and an old wagon box. Sheep Bridge is still there, but it's rotting and "it will probably fall into the canyon bottom in the near future," says a Bureau of Land Management report.

In 1882 Ebenezer Hanks, his wives Sara and Jane, nine children, and other relatives settled Graves Valley southeast of the Reef. They had left Parowan in March, and by the end of April they had diverted water from the Dirty Devil River and planted crops. In 1890 the town had a dozen families. The population grew quickly, with the residents ranching, mining coal for use on Colorado River steamers, outfitting prospectors, and trading with outlaws. Today the town is called Hanksville.

"Greenriver" (later Green River) sprang up at the Spanish Trail Crossing in 1878. It served as a relay station for mail riders on the "Star Mail Route" between Salina and Ouray, Colorado, which began service that year. Fruit growers there planted orchards and found the climate ideal. For many decades, cantaloupes and watermelons of wonderful delicacy—such as the variety developed by a farmer called "Melon Brown"—have fetched fancy prices in the eastern markets.

The town boomed when the Denver & Rio Grande Western Railroad came through in late 1882. Shortly afterward, the D&RG hired every available hand to build a railroad grade toward central Utah. Working west from Green River and around the end of the Reef, laborers with picks and shovels heaped dirt into long banks, leveling, chanting, swearing. They paralleled the Spanish Trail's route, heading for Buckhorn Draw. They made the grade, but no trains chugged along it. Competing offices of the railroad company operated at cross-purposes, and the tracks were never laid. The spur was abandoned. The railroad swung instead toward Price, Provo, and Salt Lake City. Parts of the grade remain in the desert just north of the Reef. Railroad ties and the remains of workers' camps show up here and there.

As the nineteenth century was closing, ranchers moved their cattle through the Reef between winter and summer ranges. Mail routes were worn into the desert, notably one along the Reef's front between Green River and Hanksville.

But other than dirt roads, the Reef carries few imprints of the settlers: some initials and drawings on the cliffs, a stock pond here, a gate there, the remains of a corral at Mexican Bend. They aren't much more intrusive than the nearby petroglyphs of the ancients.

10

Butch and the Old Bunch

One of Edna Robison's most vivid girlhood memories was playing jacks on the floor with a grown man. Crouched beside her was a square-jawed, sandy-haired, trail-dusty man who loved her. He probably treasured her and her sister, Dora, as the children he never had. He was Robert Leroy Parker, better known as the outlaw Butch Cassidy. Instead of ordinary six-pointed jackstones, they played jacks with twenty-dollar gold pieces Cassidy had liberated in a holdup.

"Everybody had a good impression of them, the whole gang," said Barbara Ekker. Mrs. Robison, Butch's young friend, was her mother-in-law. Mrs. Ekker is the Hanksville historian—or would be, if the town were big enough to support such a position.

Some Hanksville people say "the old bunch" when they refer to Butch and his bandits, the men known to the outside world as the Robbers Roost Gang or the Wild Bunch. Desperadoes frequently visited the store-hotel run by Edna's father, Charlie Gibbons. They liked the Hanksville people and the settlers were always glad to sell them supplies, horse feed, and ammunition.

"He'd come in with the whole gang," Mrs. Ekker said. Butch would be so eager to play with the two Gibbons girls that he'd go straight in as soon as he arrived—having Charlie Gibbons unsaddle his horse. Whenever her mother-in-law reached that part of the tale, Mrs. Ekker would interrupt, "Grandma, I wish you'd tell everybody that you were eight years old, when you tell your story!"

For many years, the Reef was a refuge for men on the run. A lot of outlaws hid out in this country, Mrs. Ekker said. Most of them undoubtedly centered at Robbers Roost, in the canyons of the Dirty Devil River and beyond. Robbers Roost Canyon begins ten air miles southeast of Hanksville, but by trail it's several times that.

A shoot-out with a sheriff is authenticated within the Reef itself, and newspaper accounts of the time insisted that rustlers thronged the Swell as well. It was rumored to be a major fortress in an outlaw trail that reached from Wyoming to New Mexico.

On August 16, 1897, the *Deseret Evening News*, Salt Lake City, quoted information in the *Southern Censor* of Richfield, Utah, that

> Mr. [Sheriff Jack] Cottrell tells of the haunts of this gang. They have stations all the way from Farmington, New Mexico, to points in Wyoming. Recent developments, of a nature not to be made public, show that the robbers carry their own mail. They have a ferry boat across the Colorado river, and are in conjunction with pals who seem to be peaceable citizens.

Newspapers of the time said Butch and many other bandits often used the Swell, sometimes hiding out for long periods there. Killers or robbers on the run would cut for the Reef, where they could choose a canyon and shake off pursuers. If anyone were foolish enough to follow, the Reef was rich in ambush points. But posses usually did not venture there.

Although some bandits undoubtedly set up camp in the Swell, it seems likely that most simply passed through it on their way to and from Robbers Roost. There, they could see anyone coming from miles away. The place was nearly impregnable.

The gangs cultivated good relations with the locals, but bandits were still blamed for the murder of an innocent sheepherder in the San Rafael Swell. According to Dee Anne Finken's research in a study sponsored by the Bureau of Land Management, a stone marker on Copper Globe Flat, in the center of the Swell, reads,

> Henry H. Jensen of May field, Utah was found dead Dec. 16, 1890. Blood and trails in the snow showed he had walked and crawled a mile after he was shot. He still held to his rifle, herding sheep for the Witbecks. It is said the Robbers Roost gang warned all sheep to "stay out of this herding mesa." He was carried out on a pack mule to the brink of Eagle Canyon to a buckboard 7 miles. He was found by Will and Otto Witbeck.

The next murder involving the Swell was on September 26, 1894. While trying to recover stolen sheep held in a corral in Spring Canyon City, Sanpete County Sheriff James Burns was shot to death by Moen Kofford and Peter Mickle. "It is said that he was riddled with bullets having been shot several times," reported the *Manti Messenger* on September 28. "The murderers took everything including guns and horses, and escaped for their headquarters in the San Rafael country." *The Messenger* added,

> A posse of nine men headed by J. T. Henrie, city marshal, left this city Wednesday night for the purpose of trying to head of [sic] the assassins in Castle Valley. If not caught before they reach the San Rafael bluffs, there will be but little use of following them. They will probably cross the Colorado and escape into the Blue mountains where a search for them would be useless.

The prediction was accurate. The paper said next week that Henrie's posse tracked the fugitives through Castle Valley and into "the breaks of Salt Wash," which borders the Swell. But they were unable to proceed farther because they had no guide.

Also finding a home in the Reef was Joe Walker, who was one of the most famous bandits of his day. He was sometimes referred to as Butch Cassidy's partner. In 1895 the forty-five-year-old Texan, who was monumentally stewed, tried to hold up the town of Price. He fled to Robbers Roost and began a career of horse-stealing and cattle-rustling.

Walker and a partner, George Lee, set up camp beside the spring just past the entrance to Spring Canyon. They were within the Reef about half a mile from Mexican Bend, near where the San Rafael River starts to head around Mexican Mountain. Thought by Castle Valley people to be part of Cassidy's Robbers Roost Gang, they raided the Price area, rustling cattle and horses. Ranchers were terrified of them.

In March 1897 they were suspected of taking three horses from J. M. Whitmore of Price. Emery and Carbon county officers set off after them, led by Emery County Sheriff Azariah Tuttle of Orangeville, who in his spare time ran the Tuttle House and manufactured lumber, lathes, shingles, and general building materials. This time the pursuers went right into the San Rafael Swell. On March 24, 1897, they caught up with the pair, surprising them at the Reef's Spring Canyon. The weekly *Manti Messenger* said:

> For two days the bandit was cornered in a narrow box canyon [Nates Canyon, which branches off from Spring Canyon] where it is next to impossible to get out when both ends are guarded, and yesterday morning the posse entered the canyon and finally came upon the fugitive. The men were separated as Tuttle, being near to Walker, dismounted because of the difficulty in getting over the rocks, and was trying to get in a position of safety where he might get his man. Walker shot him, however, before he had time to act. The ball penetrated his right thigh near the hip, and the bone was also fractured. Walker discarded his horse and was making his way on foot up the rugged mountain.

A county history written a few years later notes that Sheriff Tuttle had arrested Lee; but then Walker shot the sheriff through the right thigh, "inflicting a wound which will always cause him to be lame. He laid without assistance for thirty-six hours when friends reached him and took him home."

Why didn't the rest of the posse get to the sheriff immediately after he was shot? The *Messenger* offers an alibi with the suggestion that both ends of the canyon were being guarded —unlikely, given their distance apart. Also, the reference to a box canyon makes it clear the badman ducked into Nates Canyon, a box with only one end to guard. To reach the northern end of Spring Canyon, a deputy would have to ride through the Lower Black Box or cross the rough country behind the Reef to Black Dragon. Then he would go along the Reef and around it via Cottonwood Canyon, and finally head down behind the Reef.

The *Eastern Utah Advocate*, Price, said on April 8, 1897, "Sheriff Tuttle is rapidly recovering from the effects of the dangerous wound received at the hands of Joe Walker, and his numerous friends are pleased that his life is spared. Walker better make himself scarce around the towns of Emery county if he wants to be on earth a while."

Writing in the *Salt Lake Herald* in 1909, H. L. A. Culmer refers to this shooting:

> Within half a mile of the bend [Mexican Bend] is the mouth of Walker [Spring] canyon, so named because it was there that an outlaw named Walker shot Sheriff Tuttle a few years ago. There is a delicious spring close to the entrance of the canyon, near which Walker hid, with his horse concealed among the rocks behind him. The sheriff was killed at the first shot [not true], and Walker fled northward to the Book mountains, where he and three companions were killed by a posse in pursuit [also false].
>
> And so it goes on. The history of the place is written in blood, with the names of Butch Cassidy and other desperadoes in respectable sized letters.

In Utah, the Old Bunch is most infamous for the Castle Gate, Carbon County, mine office robbery. Cassidy and a bandit called Elza Lay had worked as ranch hands in the central Utah coal region for a few weeks. On April 21, 1897, they waited until the Denver & Rio Grande Western train pulled into Castle Gate with a mining company payroll. Suddenly, they jabbed their pistols into the ribs of the paymaster, E. L. Carpenter, grabbed bags of gold and silver coins, and pounded out of town.

One of their accomplices, who helped with horse relays after the Castle Gate robbery and may have cut the telegraph wires, was Joe Walker. The wires were snipped near Helper, south of Castle Gate. The band apparently hid behind a building as pursuers galloped past. Then they circled toward the Swell.

Using relays of horses stationed at strategic points, the bandits raced toward the San Rafael River, going into the Swell by way of Red Canyon. They dropped a bag containing $700 in silver—too heavy to bother with. They still had $7,000.

The *Eastern Utah Advocate* commented on the day following the robbery:

> The horse thieves, bandits and marauders infesting what is commonly known as Robbers Roost sixty miles southeast of Price, on the San Rafael River in Emery County, have in the past few years committed many an atrocious deed of daring, but none so bold and audacious as this last unprecedented and noisy hold-up.

So many outlaws haunted the San Rafael Swell and Reef that it was thought of as part of Robbers Roost itself. The next edition, on April 29, corrected the location of Robbers Roost: "The robbers are doubtless cooing and happy . . . in their rugged fastness on the Dirty Devil river."

Butch et al. were not able to cut the wires quickly enough to prevent word of the holdup from flashing throughout Utah. Lawmen and armed miners quickly fanned out. Posses from Huntington and Castle Gate, mistaking each other for the bandits, fired at each other in the night.

Police work was starting to benefit from technology and the opening of the West. Another posse headed by L. S. Dickinson arrived from Salt Lake City, 120 miles away. They got there so soon they must have taken the Denver & Rio Grande Western. Price residents joined them and they continued on the train to Green River. Leaving that town on horseback at 3 a.m. April 22, they "reached the crossing of the San Rafael at 7 a.m., on the road to Hanksville," opposite the Reef.

They brought along a guide to the rough country, but he refused to go farther than the Chris Halverson homestead on the San Rafael River. (It is Rey Lloyd Hatt's ranch today, at the Utah 24 crossing of the San Rafael, nine road miles below I-70.) They thought they might catch up with Butch at Iron Wash, which penetrates the Reef.

> . . . the posse pushed on to Iron Springs creek where they expected to intercept the bandits.

About noon Thursday Mr. Bacon, the mail driver overtook them and was "pumped" with much difficulty as to what information he had. He finally told as how four men had crossed the road near him about an hour after the posse left Halverson's ranch, and they had camped about five miles up the canyon the night before. The posse returned to the San Rafael crossing but by that time the bandits had a start of six hours and it was useless with jaded horses to follow them up, so Dickinson with his men returned to Greenriver.

They had discovered that the bandits rode to Castle Dale, on the northwestern rim of the Swell. They went to the San Rafael River, cut cross country to Black Dragon Wash, followed that through the Reef, then headed to Robbers Roost.

Upon leaving Cleveland the robbers evidently secured fresh horses at "Peter's spring" on the Cedar mountains, and crossing over the Buckhorn flat went down the San Rafael to Sulphur springs, where they went over into Black Dragon canyon. Going down that some miles they recrossed the San Rafael and camped at the old Tidwell ranch Wednesday night a short time. From there they proceeded next day fifteen or sixteen miles down the lower San Rafael canyon until they reached the other crossing, and then made for the Dirty Devil River and reached Robbers Roost some time Thursday evening. Their pack animal was evidently loaded with the gold and their food. It is doubtless that they are now as safe as though they had been swallowed up by the earth and thus the Carpenter holdup will probably end.

Everybody knew that as soon as the bandits reached the rough country, they were safe. The *Manti Messenger* of April 24 said Cassidy's gang "sought refuge by flying to the San Rafael Mountains."

WON'T BE CAUGHT

Mr. Carpenter [the coal company paymaster] is confident the robbers will not be taken as five-tenths of the people of that section are thoroughly terrorized, three-tenths are in league with the robbers and the balance of the law abiding citizens form so small a faction that nothing they can do would be of any use.

That wasn't quite the end of the saga. A few days later, the last posse returned to Price, telling of its fruitless search through the San Rafael and Robbers Roost badlands. Ex-Sheriff Tom Lloyd and Pete Anderson came back from a "hunt on the San Rafael" after eleven days on the trail. They traveled throughout the country from the Cedar Mountains to the Dirty Devil River, checking into the San Rafael Swell and Robbers Roost.

They found nobody meeting the description of Cassidy and Lay. But the men they did run across give us a good idea of the sorts who frequented these wild parts. Said the *Eastern Utah Advocate* on May 6,

> They encountered a number of rough characters whom they suspected were members of the Robbers Roost gang,

but these parties were always in number four and more. Most of the gang is now said to be camped in Horseshoe bend, and adjacent canyons, and at the time of Lloyd's visit there were no men at the "Roost."

The Roosters were probably at Hanksville, where Butch and little Edna Gibbons were delightedly playing jacks. One memorable night, the gang settled in for a meal at the Gibbons place. They must have arrived late from some excursion, as Edna and Dora already had been sent upstairs to bed. Their room was above the dining room.

The spavined chairs were wired together. "They were getting up from the table and Sundance went to pull his chair up," Mrs. Ekker said. "And the wire on one these chairs caught on his holster." Somehow, the gun flipped around and went off, blasting a hole in the ceiling. "They knew the girls were upstairs." Everybody rushed to the upper bedroom in a panic.

"The bullet had gone through the mattress and the pillow, and just missed the two girls. And so after that, Butch said, 'DON'T pack your guns into Mr. Gibbons' house.' And Butch always told them, 'No profanity around Julia,' the mother. And they were very polite."

Not only did Gibbons sell the bandits provisions, he even helped them by keeping their loot in his safe. "He went to Salt Lake one time to buy groceries," Jess Ekker, Barbara's husband, remembered of his grandfather. "And they picked him up in Salt Lake . . . with his money." Seems the bills were hot. That took a lot of explaining from Charlie, but they let him go.

Contrary to Culmer's 1909 article, Walker did not die immediately after he shot Sheriff Tuttle. The year following the encounter in the Reef, Walker, a Wyoming badman named Johnny Herring, and two accomplices raided Price. Again, they ran off livestock belonging to J. M. Whitmore, this time a herd of twenty-five cattle. On May 14, 1898, the *Deseret Evening News* reported,

> . . . . Billy McGuire and Bud Whitmore were held up by a gang in Box canyon and robbed of twenty-five cattle. The stock were driven off by the outlaws, along with other stolen cattle, the two men, McGuire and Whitmore, being robbed also of their saddle horses and compelled to walk.

On Sunday morning McGuire and Whitmore reached Price afoot and at once reported the robbery to the officers.

Again, lawmen followed. Again, Walker was surprised. This time it was fatal.

An eleven-man posse—including J. M. Whitmore, who had his reasons—caught up with Walker on the night of May 13, 1898. They had crossed the Green River and were in the Book Cliffs, forty-five miles north of Thompson Springs, Grand County. The bandits were sleeping, unwary, not bothering to post a guard. The lawmen dismounted and crept within sixty yards of their camp. The posse yelled for the men to surrender. At first the chief bandits were thought to be Butch Cassidy and Walker. Said the *Eastern Utah Advocate* on May 19,

> Cassidy and Walker immediately began firing and the other two threw up their hands and begged for mercy. Cassidy and Walker after emptying their revolvers started to run. Walker fell about sixty feet from the bed with a bullet through his head and another pierced his heart. Cassidy fell shortly after with a bullet through his heart.

Tuttle, who had a score to settle too, was waiting to the south to intercept the gang should they escape from the Books.

The inquest jury heard conflicting testimony from many who knew Cassidy. The jurors weighed the evidence and ruled that the dead men were Cassidy and Walker. But the two bandits who survived, known as Thompson and Schultz, insisted "Cassidy" was John Herring. The warden of the Wyoming State Penitentiary, who had known Cassidy when he served a sentence there, traveled to Price. After an exhumation, all agreed Cassidy was still at large. Legend has it that Butch managed to sneak into town and peek at his remains.

An irregular bandit city was reported in the Swell's wilderness. The danger to neighboring ranches was bad enough, but what really scandalized the *Manti Messenger* was the moral tone of the place.

On the San Rafael
Girls and Outlaws

There is a curious condition of things and withal an undesirable one over in the eastern part of Emery County just at present; a condition which has brought about and now causes considerable apprehension among the people over the mountains. There seem to be at least two fully organized and practically unhampered bands of outlaws in that region. . . . There are two combinations fairly entrenched in these impregnable mountain fastnesses: one is located toward the north, the other is southward on the San Rafael.

It's hard to imagine a gang north of the San Rafael. Most likely, the writer is confusing the Dirty Devil with the lower San Rafael, and the two groups are in the Swell and at Robbers Roost proper. At any rate, robbers obviously went to and fro in the Swell, judging by the same April 10, 1898, article:

Reports say that several herds of cattle have been driven north and a good many sold, principally at Price. . . .

The outlaws live among 'breaks,' the wildest, most rugged and inaccessible except to the initiated anywhere under the blue firmament. In recesses cut into the sides of those yawning chasms, two or three men are able to hold an army at bay. To such places all who have stolen, rustled or murdered are welcomed so that the groups are becoming augmented steadily as time goes on. They live in huts made of raw-hides, thus being . . . ensconced from the whistling winter blasts and furious drifing snow. But they are not confined to one sex. There are females forming that [motley? word unclear] combination. It is positively ascertained by parties who are in a position to know that in the one camp are two girls who seem to enjoy that novel existence and immensely comfort their male consorts.

Two women returned to the Emery County towns from one of the bandit camps. They told the names of all except two of the outlaws. The two—apparently special to them—they would never name. But they did say the killers of Sheriff Burns were among the outlaws. The only way the bands could be dislodged, the article concluded, would be by "a good big military force."

Bandits went through the Reef returning from their raids to the north. But purloined beef also seems to have come up the other direction, from Mexico, if Culmer can be trusted. In his 1909 journal he relates the tale of an alleged raid into Mexico by Tom Tidwell and his boys. It was supposed to have happened years before, when the Tidwells lived at Green River Spring beside the Reef.

He (Tidwell) was a cattle man and it is said of him that he and his boys, once at least made a foray down into Mexico, running off a big herd of cattle, most of which he sold in bunches on his way homeward. He still had a drove remaining when he reached here and hid them up on the Swell. He was followed all the way back by one of the Mexican owners, who even went up the river about a mile above the Sheep Bridge, where he was shot. . . . The spot is now called Mexican Bend.

One resident claimed to have talked to the Mexican just before he entered the canyon and advised him that he had reached a point where it would be wise to turn back. But the pursuer said, ''I have tracked them all this way and I'll track 'em to hell but what I'll get 'em.'' It was years later that the body was buried.

Soon after the Castle Gate holdup, lawmen converged on the Swell and Robbers Roost. Railroads, the Pinkerton Detective Agency, and sheriffs of several counties used telegraph and train to coordinate attacks. It was a modern sort of cooperation that the bandits could not deal with. Some of them—like Butch Cassidy, the Sundance Kid, and Etta Place—moved on to Central and South America, hitting backwater tin mines. Well into the twentieth century, the frontier remained woolly south of the border.

The San Rafael Mountains were long regarded as a safe retreat for outlaws, wrote W. H. Lever in 1898. People shunned Emery County because of that.

> But the vigilant officers of the law have made such inroads upon those dark hiding places as to almost exterminate the bands of outlaws. . . . Since then [shooting of Tuttle] some have been killed, others captured, and the band almost broken up.

Today, Hanksville folks are proud of the Old Bunch. Speaking of the Castle Gate robbery, Mrs. Ekker said, ''What tickled me is that all those ranchers that he's stole the horses from was betting on whose horse would hold out the longest!''

They think some of Butch's men may have hid out in the desert until the 1930s or '40s. One man who lived by himself near the Roost was called Old Man Carpenter. Reo Hunt, one of the town fathers of Hanksville, said Carpenter had "some beautiful guns and some good horses." He thought the old man was from the Cassidy gang. But he could get "no information whatsoever" out of him.

"He was real nice," Mrs. Ekker added. "We went down there and stayed a couple of days and went fishing."

Utah's bandit folklore is rife with stories of Butch returning. His sister, Lula Parker Betenson, insisted to the end of her life that the outlaw came back to visit the family in Circleville. For many years, the official version was that they died in a hail of gunfire from soldiers in Bolivia, where he and the Sundance Kid were raiding tin mines. But more recently, those reports were disavowed by the Pinkerton Detective Agency, their source in the first place.

Andy Moore, a rancher whose spread was near the Robbers Roost country, told Hanksville people somebody came to his ranch and borrowed a horse long after Butch's supposed demise. Something about his demeanor made the rancher suspect he was dealing with Cassidy.

According to Barbara Ekker, Moore followed the stranger's tracks back into rugged canyons, saw where the man had dismounted. Bare footprints showed the stranger had taken off his boots so he could climb the slickrock without slipping. He crawled along a ledge, dug up something, and left with it.

We were on a bench above the river near Red Canyon, a side canyon of rough, nearly vertical walls. A ranching couple—Ken Kofford and his wife, Lana, from Castle Dale—had parked their horse trailer and were saddling up beside the San Rafael River on an unusually warm day in early March. They were setting out to find their cows, intending to move them to spring grazing land.

Kofford had been ranching in the area all his life, and he said it was a hard place to make a living. He does this part-time, and also sells mining equipment and supplies.

Kofford said that after the Castle Gate robbery, Butch and his gang rode down from the high country by way of Red Canyon, instead of the easy way via Buckhorn Draw. As an experiment, a friend of his had tried to do the same thing. "He didn't get off [the high country and into Red Canyon], and then he had a hard time getting back after he got part way down," Kofford said. Still, "they swear that's how they got off—and nobody dared follow."

The cliffs at Red Canyon look too tall to scramble down. But maybe there was a way. If you were hounded by a posse of horsemen determined to kill you for the reward money, you'd be willing to take a few risks, jump down crazy places.

Kofford thinks Sid Swasey's leap had an outlaw connection too. "The story my grandmother told me doesn't jibe with the history books. There was a posse coming after him—two posses —one out of Green River and one from the west. And he jumped the river to evade them. He'd been collecting cows and sheep," and now Kofford's voice grew soft, "of other people—I don't know what's true. The story in the book is he jumped it on a wager."

Could someone do that?

"You could, but you'd really have to want to," Kofford said. You'd need a better horse, too, than the corral-bred ones around today. "You'd have to have a horse that had been out in the rough a lot. There is no way to get a run on it from the side he jumped." It's slickrock, "on both sides, and it's not level. It's just not a very good spot to be jumping horses on a wager. If he hadn't made it, he'd never told the story, because there's no way he'd live."

I remarked that I've always wondered what people who work in magnificent scenery think about it. Do they simply work in it without looking at it much, or do they appreciate it? "I like the scenery," Mrs. Kofford said. "I've seen it," he said.

They rode away on their horses, their little dog walking purposefully beside them, going toward the San Rafael River.

11

Filling in the Blank Spots

The U.S. Geological Survey showed little interest in the San Rafael Reef from the survey's founding in 1879 through the end of the nineteenth century. Bands of horse thieves and murderers were threatening enough to keep the scientists away. But by 1900 the bandits had been cleaned out. Tourists and geologists began taking an interest in the region.

Sheepherders discovered vanadium-uranium deposits near the San Rafael River around the turn of the century; they were prospected and claimed by Judge J. W. Warf. Green River residents acquired eight claims and mined them vigorously. In the fall of 1903 sheepherders found deposits in the sandstone walls of the Reef's Wild Horse Canyon.

Vanadium and uranium are often mixed in nature. In the early years, vanadium was more valuable as it was thought to be twelve times as effective as tungsten in hardening steel. Uranium was a by-product of vanadium mining—worth bothering with only if it was of superior quality. It could be used by scientific researchers, but its greatest value was in manufacturing porcelain and glass.

Cowboys like Joe Swasey sometimes hauled out bags of high-grade uranium. It was refined, then used by quacks for medical "cures." A shipment of three thousand pounds of San

Rafael uranium ore was sent to Germany by 1904. Maybe some antique Dresden porcelain figures are radioactive.

In 1905 Joseph A. Taft of the USGS stared south, looking from a peak near the junction of the Wasatch Plateau and the Book Cliffs, close to the coal town of Price. He could see "the general physical features of the whole land at a single sweeping view." Sent there to explore the economic potential of giant coal fields in the Books, Taft took no notice of the Reef and paid scant attention to the nearby Swell. In a report that year, he wrote,

> The desert plain of Castle Valley stretches away to the limit of vision toward the southwest and southeast. Between the arms of the valley toward the south the broad rugged surface of the San Rafael Swell rises in the distance.

It fell to a painter to discover the beauty of the San Rafael Reef. H. L. A. Culmer of Salt Lake City has already been quoted briefly. He was one of the best-selling landscape artists in America and was president of the Utah Art Institute for two years. His depictions of Utah's natural wonders brought him acclaim. His canvases hung in homes of the wealthy, art galleries, and public buildings. Asked to name his art teachers, the largely self-taught Culmer would reply, "N. A. Ture." He died in February 1914.

Culmer wrote in 1909 that he had been hearing stories for years about the "Silent City." That was the name that Denver & Rio Grande Railroad conductors used for the Reef, pointing out the broken country as locomotives approached Green River Station. But until Culmer, nobody had tried to tell the public about its lavish scenery.

He seems to have visited the Reef as a propagandist for a land development scheme, a project of the Green River Valley Land and Cattle Company. The San Rafael River would be blocked behind a masonry dam 185 feet high, with water let into the four valleys below by means of a tunnel through the Reef's base. Thousands of settlers would grow fruit trees and everybody would make money. Evidently, he was commissioned to paint a view of the proposed reservoir along the San Rafael River, as it would look once completed. And he pumped the project vigorously in a 1909 newspaper article. Culmer kept a diary of his trip, jotting down impressions for the article he would write.

His party arrived in Green River by train and stayed overnight. He was annoyed by the rail traffic. At that time, Green River was branching out into ranching, melon farming, and mining. Deposits of gold, silver, copper, lead, pitchblend, oil, and tar sands had been discovered in Emery County by then. According to the *Salt Lake Tribune* of 1909, farmers trekked to Sinbad at the top of the Swell and scooped oil from springs in five-gallon cans. They used it as lubricant for mowers and binders.

Culmer's adventurers drove a buckboard into the Reef by way of Black Dragon Wash, went through the canyon, then cut across the great sandstone projection of rock to the valley of the San Rafael River. The artist burned up hours sketching, photographing, and asking questions about the country. The group's wagon was wrecked on the rough trail. By midnight, when they reached the camp of reservoir project surveyors working under Chief Engineer A. A. Clark, they were on horseback. That day they made less than five miles in a direct line from the Forsmans' ranch (now called Smith's Ranch) near the northern end of the Reef. But it was sixteen miles by Black Dragon and the winding river canyon.

The reservoir site was at Sheep Bridge, where Sid Swasey had jumped his horse across the Black Box. The bridge consisted of a few thin poles eleven feet long resting on narrow ledges at the top of the Black Box. The river roared along fifty feet below, its bed thirty-five feet wide. Sheepherders crossed their flocks on that frail bridge, saving a detour of many miles, Culmer learned.

In the Reef canyons the artist was dazzled by color: cliffs sunburned black, gleaming white domes of Navajo sandstone, belts of pale green and lemon running along fluted cliffs. Nearby were orange and ocher crags, he wrote. Huge towers of Pompeiian red paled into violet and pink as they faded in the distance, line after line, spire after spire.

Black Dragon Wash he found to be superb, with a level gravelly bottom, its unbroken walls soaring nearly 1,000 feet above, sometimes bulging out 100 feet. Ferns and clinging vines hung from crevices. In his often-misspelled notes, he marveled at spires and minarets, domes and cornices of orange and brown, which rose above Indian red and maroon walls.

April 24. . . . So far we had been going Westward. Now we go several miles to the East in our discent to the San Rafael, that gorge being fortunately parallel to Black Dragon. (The latter should be called Red Dragon. It has an imposing look from above as well as below) Before descending from the high mesa we had a view in the twilight of the inner escarpments of the great Reef and hope to have a better look at it in the wonderfully rich reds and browns and the extraordinary forms. Looking Southward the prows of these separate cliffs resemble the bows of great red battleships plowing into the high mesa.

We dashed into the wind and water up to the horses' bellies and shipped a little of the river into the buck board. The team plunged to free themselves and broke the double tree in midstream although we managed to flounder them out into the willows on the shore. A pleasant half hour was spent in repairs and on we started. The road—if there was any wound around and up and down past the heads of box canyons, and in the faint light seemed as bad as a road could be and live. Their singletrees brok, kingbolt bust, etc. and after a dozen fixings we had to abandon the outfit and saddle the team, bringing in all the plunder we could carry and arriving in camp a little before midnight. The boys aproved the Jap cook we had supper and rolled into our blankets, tired but well and happy.

Monday Apr 26 [actually the 25th]. Awoke early and found ourselves in a well organized Camp. . . .

There is just one way in from the Eastern side and that is up Black Dragon Canyon. As for going up the San Rafael Canyon, that is considered quite an achievement on foot or horseback at the lowest stage of the stream, and is quite impossible in the Spring time. It involves leaping your horse from rocky ledges into deep water and many a quick pitapat over quicksand down in the dark boxes of the canyon.

According to Culmer, the trail up the canyon of the San Rafael was reputed to have more thrills to the mile than any other "in the universe."

The dam project was abandoned as infeasible, and no remnant exists today. The tunnel was never drilled through the Reef. The expected thousands never showed up to farm the benches.

But the Green River region was growing anyway. When Culmer visited, the town's population was 1,100, and the town had an assessed valuation of $320,269. Residents were demanding river improvements. In 1910 the U.S. Army Corps of Engineers cruised along the Green and Colorado rivers, weighing the possibilities of navigation improvements. They outraged townsmen by recommending against dredging the Green.

The next year, Frank L. Hess of the USGS spent two days in the Reef investigating a sulfur deposit next to the San Rafael River. At the same time, the survey's Charles T. Lupton was mapping along the Swell's west flank in Castle Valley. Hess detailed his findings on the sulfur discovery in 1913—the first USGS report of a trip within the Reef.

He investigated a sulfur deposit "18 or 20 miles west of the town of Greenriver." The sulfur spring was five miles within the canyon, where it widens to a quarter of a mile across, placing it near the Lower Black Box. The deposit lay "in limestone debris through which rise a number of springs carrying large volumes of hydrogen sulphide gas from which the sulphur has probably been formed," Hess wrote. The smell could be detected from at least a mile off. The deposit seemed too small for profitable extraction, he concluded. It was a strip only 100 or 150 feet wide and 750 feet long. "Sulphur deposits not accompanied by springs are reported to occur near San Rafael Swell 5 to 6 miles above the ones described," he noted, and others were fifteen miles farther to the northwest, on Cedar Mountain.

Hess could not resist admiring the Reef's striking formations.

> San Rafael River flows southeastward across the northern part of the San Rafael Swell and has cut a deep canyon with nearly perpendicular walls a thousand feet or more high which are in places impressively beautiful. Broad and narrow bands of red, white, and buff alternate in the sedimentary rocks of the walls, and with the bright blue of the sky and the green of the cottonwoods and brush on the floor of the canyon produce very striking color effects.

Lupton and W. R. Calvert visited the nearby Red Plateau in August 1911, and a little later Lupton penetrated to the Swell's interior with W. C. Mendenhall. In a 1916 USGS bulletin, Lupton wrote the best description of the Swell's geology up to then:

> The most prominent feature of the San Rafael Swell is a series of odd-shaped sandstone forms which encircle an area in the heart of the Swell, locally known as 'Sinbad,' which is 40 to 50 miles long and 10 to 20 miles wide. These fantastically eroded forms are remnants of the outcrop of a massive cross-bedded gray Jurassic sandstone about 800 feet thick. It is practicable to cross the Swell at only a few places on account of the almost impassable barrier formed by this sandstone rim. Nearly vertical scarps and canyon walls 300 to 500 feet in height are common. Low hogbacks formed by resistant beds in the strata overlying this sandstone, the upper surfaces of which produce dip slopes of varying extent, depending on the inclination of the beds, encircle this belt of rugged topography. Badlands are common, especially near stream courses.

Roads were starting to crisscross the Swell. Lupton said a road from Castle Dale ''follows closely the route of the old Spanish Trail across the north end of the San Rafael Swell to Green River, the easternmost town in Emery County.''

A road from Castledale through Buckhorn Flat and along Buckhorn Wash also leads through 'Sinbad' to the desert. From Emery two roads to the east have been constructed. One road 20 miles in length leads through Rochester and Dry Wash to the Globe Copper Mine [in the center of the Swell]. The other leads to the southeast about 18 miles to a supposed oil field on Salt Wash, 2 miles above its junction with Muddy Creek.

In 1921 oil companies exploring in Sinbad built a road from Buckhorn Flat down Buckhorn Wash to the San Rafael River. They erected a bridge there and continued the road on south. James Gilluly said in a 1928 USGS bulletin that the route was described as ''practically never used'' but passable by automobile. The bridge was washed out by then; however, the San Rafael usually could be forded. He added that a recently built road through Black Dragon Wash was badly washed out but could probably be repaired at comparatively small expense. A road was built some years ago from Rochester to Horn Silver mine, a copper prospect on the Reef, but it is in very poor shape, as is the road from Emery to Caineville, which was built by oil men about 1920. . . . All these roads are but little more than winding trails along which a vehicle can be moved only with difficulty because of washes, loose sand, and rock ledges.

The road building was prompted by an "oil excitement" in the San Rafael Swell between 1918 and 1922. Although no great gushers of black gold spurted from drill rigs, the region's potential began to interest the U.S. Geological Survey. Starting in July 1924, the survey's E. M. Spieker began mapping the Swell, focusing on oil possibilities. His map was to cover all of the Swell except part of "the eastern margin," that is, part of the Reef.

Surveyors in that period used the plane table, a tripod with a table on top, on which maps could be prepared in the field. An alidade—a movable telescope connected to a straightedge—was placed on the top of the plane table. With the straightedge, lines could be drawn on the map reproducing the telescope's exact alignment.

Spieker withdrew from fieldwork in August, and the 29-year-old Gilluly was put in charge. He continued to map until the project was completed in September 1925. John B. Reeside, Jr., helped Gilluly by spending several weeks studying the stratigraphy of the Swell in 1924, revisiting parts in 1925.

No permanent settlers lived within the area surveyed, Gilluly noted in a report, although attempts at dry farming had been made at Buckhorn Flat, Summerville Wash, Fullers Bottom, the Lockhart cabins, and at Joe Swasey's cabin in Sinbad. "But lack of moisture has discouraged the attempts, and all had been abandoned," Gilluly wrote.

Water holes are sparsely scattered over the area, and most of them, except a few in pockets in the sandstone along the top of the Reef and near the south end of Sinbad are unsuited to the use of man, though stock will drink from them. The water of both San Rafael and Muddy Rivers is sometimes so concentrated that even stock will not drink it, but this happens only during the very hottest and driest periods. Throughout the field work except that in the southern part of Sinbad it was necessary for the party to haul from the towns in Castle Valley all the water used for drinking. The water from some of the Cottonwood Springs is potable, and those of a few other localities probably are at times, but none are free from alkali and most are better avoided.

They measured sections of cliffs throughout the area, from south of Muddy River to the Sinbad and Black Dragon Canyon. The partners laboriously recorded every layer, sometimes for cliffs more than a thousand feet tall. At times the work was so detailed that layers are listed in inches.

Speaking of the Waterpocket Fold, later to become the heart of Capitol Reef National Park, Gilluly and Reeside wrote that it is "a district remarkably resembling the San Rafael Swell in topography."

Gilluly declared the Reef impassable, and he was probably glad the township he was assigned to map did not take in the southern part of the Swell. In places, he wrote, the Reef is

. . . one nearly sheer cliff, although generally the cliff is broken by one, two, or three benches. From the top of these walls the country slopes away from Sinbad on all sides—steeply on the east and south, so that these parts of the Reef are striking hogbacks that plunge directly into the general plateau surface with only very minor accompanying outer ridges. . . .

The canyons of the San Rafael and Muddy rivers are very striking. The San Rafael flows southeastward across the Swell, without regard to the varying resistance of the rocks it encounters, carving winding canyons as much as 500 feet deep through the outer hogbacks, 1,800 feet deep through the Reef, and 800 feet deep in the Black Box, at the north end of Sinbad. . . . At the east end of the Black Box it swings sharply northeastward, emerges from its canyon into an open valley, curves with a radius of about a mile through nearly a complete circle, the Mexican Bend, and again trenches a box canyon several hundred feet deep and in places less than 40 feet across at the top. Below the canyon it swings to its regional trend and flows out of the area to join Green River, about 35 miles away.

Gilluly skirted most of the Reef, although he entered Spring Canyon, Mexican Bend, Black Box, and drainages leading into the ridge at several places. He mapped parts of Bell and Chute canyons and the tip of the Moroni Slopes. The rest of it was out of his territory.

Then, in 1935, into this desiccated realm of cliffs, foul springs, and bad roads came the U.S. Geological Survey's Charles Butler Hunt. Like Gilluly when he started, Hunt was only twenty-nine and the chief of an important expedition. He set out to map the remaining uncharted country of the San Rafael region.

12

The Last Mule Expedition

An animated man of seventy-eight who looked as if he were in his early sixties, Charles Butler Hunt sat in an easy chair near the living room window. We were in his white, ranch-style home in Taylorsville, Utah, on a Sunday in late 1984. ''It was all pack train work in those days,'' he said. ''It was a wild piece of country, in an area the size of the state of New York without any railroads, and a third of that area had no road of any kind.''

He was remembering the years when he made the first topographic map of the southern part of the San Rafael Reef, starting in 1935. They used strings of twelve or fifteen horses and mules—the last time the U.S. Geological Survey sent a big mounted expedition into the wilderness. It was the end of an era that began with Powell.

Then as now the main exception to the roadless desert was Utah 24, the highway paralleling the Reef from Green River to Hanksville. When Hunt was there, the Civilian Conservation Corps had recently improved the dirt road that later became Utah Highway 24. Mapping the Reef was the first monumental challenge tackled by Hunt's USGS expedition, which spent five seasons in the region, through 1939.

From the start, the project was a difficult one. ''The Reef of the San Rafael Swell, the Capitol Reef, and the Waterpocket Fold are formidable obstacles to travel of any kind,'' Hunt wrote

143

in the 1953 USGS professional paper that reported his studies. "Horses can be taken into them at only a few places and only a few of the canyons through them are passable."

Hogback ridges, known locally as reefs, are prominent and spectacular, he observed. They include the San Rafael Reef, Capitol Reef, and the Waterpocket Fold.

They are formidable barriers to travel and can be crossed at only very few places, even on foot. Their surface is mainly bare rock and virtually all of it is waste land.

Broad strike valleys lie on each side of the hogback ridges . . . and they are connected by only a few widely spaced narrow canyons through the ridges. Many of these connecting canyons are too narrow or too rough for horseback travel. Boulder Canyon, for example, which crosses the hogback ridges of the San Rafael Swell, is about 300 ft deep but its sides are so close together that a boulder fallen from the rim has lodged between the walls without touching bottom. One does not need to stoop much to walk under it, but until it is dislodged, horses cannot be taken through the canyon.

Hunt was already a USGS veteran at the time, having worked as a field assistant in 1929 in a survey through what later became Arches National Park. Next he was assigned to New Mexico, Montana, and Kentucky. He was based in Washington, D.C., when the Henry Mountains assignment came up. He got it because he had become interested in problems of volcanic rocks while at Mount Taylor, New Mexico.

The classic study on the Henrys, which established the importance of volcanic upthrusts in the creation of such ranges, was performed by Grove K. Gilbert of Powell's survey. Powell had glimpsed the Henrys (which are just south of Hanksville) during his second expedition. He guessed that lava bulging between sandstone strata was important in the mountains' formation. In 1875–76 he sent Gilbert to check it out.

Now Hunt was supposed to update Gilbert's work and prepare the first good topographic map of the region. But before he got to the Henrys he was to chart areas that were adjacent to Gilluly's assignment—including San Rafael Reef.

That's where they began in the first season. Horses and mules carried the gear, and the crews camped in rugged canyons. Hunt and his assistant did the grunt work, scrambling over the Reef, sketching formations, triangulating, calculating elevations and angles, mapping layers and crests and dips and canyons. They mapped North Temple, South Temple, Wild Horse, Crack, Chute, Little Wild Horse, Bell, Cistern [called Boulder in the report], and Muddy Creek canyons, as well the Reef itself.

After they finished with the Reef, the team moved south to the Henry Mountains. Altogether, the geologists spent about eighteen hundred man-hours in the field.

Hunt remembered his chief packer, Charlie Hanks, with great fondness. "He was one of the old-timers and it was a great opportunity for me. He was very much my senior. He was old enough to be my dad. But he was a complete cow-puncher, and he took care of our string of horses—and the geologists," he laughed. "Both being tenderfeet, I might add."

Hunt did not work inside the Swell, as Gilluly had done the main mapping there. "My mapping ties onto the south end of Jim's mapping. If you remember his map, it does not quite go to the Reef on the south end of the Swell."

"So did you go into the Reef?"

"I had to go across the Reef to tie into his mapping. My map extends across the Reef in the San Rafael Swell."

They started at a seep near Temple Mountain called Buckskin Spring. "And then we extended that mapping down to south of where the Muddy River comes through, and on down to the Fremont River at Caineville; carried that fold down around to the Capitol Reef, and then on down Waterpocket to the Colorado River."

Hunt consulted G. K. Gilbert's original notes of sixty years before, written in several small notebooks. They were valuable because there were no good maps of this section. The only topographic map available was one issued by the Powell survey, showing the entire state of Utah. It had few details in the San Rafael country. Hunt and his men were recording this region on a scale of one mile to the inch; if they had mapped the state at that scale, the chart would have been more than thirty feet long.

The geologists would set up triangulation flags, locating each by sighting on other landmarks whose positions were known, such as the several peaks of the Henry Mountains. As they worked their way along the Reef, they'd take direction bearings from these flags, or measure distance and angles to them. Then they could pinpoint their location. That was literally how they indicated where they were: by the prick of a needle on the mapping paper. They'd draw rays on their charts to points of interest, move to another location, and sketch in the topography between locations. They would sketch and take notes as they moved, measuring and calculating altitude as they went.

How did they manage to map along the Reef?

"On foot. You can't take a horse along the Reef. Two of us mapped it. It was by plane table. . . . We would go to a canyon by horse, and Charlie Hanks would then take our horses back to a pack camp."

As they walked along the Reef, mapping geologic boundaries, they had to cross any canyons that cut through the ridge. "Did you walk on the reef itself?"

"Oh, yes. . . . Charlie Hanks had to estimate how many of these canyons we could cross in a day. He would drop us, then pick up our horses and move on down to where he thought we would come out. We were good for only about one crossing in a day, with the distance that we had to travel along the top of the Reef. . . . The only way you can get across those canyons was to climb down along the Kayenta Formation. Then you gotta climb right back up on the other side, which isn't very far. And you start over again."

It was not a matter of walking straight ahead and sketching the formations. The men worked slowly. "I would carry the stadia rod and I had my assistant manage the plane table. I would go ahead and he would shoot me in on the other side of the canyon." Once across one of these steep-walled canyons, Hunt would find himself with nothing to do but sit and wait for his assistant to cross. "Then he would go beyond me and backsight to the stadia rod for his location. And then he would have to sit while I walked past him." In addition to noting the general topography, as they walked on the Reef they were mapping the positions of two formations, the top of the Wingate and the base of the Navajo sandstone.

They mapped the inside curve of the Reef, along the Reef's

crest, and on the outside of the great ridge. "So we caught it three ways," Hunt said. "That's no different from what Jim Gilluly did. You look at that Reef on his map, and it's the same on my map: you can figure that every one of those geological boundaries are a geologist's footprints."

He recalled the big boulder that had fallen from the rim in Cistern Canyon. That was impressive, because the cliffs were so close together the rock wedged between them above the floor. "And somewhere along that canyon—I can't remember whether it was above or below the boulder—I have a picture of one of the geologists standing in the bottom of the canyon with his hands reaching out and touching each side of the wall." A drawing was made from this vertical panorama, and incorporated in USGS Professional Paper 228, Hunt's report.

Come evening, the weary geologists would hike down the Reef, deciding they had covered as many knobs and ravines as they could that day—and there they'd find Hanks had set up a new "spike camp." Base camps, which were more elaborate than these overnight sites, were accessible by car. They were home to the four geologists, the packer, and the cook. The geologists would move from these by pack train. "Depending on the weather, we might do without tents. We lived outdoors repeatedly," Hunt said. They ate mostly canned food, considered good eating in the depths of the Depression.

They heard lots of coyotes and saw a few deer and a lonesome rattlesnake or two—but no remarkable wildlife, no mountain sheep, even though Hunt recognized the Reef as good mountain sheep habitat.

After leaving their first camp, which was at Buckskin Spring near South Temple Wash, they worked slowly toward the southwest. "And when we moved down to camp near the Muddy River, Charlie Hanks had to come with me with the cars, because he was the only one who knew how to get back up past Factory Butte to the Muddy River, where we went to camp," Hunt recalled.

"So we sent the cook and one of the geologists to bring the horses around. And the way Charlie instructed them to come was to go up Wild Horse Canyon and come around on the Triassic to the Muddy River, and come down the Muddy River and he would come right to our camp, with the string of horses. . . . I guess we had about 15 horses."

On the overnight trip from Temple Mountain one of the horses got away. That kind of mishap never happened when Hanks moved the string, said Hunt, but when the cook and the geologist moved the camp things went wrong.

"Well, they described about where the horse had taken off, and so Charlie packed up next day and took a second animal with him with a camping outfit, because he didn't know how long he was going to be tracking down a lost horse." He left right after breakfast and was back in camp with the runaway before the surveyors returned in the late afternoon.

"I asked Charlie, 'How in the world did you track down that horse?' He said, 'Oh, he didn't go up through the Triassic. He went up the back side of the Reef to Wild Horse.' And he said, 'I saw the horse tracks coming down Wild Horse.'

" 'Well,' I said, 'then you just followed his tracks.'

" 'Naw,' Charlie said, 'I took a short cut on over to the trail from this spring [Buckskin Spring] . . . went down to Wild Horse Spring. Oh, I figured the horse would hang around that Wild Horse Spring for a while, and then he'd head back to where we'd camped before. I just figured I'd go where the horse would go.' "

That's where he found the horse, walking back to Buckhorn Spring.

According to Hunt, Hanks could figure the movements of men as accurately as he could those of his equine charges. This is shown by the story of what happened to the two horses that carried supplies for a man who came down with appendicitis. The fellow returned to civilization, leaving his horses behind.

"When you're working the pack string in that country, you've got to haul in feed for the horses. And each man has to have two horses, because the feed is not good enough for a horse to sustain itself, working daily." They packed 300 pounds of oats per month for each animal. "The logistics add up to being a lot of oats," he said.

Some of the horses belonged to the U.S. government and some were rented from a Green River rancher, Sam Adams.

Hunt decided to send Hanks to Green River to find out from Adams where they should deliver the two horses that were no longer needed. "We can't afford to be hauling in for two horses that we're not using."

"Charlie came back from Green River and he said he didn't get to see Sam Adams because Sam Adams had left that morning for Rabbit Valley, which is up in the Loa Country, in the High Plateaus. I said, 'Good God, Charlie, Sam's going to be—what?—a week getting to Rabbit Valley.'" Worse than that, Adams would spend another week visiting the valley and yet another in returning. Hunt's expedition would have to feed two useless animals for a month.

"Charlie leaned back and he said, 'Well,' he said, 'I figure, Sam, tonight he's probably down around the San Rafael [River]. Tomorrow night he'll probably stop at Garvin's—that's on Temple Mountain Wash. . . .

"'Let's see. Tomorrow night he'll stop at Garvin's. Then he'll go to Hanksville and he'll stay down at Andrew Hunt's.' Andrew Hunt had the ranch right by the Muddy River in Hanksville.

"'He won't get away from Andrew's very early. He'll get up to Hanksville and he'll be seein' Mort and Neelis. And I think if I go down here to the road about three o'clock Thursday I'll see Sam.'

"And so help me, he only had to wait an hour!"

Hanks and Adams visited for a bit, and Hanks asked what should be done with the horses. "Sam said, 'Just turn 'em loose.' So Charlie took them back to this spring where we had started." The horses were freed at Buckskin Spring, where Adams could collect them at his leisure.

Hanksville was named for Ebenezer Hanks, and Charlie Hanks's family made up much of the town's population. During the expedition, though, Hanks lived in Green River. Hunt's geologic report credited him as playing "a leading role in the history of the region." He was packer and guide for all five seasons.

George Wolgamot, who owned the Trachyte ranch south of Hanksville, worked with the field parties in 1937–39. "These two men proved most valuable guides because of their thorough knowledge of the country and the handling of saddle and pack animals in the desert," Hunt wrote in his report.

He noticed that several of the Reef's canyons meander as if they were gentle streams crossing broad valleys. Like Powell before, he realized such windings are inherited from more ancient levels of the stream course, with the stream gradually working its way down.

Caineville Reef was a structural double to the San Rafael Reef, but in a geologically higher formation. "The Capitol Reef is identical to the reef around the San Rafael Swell," he said.

By 1939 Hanksville had fifty-seven adults and sixty-five children. Mail came through three times a week by motor stage from Torrey, near Capitol Reef. Hunt wrote in his report,

> A store in Hanksville keeps a small supply of groceries, gasoline, and oil; private homes there provide overnight accommodations. Hanksville has an elementary school, but the nearest high school is at Bicknell, 50 miles west. The nearest electric power, telephone, medical services, and garage facilities are at Green River, 60 miles north of Hanksville or in the towns of Rabbit Valley that are an equivalent distance to the west.

"Were they into mining, mostly?" I asked.

"No, mostly ranching. There was a little mining and prospecting on the side for vanadium in those days and for gold in the Henry Mountains—placer gold."

While I gobbled rich brownies that his wife, Alice, had just baked, Hunt unfolded treasured photo albums he had kept for half a century. "Camp West of Hanksville" shows the team's base camp. A two-photo panorama pasted together, it's a view of four tents, grazing horses, and a mighty formation rising in the background. "Crack Canyon, in San Rafael Swell" is a vertical panorama from the heart of the Reef, dwarfing the geologists at the cliff base. In "1935, Camp at Muddy River in San Rafael Swell" a pack train moves off toward the cliffs, two men on horses and half a dozen loaded mules, Hunt's horse sticking its ears into the foreground. "Reef of San Rafael Swell, 1935" shows two riders emerging from shadows, the rugged cliffs rising around them.

Hunt does not recall that much mining was going on in the Reef when he was there; at least, not much for uranium. "Back in those days, in the '30s, the only interest was in vanadium," he said.

Although the ductile metal was slightly radioactive when found with uranium, it was still used as an alloy in steel manufacturing. "In those days, they had to pay a penalty, because there was uranium mixed with the stuff. Nowadays, the same deposits are mined for uranium and they get a penalty because there's vanadium mixed with it," he said. "The two are very difficult to separate in the treatment of the ore."

Practically no mining was carried out in the San Rafael Reef when Hunt was surveying it. "There was a little prospecting for vanadium down at the southern end of the Henry Mountains, down around the Tickaboo country. And there was a little activity at Temple Mountain, but I can't remember what the interest was. . . . But once in a while, a cowboy would get bored with the cows and go out and knock off a few pieces of high-grade and bring it in. And that would be called mining, in the 1930s."

Just before World War II, Hunt worked at locating strategic minerals, notably surveying manganese deposits on the Colorado Plateau. Then, when the war started, he was put in charge of the Military Geography Unit. He predicted ground conditions in areas to be invaded, read geologic maps, and interpreted terrain for the engineers.

After the war he was appointed the regional geologist for the USGS in Utah, headquartered in Salt Lake City. The family lived in Alpine while he traveled through the state, working on geology as well as performing administrative duties. He studied part of Utah Valley and the beds of Lake Bonneville.

His report on the Reef and the Henry Mountains came out in 1953. The importance of his work in southern Utah was recognized immediately by geologists. Eugene M. Shoemaker, the USGS expert who was interviewed in an earlier chapter, wrote in a 1956 report about features of the Colorado Plateau and uranium,

> Present-day concepts of the structure of the mountains in the central Plateau are due largely to Hunt (1953), who

mapped the Henry Mountains in detail. Hunt has shown that each of the Henry Mountains is underlain by a broad structural dome from 6 to 15 miles in diameter.

Hunt is still so busy with geology I had a hard time catching up with him. The first couple of times I tried for an appointment, he and his wife were off haunting the Henry Mountains, retracing the footsteps of his hero, G. K. Gilbert. Hunt had recently published a book on Gilbert's geological journals. He keeps in touch with the Hanksville folks and feels at home in that town.

After he retired from the government in 1961 with thirty years' government service, he taught at Johns Hopkins University, Baltimore. When they returned to the Henry Mountains with a group of Johns Hopkins students in 1961, Mrs. Hunt— who had earned a master's degree in archaeology—studied Fremont remains in the Henrys' Bull Creek flood plain.

Mrs. Hunt also wrote a study on Death Valley archaeology and a volume on the ancient people of the La Sals, while Hunt worked on the geology of those areas. But she was much too modest to consent to be tape-recorded by me. Hunt had to chuckle at her reticence. "To hear her talk, she ain't done nothin'."

13

Folks Who Live There

"See, Charlie Hanks and I worked for Charlie Hunt when he was doing that survey," said Reo.

Conrad and I were trying to warm up in Barbara Ekker's double-wide, brown and white trailer in Hanksville on a numbing November morning. After shivering all night in the Reef, we were as grateful for the hot coffee as we were for the interviews she had lined up.

The first thing we noticed about Barbara Ekker's yard was her weather station. From this box of white slats on stilts, she reports Hanksville conditions. Sometimes it's the coldest spot in Utah. After all, this is a desert country of extreme temperatures.

That day, two deer heads were propped on top of the gauging station and the door was open. The bucks were bagged during the hunting season by her husband, Jess, and son Justin. They were left there to show them off, Barbara said. A couple of antlers from some previous season also decorated the station.

Pies steamed on a counter, and two boys sprawled on a couch watching football players crash across a large color TV. A wood stove warmed the living room.

Reo Hunt (not related to Charles B. Hunt) is a short, burly, ruddy man with a big grin. He was in his sixties, but exactly where was an unknown—he said only that he was "too damned

153

old." Stories are told that some of his equipment was vandalized by radical environmentalists.

His business card reads on one side, "HUNT'S SERVICE INC. Oil Field Locations. Hot Shot Service Welding-Wrecker Service. Rental of: Tools-Equipment & Mobile Housing 24 Hour Service." The flip side says, "BUSINESS built on SERVICE. Used Cars—Land—Whiskey—Manure—Nails—Flies—Rocks—Flyswatters—Hippies Tamed. . . . Watermelons—Bed Pans —Tequila—Baby Sitting—Scoop Shovels—Tigers Tamed—Bars Emptied—Computers Verified—Orgies Organized—Wading Boots."

Reo arrived in Hanksville in 1928 from Kenilworth, near Price. Soon afterwards, when Charles Hunt's expedition came mapping, he was one of many Hanksville residents who helped Charlie Hanks, Hunt's packer. At the time, the USGS scientists were camped at Garvin's, the ranch at the junction of Utah 24 and the South Temple Road.

"I was just a kid then, quite interested in learning something about geology. I didn't get a chance to go to school," he said. "And you'd ask Charlie something and he wouldn't tell ya. But this other cook, he noticed it. And he said, 'Hey, Reo, say, I'll tell you—if you want to know something about some particular place we've worked during the day, when you get in at night and Charlie's doing his notes,' he said, 'don't ask him. Argue with him. Disagree with him.' And he was so right. If you disagreed with Charlie, he'd go right down and tell you everything about it. And it took him quite a little while to catch on to what I was doing. Then he took quite a time, and he taught me quite a little bit about geology."

Other than guiding geologists, how do people in Hanksville make a living?

"We steal from each other," Barbara said.

"Lots of minin'," said Donald "Bud" Hanni.

"Lot of mining," agreed Jess Ekker. But with the uranium boom over, he said, "it's pretty damn tough. . . . In the winter we don't have much here at all, really."

Jess's family has lived in Hanksville nearly since the town was founded. His father was a miner and cattleman, and Jess "mined up there for years and years" at Temple Mountain. He has always lived in Hanksville except for time at school and in the navy.

In the 1980 census Hanksville's population numbered only 361. This remote town's economy depends on tourists driving through toward Lake Powell or Capitol Reef National Park. Several gas stations and one motel, the Poor Boy, bring in dollars.

But during the uranium boom of the 1950s the town was in its heyday. Of course, the earlier uranium-vanadium economics had reversed.

At that time, Hanksville had 536 registered voters. Barbara remembers that distinctly because she was the voter registration agent. "I mean, we could have swung the election in the whole county. That whole Red Rock trailer park was full of rig people, and every trailer park in town, every rental, was filled up. . . . You know, people'd say, My God, who's that downtown?" So many strangers were in town that the post office ran out of boxes.

Reo Hunt was involved with Vernon Pick when Pick made his strike at Hidden Splendor, the Delta Mine which is just inside the Reef where the Muddy River goes through. "When he took the first load of ore that he took out of Hidden Splendor up there, he put it in my pickup. I lent him my pickup. And that pickup load brought him thirty-two hundred dollars."

"I'll tell you what he done," said Jess. "Went in there and he shipped, oh, I think around a million and a half, two million dollars worth of ore . . . and he sold it. Got a good buy." A big company paid Pick $9 million cash for the mine, Jess said. "He just picked that $9 million up and went to California, and built him a house back away from everybody." Eventually, the mine was closed, the ceiling collapsed. "I mean they left a lotta, lotta ore in there," he said.

Before the uranium boom took off around 1948, when the United States started testing and stockpiling nuclear weapons in a big way, Hanksville lived on cattle ranching and placer mining. Some areas in the Henry Mountains have gold, although the lack of water makes mining difficult. Reo hauls loads of rich dirt to his home in Hanksville, where he uses an extracting machine to recover gold.

But with the mines shut down and the cattle business in a

bad way, Hanksville is hurting. He thinks mining will make a comeback if they can "get rid of a few of these ecologists."

He then asked bluntly about my intentions about the San Rafael country: "What are you tryin' to do, make a wilderness out of it?" I had come a long way and suffered from the cold for these interviews, and I was not about to abort now. So I fibbed.

"No, I'm just doin' a book."

"We'll get rid of you right now, if you are," Barbara said.

"Yep," Reo laughed. Obviously, they were joking.

"I don't know what's going to happen when these environmentalists get their way," Reo said. "And they've got the livestock [grazing] cut down a good ninety or ninety-five percent now."

"Where's that?" I asked.

"All over," Barbara and Reo answered in unison.

"All over," Reo said again. "They've canceled permits. You see, this is government range or federal land, the majority of it is. And they've got 'em cut down at least ninety or ninety-five percent right now."

"Why's that? What is the excuse or reason?"

"Just because they're so stupid," he laughed. "Oh, the range's overgrazed, to hear 'em talk. It's just so badly overgrazed.

"Well, before we ever got here—before white people ever hit this country—there were buffalo, antelope, deer, wild horses—and there was livestock, everywhere. When we came, when the white man came here, they run the Indians out and they also run the buffalo and a good share of the deer and antelope.

"Then the Bureau of Land Management killed all the wild horses. I mean they shot them, on the pretense of making more feed for livestock. But at the same time, they kept cutting the permits on livestock. Well, they've got it down now to where there's very, very, very few head of livestock. . . .

"And the stupid damn fools. Any time you raise anything on a piece of land, you have got to put something back to pay for what comes out growing. If you don't, your growth will just diminish every year, until eventually nothing will grow. When the livestock was there, they'd eat what grew green every year, they put their droppings where they'd eat it. The rain'd come along, soak it back in the land, and, it was fertilized—it'd grow again next year."

But now, he said, "They've got to have wilderness here, wilderness there. And wilderness means getting rid of all the livestock. They can't step in a pile of cow manure, that's dirty. If we let 'em manage the way they are going today, thirty years, there won't be anything growing out there."

As an example of the idiocy of the government men, Reo cited the demise of thousands of mustangs that roamed around this region. They were the reason for names like Little Wild Horse Canyon, Wild Horse Canyon, and Wild Horse Butte.

"During the war, they furnished the shells to shoot 'em," said Jess. "But I can't understand that, you know. And then they let these riding clubs come here, ten or fifteen riders. And they wouldn't just go out there on horseback and rope 'em; they'd take planes and run them so much until they couldn't run no more, and then they'd rope them, see. But, God Almighty, you know, they just packed 'em up."

"The Reef is the same thing, what you've been studying up there," Reo said. "There are natural resources up there unlimited. . . . There is grazing. There is uranium.

"There is oil. You can go in some of those old mining tunnels up there on that Reef, and the oil has run just out of the cracks and filled the old tunnels up—"

Me: "No kidding."

Reo: "—with straight oil. I can take you to two or three of those mining tunnels that have been driven back in there, that you can see where the oil comes right out of the cracks in the roof, settles in the old tunnel."

Barbara pointed out that one of the problems with the Temple Mountain ore is that it contained too much asphaltlike material, so it couldn't be processed easily.

During the uranium boom, miners lived "all over" the Reef area. The camp near North Temple Wash was called Magliaccio's. It was a big camp, with 150 residents around 1954. Generators provided electricity. Jess's mother and his stepfather, Harry Phillips, had a business drilling air holes into uranium mines. During the summers, families would live with the miners. At other times, when the children were in school, the men "bached it."

At first, miners used carbide lamps for underground lighting and sometimes had to haul ore out in wheelbarrows or a "Mexican drag line."

"You was pickin' it out by hand—hand drill," Jess said. "And then just take the richest you could get, you know." The ore might be yellow or "black, real coal-black."

The mines were in many parts of the Reef and Swell. In 1968 a survey commissioned by the Atomic Energy Commission produced maps that pinpoint at least twenty mines, all of them abandoned today.

Uneva was the name of a shaft that burrowed into the Reef a mile and a half below Spotted Wolf Canyon, the canyon now bisected by Interstate 70. The "Temple Mountain Collapse Structure" was loaded with mines. Around Temple Mountain were the Vanadium King Mine; Vanadium King 1; Vanadium King 5; North Mesa; North Mesa 1, 2, and 5; and Camp Bird. Fumerol was just below Camp Bird. Camp Bird 12 was in South Temple Wash. Black Berry was on the southwest side of South Temple. Near Chute Canyon were the Desolation and Virginia Valley mines. At Little Wild Horse Canyon were mines called Little Wild Horse 3, Little Wild Horse 6, and Little Erma 2. Bell Canyon had the Cistern Mine. The Delta Mine was the major excavation in Muddy River Canyon.

"It is always advisable to ask at Green River, Temple Mountain Junction, or at mining camps about the condition of roads within the swell. Extra water, food and gasoline should always be carried," the AEC report cautioned.

Long before the boom Virginia M. Harris ran a way station along the Reef, beside the road from Hanksville to Green River. You could water your horse and get a bite to eat there. That's why the canyon is called Old Woman Wash.

When the mines opened, U-24 was paved between Green River and South Temple Junction, as was the road through the Reef toward Temple Mountain. Trucks could haul uranium ore to the railroad. Sometimes the trucks ran twenty-four hours a day. At South Temple Junction, a service station, restaurant, and bar were opened for the miners. On the other side of the Reef the camp had a large garage with maintenance sheds.

Troops of cats wandered through camp. "Every time you'd get a rag out of the old rag box, there'd be a cat and a bunch of kittens," Barbara said. One fellow was determined he was going to rid the camp of them, "so he went and took them all and scrubbed their rear ends with sandpaper and put battery acid on them." They disappeared for a long time.

"Were you ever worried, you know, about working around uranium? Did that scare you at all?" I asked.

"We always tell the story about Jess's dad," Barbara said. "They told him, 'Now if you work around this uranium, it's going to make you sterile.' And I said, 'He had 12 kids. I'd hate to see him if he hadn't worked around uranium.' "

By 1963 the Temple Mountain boom was over. Mines were not producing as much, and the price of uranium kept dropping. Miners shifted south, toward Shoot-a-Ring Canyon and Ticaboo on Lake Powell.

Shitamaringe is the canyon's original name. But that never would have passed the scrutiny of the Board of Geographic Names. So when Hunt's crew was mapping in the Henry Mountains they decided to call it Shoot-a-Ring, attempting to keep the name as close to the original as possible. Some Hanksville people visited the USGS camp, looked over the field maps, and hooted, "Shoot-a-Ring! Shoot-a-Ring! You goddam sissy."

When I visited Hanksville, the uranium project at Ticaboo, with its 500 residents, had recently closed.

Barbara believes the accident at Three Mile Island ruined the uranium industry, as it resulted in cancellation of many contracts to build atomic power plants.

"I think that the news media and a bunch of these ecologists are backed by either Russia or Cuba. Now I'm sure of that. I'm just positive of it," Reo said.

Bud Hanni became superintendent of a uranium mine when he arrived in Hanksville from Ely, Nevada, back in 1954. A strong-looking man of seventy, he spoke with a slow drawl like John Wayne's. Around 1966 he and his wife, Millie, lived in Chute Canyon, building the small tin shack there.

"She's a good miner too," Barbara said.

His mine was high on the Reef's rim, and he had to build a road up to it. He still has some claims there.

"Had a spring there," Bud remembered of Chute. "Had a little spring down in that creek that I always dug out." Unlike other water holes in the Reef, the water was pure. "Most of the time back there for, oh, almost twenty years, I hauled water in a barrel."

Bud used to hunt deer in the Reef. "There used to be a hell of a lot of deer back there, but there ain't none left today," said Jess.

Bud remembered that a man was killed in a mine accident just below Greasewood Wash in 1955.

Reo said two prospectors were poking around near the Delta Mine, east of the Moroni Slopes, where the Muddy River goes through the Reef. "They were there in the wintertime. They plunged through the ice on the Muddy and got wet. They'd wet all their matches and everything. And it looked like they just huddled under that ledge and froze, tryin' to keep warm." Their bodies were discovered four or five days afterwards. "That's what happens when you get people out in the country like this that don't know what they're doin'," he said.

"Reo pulls them out of the Muddy and the Poison Springs all the time," Barbara said.

"Yeah, I pull them out of the Muddy. And some damn fool gets out there lookin' at the scenery and falls off the ledge, and I have to go take and pack 'im out."

Bud had yet another version of Sid Swasey's leap. "The story I heard, Swasey had this kid—a big kid. That kid, you'd tell him to kick a cactus and he would with his bare feet. He's the one that jumped that."

"He made him jump over it," Barbara said.

Bud had us drive to his place so we could see his buffalo head. For fifteen or twenty years he'd put in applications for a permit to hunt the Henry Mountain buffalo herd. Finally, his name was drawn for the 1983 hunt. Now the head was back from the taxidermist's, a thousand-dollar mounting project.

He lived in a snug yellow clapboard home. Across the yard was his storage area, a century-old house of wood slats over adobe onto which a leaning cottonwood threatened to collapse. The head was still in the camper shell on his new pickup.

He opened the back window and hauled the buffalo remains onto the tailgate, a gigantic, soulful-eyed head lifting its muzzle to the window. Bud stood proudly holding one horn, smiling beneath his gray moustache. The trophy was mounted from the neck up, half as tall as he was and exceptionally massive. He told a story about a fellow who kept blasting away at the herd, thinking he was missing. Then four of the beasts dropped. The hunter had to pay a stiff fine.

14

Protective Gestures

Two currents run through the history of the San Rafael country. One is toward protection.

The earliest writing that shows off the wonders of the San Rafael Reef and implies that this country is of national park quality is an article by H. L. A. Culmer, the artist who visited it in 1909. "No adequate description has ever been given of the wonders of the San Rafael Swell," began his report in the *Salt Lake Herald* of May 9, 1909.

> Although its [the Reef's] northern ramparts are plainly in view from the trains of the Denver & Rio Grande railway, as they approach Green River station, and where they are pointed out to tourists as the Silent City, no attempt has hitherto been made to impress the public with its great scenic features. Yet they are of a character so imposing and extraordinary that in any other state they would be exploited far and wide, bringing thousands to see them from every land and adding to the fame of Utah as one of the greatest scenic states in the Union.

A trolley line from Green River into Black Dragon Wash and then to the San Rafael Canyon could be established to serve tourists. Casual visitors otherwise might find the going too difficult by buckboard. After all, the wagon Culmer took into the Reef was still scattered around the desert, knocked to pieces by the rough road.

It is quite within reason to believe that before many years have passed, this new wonderland will be a popular resort for tourists; because a reservoir with 185 feet head and a line with hundreds of feet more fall has great power possibilities, and a trolley line from Green River City to Mexican Bend has already been seriously considered in connection with the power plant.

Nature has not been niggardly in the bestowal of scenic attractions upon this state, but those wild combinations of monumental rocks and lovely plain, like the bridge country and the upper valleys of the Rio Virgin [today's Natural Bridges National Monument and Zion National Park] are far away from railroads and require days to reach. But Black Dragon canyon is within an hour's trolley ride from Green River City, and in some respects will compare with any of them.

Culmer said a few thousand dollars' worth of bridges and roadwork "would carry the traveler easily and safely into the heart of this wonderland, and from there horse trails in every direction would take him into a world of mystery and delight."

However, little attention was paid to the natural beauty of the San Rafael country until Interstate 70 bisected it. Surveying for the highway began in 1962; two lanes were opened across the San Rafael Swell between Fremont Junction and Green River on November 5, 1970.

In 1965, while preparation work was going on, the Bureau of Land Management examined potential recreation sites in the Swell. In the freeway corridor the BLM identified twelve campgrounds, two overlooks, a picnic site, and a historical site. None were near the Reef, and at that time none had been developed.

Since then, improvements have been made at the primitive campground at San Rafael Bridge, where the road to Mexican Bend takes off from the Buckhorn Draw Road. Explanatory markers were erected at the damaged Buckhorn Draw pictograph. A little road work has taken place at the Swell's Wedge Overlook, a high vantage point just above Buckhorn Draw, offering a view of the Little Grand Canyon below.

BLM and state officials met on August 18, 1970, to explore strategies for planning land use in the corridor of the I-70 freeway. They agreed they did not want "strip development" to occur along the highway. A committee from this group recommended to Utah's then-governor, Calvin L. Rampton, that only one service center be established between Green River and Salina. It would have a service station, restaurant, motel, and campground at the Moore Interchange, on I-70 about five miles within the Swell from the west. The complex was never built.

When the freeway opened recreationists immediately discovered the Swell. Motorcyclists gouged trails, breaking slickrock, covering hills with tracks, scaring livestock, disturbing bighorn sheep. They have caused erosion that will never heal where tracks broke the fragile desert cover of cryptogamic soil. Pictographs were shot up and scribbled upon.

In 1972 the Institute for the Study of Outdoor Recreation and Tourism at Utah State University, Logan, launched a survey of the Swell's ability to attract tourists. The authors, Assistant Professor Lawrence Royer and research coordinator Michael J. Dalton, believed development had to be directed if the great natural values were to be protected. Developing tourism was the unabashed objective of the report.

"It is the last remaining large and highly scenic area of canyon country to be administered by the Bureau of Land Management," Royer and Dalton wrote in a cover letter.

In many ways, the early situation in Canyonlands National Park basin resembles the present San Rafael Swell situation. Both areas were initially lacking in surfaced roads. Both areas possessed an adjacent federal highway through route. Both areas are superlative scenic areas. A major difference is, of course, that the Canyonlands National Park area has received formal status as a national park.

During their investigations, the authors heard that the San Rafael Swell "is of national park system caliber." They examined it, compared it with the other Utah units of the National Park System, and concluded, "this is indeed the case." But they didn't recommend establishing a new park. Instead, they called for setting up a National Conservation Area. If the BLM could not be strengthened by statute so it could protect such an area, they said, then "the creation of a San Rafael Swell National Park or Monument should be seriously considered."

Royer and Dalton proposed varying levels of development. Among other recommendations, they called for surfacing the road from Castle Dale, down Buckhorn Draw, and to South Temple Wash. Then a tourist facility could be built at the mouth of Buckhorn, the authors said. Paving the sixty-nine miles from Temple Mountain to the head of Buckhorn should take precedence over all other scenic road proposals in Utah, they thought.

A tourist complex could be built at Tomsich Butte, near the western boundary of the Swell where I-70 goes through. A resort-guest ranch was proposed for Hidden Splendor, on the Muddy River just inside the Reef. Several areas should be closed to off-road vehicles. Access could be provided from the freeway to Black Dragon Wash.

The same year, the BLM's Price District began studying the Swell for special protection. "What prompted it in the first place was the highway itself, going through a unique area, in my estimation," recalled Glenn Freeman, who was then the BLM Price District manager. Today, he is manager of the Lewiston, Montana, District. He said there were few facilities to enable the traveling public to enjoy it. "I think also there was a need to identify the multiple uses in the area and legitimize them, because the bureau at that time was still pretty much a grazing service. I think that was a first attempt at providing a multiple-use plan for a unique area."

Paul L. Howard, then the BLM's state director, appointed a team to develop a long-range plan for all resources affected by people using I-70. The study area was a 665,137-acre rhombus bordered by the San Rafael Reef on the southeast, the San Rafael River on the northeast, Molen Reef on the northwest, and Muddy Creek on the southwest.

Public meetings were held in the local towns. Early in 1973 the BLM Price District office issued its recommendations. The study, written mostly by Price District staff under Freeman's direction with assistance from the BLM state office staff, advocated special management for a 630,000-acre region of the Swell. It would be a National Conservation Area.

The district said the Swell "has a high recreation potential and . . . has the quality and use types typical of the nation's great park lands. However, the area is also potentially valuable for energy-related and other minerals.''

The influx of travelers on I-70 has created people management problems. Some people are camping along the right-of-way, cutting the fences, indiscriminately using the country with off-road vehicles, littering and causing general safety hazards and sanitation problems that are deteriorating aesthetic and environmental values.

The study team estimated 80,000 visitor-days were spent in the Swell in 1971, shortly after the freeway opened. Conflicts were developing: in that year, the Swell provided 22,400 animal-unit months of livestock grazing in thirty-one allotments, used by seventy-six ranching operations.

Highlights of the proposals were:

—All lands within the area should be consolidated within one agency's ownership, and managed to protect aesthetic quality. Any changes in the natural environment should be carefully considered on the basis of need.

—Unnecessary trails across the desert would be closed and revegetated.

—Mineral claims would be banned from a "Visual Corridor and Service Zone" of 100,000 acres, mostly along I-70.

—Camping in any one spot would be limited to sixteen days or less.

—Coal Wash, in the northern part of the Swell about ten miles southwest of San Rafael Campground, should be a primitive area. So should the Mexican Mountain region.

—Rangers should patrol the desert to protect visitors, gather information, help anyone in trouble, and enforce rules. An interpretive program would explain and give information about the Swell's archaeological, historical, ecological, and cultural features.

—The I-70 visual corridor, the Swasey Cabin area, the San Rafael Campground and the vicinity, and primitive areas should be designated as recreation lands. That would help let the public know about these resources. The BLM should provide camping facilities adjacent to I-70 near Ghost Rocks in the Swell.

—A campground, restaurant, store, and service area could be built a few miles east of Head of Sinbad.

—All vehicles should be confined to designated roads and trails. The BLM would close any "not designated for use."

Indiscriminate off-road vehicular use would reduce the vegetative cover and compact the soil. This would then result in erosion of soil particles. Roads and tracts in fragile areas must be kept to a minimum if the area is to be rehabilitated.

Toward the center of the Swell, the district endorsed building the proposed Moore Interchange, allowing access from I-70 to the heavily mineralized western part of the Swell and to the towns of eastern Emery County and Utah Highway 10. The westbound lane in the Head of Sinbad area should be built within fifty feet of the existing lane, instead of half a mile from it, to reduce the aesthetic impact and the vandalism danger to the nearby pictographs.

District planners called for rejecting the state's application to select federal land at Moore Interchange, saying it would be contrary to a proposal for the BLM to acquire state land in the I-70 scenic corridor. Whether to develop facilities at the interchange was left undecided.

All these recommendations were made by the BLM's Price District and passed along to the public by Paul Howard.

Following up, in October 1973 the BLM formally proposed to designate a 630,000-acre region of the Swell as a National Conservation Area. It suggested withdrawal of 100,000 acres bordering I-70. Changes this sweeping would require an act of Congress.

Why was this proposal made? Howard remembers that the BLM had long recognized the San Rafael region as a unique area. "When I first came here, the Price District had identified that region as a kind of special area. We were trying to get some recognition for it," he said. Nothing ever came of the effort. Controversy over coal in the Kaiparowits Plateau took priority about then. Apparently, nobody lobbied Congress on establishing a national conservation area.

Ironically, one monkey wrench in the machinery was a supposedly protective law, the BLM Organic Act of 1976, properly known as the Federal Land Policy and Management Act. In it, Congress ordered the agency to abandon its traditional role as land disposal agent and begin conserving important natural resources. Wilderness Act provisions were now to apply to the BLM's holdings.

The Wilderness Act, passed in 1964 for the Forest Service's wild areas, had resulted in designation of millions of acres of forest wilderness. The BLM had a few primitive and natural areas, but no wilderness areas. With the new mandate, the BLM began reviewing the wilderness suitability of its gigantic holdings—twenty-two million acres in Utah alone. And the conservation area proposal was lost in the shuffle.

In 1977 a few hikers and environmentalists formed the San Rafael Coordinating Committee. The group was headed by Peter Hovingh, a Salt Lake City biologist and conservationist who started exploring the San Rafael in the 1960s. The committee campaigned hard to protect the entire Swell, including the Reef.

Hovingh was worried about new power plants near Huntington, Emery County, a possible upsurge in uranium mining, a proposed power line corridor, and off-road vehicles. "Off-road vehicles can 'overgraze' much more readily than cows," he told me at the time. "Off-road vehicle people will do damage when they leave the roads. When you run over the desert range you're going to do damage."

THE SAN RAFAEL REGION
A National Park or Destroyed Rangelands?

That was the heading on a four-page brochure the committee issued, with funding from Public Lands Research. The BLM considered the Swell to occupy 630,000 acres, but Hovingh's group thought it was much larger, including adjacent areas that had to be protected or the Swell would suffer too from the impacts of development.

"At the time that came out, some oil companies and uranium companies were staking out huge areas of claims within the Swell," Hovingh said. The claims were mainly in Upper Buckhorn Draw and the flat lands of the Swell. Uranium deposits near the Swell's Buckhorn Well were only twenty-five feet below the surface. Conservationists imagined gigantic drag lines crashing through the thin desert crust at Buckhorn Well.

The San Rafael Critical Area is a highly scenic area with a rich geological and historical past and high biological interest untouched by man. . . .
Mining in the past has had only a limited impact on the region. Future mining will cover square miles of leases. Mining activities must be strictly controlled and all leasing programs should be stopped until a firm management plan of the region is completed.

The committee's solution was to propose a mix of state and federal actions to protect the Swell. An alternative suggestion was to transfer the San Rafael region to the National Park Service as a new park, recreation area, national monument, or additions to Canyonlands and Capitol Reef national parks. "This action would give the area its greatest protection, greatest land-use restrictions and would be very unpopular in the growth-oriented state of Utah." Many Utahns already wondered why parts of the San Rafael weren't in a park, wrote the coordinating committee. If a San Rafael National Park were established, the federal government would "fill in all dangerous and historical mines. Recreation would be restricted to non-machine use," according to the brochure.

When the brochure hit the newspapers, S. Gene Day, then the BLM's Moab District manager, invited Senator Jake Garn, R-Utah, to fly over the Swell with him. Reporters—including myself—went along on the flight, December 20, 1977. Garn piloted a helicopter.

We watched spellbound as the landscape unfolded before us, with its towering mesas, sheer red cliffs, secret canyons and gullies, flat ranges, dry washes, sandstone spires. Striking canyons kept opening below, as we went chopping over tall fingers of rock that pointed up for a hundred feet. We veered around sheer cliffs, watching dark green dots of juniper that clung to talus slopes. We saw surprising stands of big pinyons tucked in pockets of the cliff. The light snow looked like a thin layer of plaster on the undulating rock floor. It seemed smooth, hard, dry. In places, patches of orange sandstone showed through. Flying past Mexican Mountain, we headed toward Window Blind Peak in the Swell, then over the extremely rugged landscape of the Wedge.

At the end of the day, Garn said the government should not "lock up" huge regions for one special interest or another. It was necessary to consider grazing, mining, aesthetics, and other values in managing the Swell, he said. "There's room for some primitive-type or wilderness areas," Garn said. The senator could not estimate which part of the mix should be in multiple-use management and which part should be preserved.

Day said much of the Swell is "definitely national park character." But with five national parks already established in Utah, he questioned whether the state needed another. "I personally feel that the San Rafael Reef is superior to Capitol Reef, as far as visual considerations," he said.

Three months later, Hovingh broadened the coordinating committee's attack, demanding protection for land owned by the state within the Swell. He wrote Governor Scott M. Matheson, "For several months now I have been trying to find out what is the state of Utah's position on the highly unique San Rafael region. I can find no position." He accused state officials of promoting industrialization projects near highly scenic areas.

Perhaps the State Land Board should also be beefed up and actually start administering its public lands for long term yield instead of the present pay now, bail out in the future philosophy.

Our only other choice is to make the San Rafael region a National Park. This would not be fair to the other public lands that are suffering from erosion.

Today, he thinks the campaign forced BLM managers to take the area more seriously, "because they realized they may have had a jewel." He insisted that the whole Swell should be protected: "What should be done is greatly restrict the ORVs to the highways and the roads, and probably remove the cattle from the rivers . . . and keep mining under control."

An advantage of park status is that highways would be managed. A park would allow use of roads while preserving the integrity of the land, he said. "There are problems with parks too. They tend to be recreation-oriented."

Whatever alternative is followed, Hovingh wants it all protected. "The center of it is just as important." Near Interstate 70 you can see drainages going four directions, he said.

Dan Cortsen, the Salt Lake environmentalist who took the photographs in the brochure, does not want to see the region become a national park because of the development that would entail. It could be protected as a BLM primitive area, he thinks. He has been hiking the desert country from Temple Mountain to the Muddy River for many years. "I get there every chance I get," he said.

Late in 1985, a few months before the BLM was to announce its draft wilderness recommendations, officials of Emery County tentatively seemed to support creating a national park in the northern Swell and part of the Reef. Since all of the Swell and Reef are in Emery County—with the exception of the toe of the Moroni Slopes, which sticks into Wayne County—these officials carry weight in deciding the future of the region. The land is almost all federal property, but tradition and policy deal a strong hand to the locals.

The 210,000-acre park would reach from Eagle Canyon on the west, through Buckhorn Draw and the Wedge Overlook, and end at the Reef above I-70. Black Dragon Wash was to be part of it.

The park proposal captured the interest of the Emery County Development Council, based at the county seat, Castle Dale. County employees envisioned paving the Buckhorn Draw Road, the route to the Wedge Overlook and the rough road along the San Rafael River to Mexican Mountain.

Development council members flew Rep. Howard Nielson, R-Utah, over the region. He liked the park idea, too. "I am interested in it," he said. "I indicated that it does have national park character. The only question I had was, did it have sufficient diversity to qualify as a national park? I am certain it would qualify as a national monument with no problems." Nielson said he was impressed with the Reef, "because to me it's the most unique part of it." The problem is, he said, I-70 bisects the Reef itself. He did not know of another park cut by an interstate highway in quite that way.

Wes Curtis, chairman of the development council, said, "What we're really looking for is an alternative to the wilderness proposals made in that same area—the Mexican Mountain Wilderness Study Area and the Sids Mountain Study Area." Curtis questioned including both sides of the Reef in a park proposal because people might think they'd seen the park when they only drove through on the freeway. "We may end up including part of that eventually," he said. For now, it seemed too spread out to be easily managed, and ranchers might object to extending the park. But wilderness might be a good designation for the rest of the Reef, he said. "We're just starting now the legislative process of getting a bill put together, getting it written, taking it to Congress."

The background to that startling movement was that the Utah Wilderness Association had been negotiating with Curtis and county commissioners about protecting the San Rafael country. The association had clout because the previous year it helped draw the final lines in Utah's Forest Service wilderness bill.

James Catlin, conservation chairman of the Utah Chapter, Sierra Club, also supported the park proposal—as far as it went. "I think this is very positive, that the Emery County Economic Development Committee and the county commission are making long-range plans for a durable, sustainable economy that favors locals and recognizes the limitations of the extractive mineral industry," he said. But Catlin pointed out that some of the best parts weren't included, like the Moroni Slopes, North Caineville Mesa, and Factory Butte. He called the proposal north of I-70 "very modest." A larger, more representative area should be considered, he said.

The *Deseret News* greeted the plan with an enthusiastic editorial: "While some people may boggle at the idea of another national park in Utah . . . it can be argued that Emery officials are too modest in their approach." The *News* advocated including the rest of the Reef, with its spectacular hiking country. The paper was glad, too, that local officials had suggested the park themselves.

Then Utah's new governor, Norman H. Bangerter, knocked the park idea for a loop, saying the local support only showed how much Emery County residents feared wilderness designation. On November 13, 1985, the county held a public hearing on the idea. The overwhelming response was against creating a park. The county commission fell in line with Bangerter and the locals and backed off. In January 1986 the commissioners wrote to everyone they could think of—Bangerter, the Utah congressional delegation, state legislators, environmentalists, Bureau of Land Management officials, four neighboring county commissions, and state agency administrators. They took themselves right out of the park business.

Miners were worried about losing their leases for quarrying stone, gypsum, tar sands, and other resources, the commissioners wrote. Hunters and ranchers fretted over losing their privileges. "The ORV community response . . . was one in favor of maintaining the status quo and working within the current system to come up with solutions and management alternatives for use of the San Rafael Swell."

Others brought up the fact the Clean Air Act requires the strictest protective designation, Class I, for the atmosphere above a park. That might restrict future industrial growth outside the Swell, commissioners feared.

> . . . the Commission has concluded that it cannot support any designation upon the San Rafael Swell by any agency that would result in restrictive and exclusionary management practices being employed beyond those multiple use and sustained yield practices currently employed by the Bureau of Land Management.
>
> The Commission firmly believes that current BLM management, which incorporates local citizen input, is sufficient to both utilize and protect resources of the Swell. Any further enhanced federal control . . . is viewed by the Commission as a contravention of the principle of New Federalism which presumably was to return power and authority to the states from the federal government. Restrictive park, monument, or wilderness management has to be viewed by the Commission as preemptive of local abilities and prerogatives to manage the lands for sustained yield, for preservation of the resource and for multiple beneficial use. . . .
>
> The Commission acknowledges that there are extraordinary opportunities for recreation in the Swell, but feels that outstanding examples of Southeast Utah geology are already captured in existing state and national parks. Therefore, additional park, monument, or wilderness designations in the Swell are seen as being redundant and unwarranted.

The letter ended with an offer to enter into a dialogue with the BLM about setting up some kind of "stewardship management option" or other multiple-use management program to involve "different interest groups."

A counter-proposal was detailed in a June 1986 *Salt Lake Tribune* "Common Carrier" article. Charles B. Hunt, the retired geologist, called for setting up a Scenic Eastern Utah Park. Centered along the Colorado River, it would take in about 20 percent of the state, including the western part of the San Rafael Swell. The park would absorb the present parks, national forests, and recreational areas. It would be governed by a lands authority made up of federal, state and county officials. Visitors would enjoy it via new light-duty roads.

In the meantime, BLM wilderness studies were winding up. During August 1985, in hearings both at Castle Dale and Salt Lake City, officials of Emery County delivered slashing attacks on the idea of wilderness.

The BLM had proposed wilderness protection for most of the Reef, although little of the Swell would be designated as wilderness. Black Dragon Wash was not in any wilderness study area, nor were the Moroni Slopes.

A newsletter called *ALERT*, issued by the National Parks and Conservation Association in April 1986, called for nature supporters to attend public meetings on tourism scheduled by the southern Utah Five Counties Association of Governments. They were poorly publicized in the northern part of the state.

Terri Martin, the association's regional representative, Salt Lake City, wrote that unrestrained and uncontrolled tourism development "can scar Utah's scenic beauty with unsightly developments and careless use of the land." She listed eight recommendations, including the use of shuttle buses in Zion, Arches, and Bryce Canyon national parks, establishing carrying capacities for parks to avoid overcrowding, and opposing industrial development next to parks and other natural attractions. Another recommendation was to designate more national parks and wilderness areas in Utah, not only to protect deserving areas, but to avoid overcrowding of existing attractions. She urged conservationists to list their own examples and suggested that two good ones are a Great Basin National Park in Nevada and a San Rafael National Park in Utah.

Although hopeful attempts have been made toward protecting the Swell in the past eighty years, no strong action has ever come from the federal government. In the meantime, the forces lined up against protection of any more land in Utah grow much stronger every year.

15

Threats

The riptide of exploitation runs deep, and it's faster than the protectionists can swim.

A good example is the hideous drill pad Utah officials permitted to be carved out of a section of state land, destroying the topography near the South Temple Wash pictographs. Some of the other projects might suddenly fester into major damage—for instance, if a large oil deposit were developed.

Much larger projects could be pushed through on the holdings of the federal Bureau of Land Management, which includes nearly all of the San Rafael region. Most claims dating to the years before the Federal Land Management and Policy Act have expired in wilderness study areas, and new mineral claims have been filed since then in the study areas. Under the act's rules, development would be subject to tough protective stipulations, if the areas are not rejected as wilderness; however, many claims have been filed on parts of the San Rafael Swell that are not in wilderness study areas. Most of the Swell, the Moroni Slopes, and two chunks of the Reef are not even in study areas.

Conservationists may believe the simple operation of wilderness rules will protect BLM land in the San Rafael Swell. That's understandable, as the law seems clear. In the fine phrases of the Wilderness Act, wilderness is a place "the earth and its community of life are untrammeled by man, where man himself is a visitor who does not remain." But the law is not protecting the Swell, for most of it is not a candidate for wilderness. To qualify, a region must be without roads—and that's a subjective judgment in a desert where anybody can lay down tracks that don't erode.

Although most of the Reef is proposed for wilderness, some parts are left out. Parts that are proposed have never been properly protected from off-road vehicle abuse. At times, wilderness rules themselves provide only flimsy protection. The Federal Land Policy and Management Act makes it clear that protection is "subject, however, to the continuation of existing mining and grazing uses and mineral leasing. . . ."

Three wilderness study areas were designated in the Reef as part of the process that could someday lead to congressional designation of wilderness there. From the north, they are Mexican Mountain, San Rafael Reef, and Crack Canyon. At the Mexican Mountain Wilderness Study Area, the BLM says up to a thousand tons of uranium oxide is present. A total of sixty mining claims, mostly for uranium, are active in the San Rafael Reef Wilderness Study Area. At the southernmost study area, Crack Canyon, 502 active claims cover 4,780 acres, nineteen percent of the study area.

Federal rules allow claims located prior to wilderness designation to be worked, with operations regulated with an eye to preventing "unnecessary or undue degradation." If not developed within ten years of issuance, claims usually expire. Additionally, a federal court ruling in Salt Lake City held that reasonable access to claims must be guaranteed even if that damages wilderness values.

Mineral claims and leases blanket much of southern Utah. For example, the Crack Canyon Wilderness Study Area is undercut by oil and gas leases on 13,955 acres, filed after passage of the Federal Land Management and Planning Act in 1976.

The worst threats to preservation of the Swell are a salinity-control project proposed by the U.S. Bureau of Reclamation; off-road vehicles; uranium claims; and a potentially huge tar sands industry.

SALINITY CONTROL

The U.S. Bureau of Reclamation has recommended that Congress authorize construction of the Dirty Devil River Unit of the Colorado River Water Quality Improvement Program. This is a double-barreled project, with a small part in the Swell below Interstate 70 at Muddy Creek and a larger part adjacent to the Moroni Slopes.

The project is one of a host being studied, with the aim of reducing damage to agriculture caused by the saltiness of the Colorado River system. "The high salt concentration in the Lower Colorado River Basin adversely affects more than 17 million people and about 1 million acres of irrigated farmland in the United States," says the bureau's environmental assessment on the project. "Affected most severely are municipal and industrial water users in the Las Vegas, Los Angeles and San Diego areas and irrigators in the Imperial Valley of southern California and in Arizona who experience economic losses."

The problem is, as farmers irrigate more and more land, salts leach out of the soil, work into the aquifer, and reach the Colorado, where they glide on downriver to damage crops there. Yields fall, and the soil has problems with leaching and drainage.

Reclamation economists calculate that for every ton of salt added to the Colorado River system, economic damages of $52 will occur. That counts every conceivable type of damage: increased water treatment costs, accelerated pipe corrosion, the need to use more soap and detergent, and even "drinking water palatability."

To correct this, the bureau has cooked up a series of possible projects including the one planned for the Moroni Slopes, called Hanksville Salt Wash, and the one in the Swell's interior, called Emery South Salt Wash. Both would work in similar ways. Naturally saline water would be collected in fourteen wells so it could not flow into the Colorado River system. The wells would be spread out over eight and a half miles of Salt Wash next to the Slopes, with wellheads protruding four feet above ground. Then an underground pipeline would convey the water to a treatment plant. It would eventually be injected 3,400 to 3,700 feet underground into a layer of Coconino sandstone. There it's supposed to stay and not bother the Imperial Valley.

A sand filtration system would also be built. Pumps and offices would be contained in a one-story building. An evaporation pond eleven acres in size would be constructed, along with an equalization basin of 1.25 acres.

Most dramatic is the power line that would be constructed along thirteen miles of dirt road that goes by Factory Butte. Set 300 feet back from the road, it would cross Salt Wash and hang there, dark wires against the sky, next to the Moroni Slopes. The road itself would be upgraded.

All this would cost $8.1 million. Computed on an annual basis, using a formula that takes into account interest, operating costs, and construction expenses, taxpayers would pay $1.3 million every year to operate this object for its fifty-year life expectancy.

Hanksville Salt Wash is expected to reduce the Colorado's salt load by 14,300 tons of salt per year—just a shaker-full, compared with the Colorado's volume. Each ton of salt will cost ninety dollars to remove. Meanwhile, if that same ton of salt is not removed, it will hurt the farmers, bathers, pipe-replacers and people who don't like a salty taste in their water by—how much? Fifty-two dollars. The project would cause a net loss of thirty-eight dollars for every ton of salt it removes.

Unbelievably, that won't kill the project. For most federal water reclamation projects, a positive cost-benefit ratio is a legal requirement, or they can't be built. That is not the case here. Federal laws have established a national policy to prevent degradation of water quality. According to the Bureau of Reclamation's environmental statement, this policy is "governed not by traditional economic evaluation but rather by accomplishing the objective at the least cost." So it doesn't matter how expensive such a project is. What is important is how one possible salinity control unit stacks up against others; the better ones may well be financed by Congress. And some bureau experts say Hanksville-South Salt Wash is one of the more cost-effective of the bunch.

Reclamation's final environmental assessment of the project mentions short-term scenery impacts, such as that caused by construction activities. But it does not say anything about long-term scenery impacts. Instead, in July 1986 Bureau of Reclamation officials signed a finding that this project would have no significant environmental impacts.

They had to make that finding or they would have been forced to write a full-blown environmental impact statement. That would have entailed hearings and review by the Environmental Protection Agency. By filing a finding of no significant impact, the assessment is the last document in the study. No hearings were held, and nothing will be submitted to the EPA.

It is true that the Moroni Slopes—the end of the Reef—are not lovely. The sunlight does play on the high gray sandstone and pink-striped Morrison formation hills, casting interesting shadows, highlighting fine textures. But to most people who venture there, the Slopes and Salt Wash must seem a harsh badlands where the sun blasts furiously and the wind never stops blowing. Yet to a person with eyes adjusted to finding the worth in a landscape or face, it's not prettiness that counts. It's honesty, or a memorable look. For the Moroni Slopes, most of all, it's the untouched desert. The scene here is striking.

The United States Bureau of Reclamation is on record. It feels that destroying the natural character of these rugged badlands has "no significant impact."

OFF-ROAD VEHICLES

On a spring weekend the Hanksville convenience stores—gas station-quick shop combinations—are busy selling sandwiches, soft drinks, beer, and gas to motorcyclists. Nearing the self-serve island, you idle in roasting heat behind a pickup with a three-wheeler in the back, which is itself behind a van towing two dirt bikes in a small trailer. Somebody talks on the pay phone outside the store. A Jeep starts and drives onto the road; the rest of the line jolts forward.

Girls wander around in skimpy tops. Deep-fried young men in cowboy hats lounge beside their trailer, waiting for a pump. One motorcyclist says to another, "I've been with those other drunkers." He was drunk last night and the night before that and the night before that, he says.

Inside the Black Oil Company store, so many ORVers stand by the cash register that they're bumping each other. One says she's from Salt Lake City. Sometimes the shops run out of popsicles.

The most immediate danger to the San Rafael country, particularly the Reef, is destruction by these off-road vehicle drivers. The BLM is updating its management framework plans which, in the event of a miracle, could ban such vehicles. Yet in the years of environmental concern over the San Rafael country, so far the BLM has done next to nothing to curb them. In fact, it encourages motorcyclists and has never chased them from the wilderness study areas.

A friend of mine who lives near Capitol Reef National Park once complained to a BLM official about ORV damage to the clay hills on both sides of U-24 south of the Moroni Slopes. He was told, "Well, they have to have someplace to ride."

This friend wrote to me in 1985, "There's no saving that area now; it's pretty well shot now, esthetically at least. We were out there on Easter weekend and saw hordes of bikers (heard them, too, miles away.)" He added, "I've wondered when they would start fanning out to the north. Two days ago we were out on the Factory Butte road and saw tracks all over the place, miles north of the highway area—even in Salt Wash along the Reef. Both bikes and 4WD [four-wheel drive vehicles]."

All through the Swell's Buckhorn Draw and its little side canyons, on a warm weekend, anywhere between a handful and scores of bikers rampage. They buzz across hills with a deafening, whining, metallic shriek, lifting long clouds of dust. You see families with their campers parked beside steep brown hills, so the kids can tear up and down them with motorcycles. Hundreds of ridges are lined with tracks. On the steep incline where the road from Castle Dale drops toward Buckhorn Draw, tracks show where a truck or Jeep plowed up at an impossible angle, and you wonder who would dare do such a thing. You wonder why, too.

Cyclists congregate so thickly in Buckhorn Draw that they have begun to move out, seeking new hills to climb. The Reef is being subjected to more and more motorcycling. In the lonely canyons, tire marks remain on slickrock and along benches, scarring naked hills.

For years, organized motorcycle convoys have roared out of Goblin Valley State Park, just south of the Reef, cutting through at South Temple Wash or North Temple, then continuing along the trails behind the Reef. A state brochure illustrating Goblin Valley had a photo of a smiling group of cyclists riding beside the Reef on the other side of the ridge from the park.

The Utah Division of Parks and Recreation has conducted big groups on hundred-mile motorcycle treks in the Swell and beside the Reef. Before the weekend cycle outing of April 30—May 3, 1984, Max Jensen, the department's regional supervisor, said, "We're not taking these people actually off the road. We certainly don't want to cause any environmental concerns whatsoever." Gene Nodine, BLM district manager in Moab, pledged that officials would watch carefully to make sure that cyclists did not get into any of the fragile desert canyons in wilderness study areas. But these pious intentions were blown away by the insensitivity of many ORVers. A letter to the editor of the *Sun-Advocate* in Price said the planned ride would be boring. "If anyone is interested in a real trail ride to see the areas that are closed, look for the sign of the Phantom Seagull on the way in." way in."

Around the middle of the next month, I came upon a great clutch of Colorado motorcyclists at the entrance to South Temple Wash. They said they had been going to the area for four or five years, liked to drive around the old mine dumps, always checked in with the ranger at Goblin Valley, and never had any trouble. I took a photo of their camp, and it shows a man riding his cycle on part of the Reef.

In the summer of 1984 the BLM's Price office announced it was considering a proposal by motorcyclists to designate thirty miles of motorcycle trails adjacent to the Reef. Two of the five trails would be along dirt roads and gullies that are the borders of San Rafael Reef Wilderness Study Area. The trails would be marked with painted cairns and signs, with information posted to tell bikers to stay out of the wilderness study areas.

I noticed signs to guide motorcyclists were already set up on the route beyond North Temple Wash in November 1984, long before any decision by the BLM.

The BLM pared the project down to a "fewer trails alternative," in which seventeen miles would be dedicated to bikes, instead of thirty miles. Motorcyclists were supposed to follow existing unmaintained dirt roads, wash bottoms, and ridges.

In December 1983 biologists with the Utah Division of Wildlife Resources spotted a dozen bighorn sheep in North Temple Wash. "Desert bighorn sheep also occur in the San Rafael Reef east of the proposed trail system," said a BLM environmental assessment. "Development and use of the proposed [longer] trail system would probably restrict or inhibit bighorn expansion," the assessment continued. The "fewer trails alternative" would have similar, but reduced, impacts on the great wild sheep. Intermittent use of the trails,

> such as that which would take place on the proposed motorcycle trail system, would be startling and loud to the animals. . . . Desert bighorn sheep already using the affected area would probably abandon that portion of their range. Current expansion of the range probably would not continue in the affected area.

Originally, a segment of trail was to intrude deeply into Iron Wash, where waterholes are essential to the bighorns' survival. That part was deleted in the final paring down. But the North Temple Trail was kept in, even though bighorns were spotted there. The BLM approved the trails system, giving the go-ahead for posting of signs in a 1986 agreement with the Pathfinders Motorcycle Club Inc. Either side can cancel the agreement with ninety days' notice.

A few friends and I hiked through Wild Horse Canyon the weekend after Easter 1985. This lovely wash, within Crack Canyon Wilderness Study Area, is a main target of off-road vehicles. "I wanted to take a quiet hike," said Jean Cassidy, "but all I got was Joe Bauman complaining about motorcycles!" I wanted a quiet hike, too, but all I got was an eyeful of destruction of a canyon I've loved for many years.

Near the entrance a long trail of knobby mud showed where a cycle had cut across a slickrock shelf just off the wash floor. Where it launched itself from the shelf, the frame hit hard, biting a big semicircular chunk from the shelf. Sandstone fragments were scattered beneath the gap. Deeper in, where a side canyon heads into a box, motorcyclists have funneled through a narrow place above the junction. For a long stretch, they've worn a trail inches deep into the fragile soil.

While hiking toward a low Fremont-type rock wall in an alcove, my friends came across another motorcycle trail that stretched beside the cliff, actually at the top of the talus slope.

Wherever wheels spun on the buff or pink slickrock floor of Wild Horse, there was a black streak. Because the canyon has been abused for years, in some places we found streaks upon streaks, layers of damage.

Even if all bikes were cleared from the canyon forever, for a long time we'd see where they peeled out of the ravine and roared up and down little hills at the sides. We'd see where they gouged the crust and ran over plants.

On Memorial Day weekend 1984, Cal Grondahl and I camped at Black Dragon Wash, witnessing a mechanical herd in action. Dozens of bikers were camping at the turnoff from I-70. They had campers, pickups, motorcycle trailers, bikes. Families lived in a city of trailers and tents. We set up beside the Reef, a mile or so away from the bikers.

Cal's father, Melvin, hiked with the two of us toward Black Dragon overlook. A deep white gouge on the Reef showed where someone had just driven a motorcycle onto the Reef itself. The frame had scraped the sandstone. From the top, the sunset gave us a calm moment. Shafts of golden light cut through the evening haze, illuminating sections of the cliffs and the great bowl in the wall below. Cal and his dad and I went lower now and rested on a ridge of the Reef, talking, looking at sunlight on far-off buttes.

Then, ten motorcyclists roared through our camp. Most drove three- or four-wheel all-terrain vehicles, although a couple drove traditional dirt bikes. We watched them make a road. They cut from the main trail through Black Dragon Wash, then north, crossing a virgin stretch. The first headed off from

C. BERT 85

the path, winding and bouncing over the sagebrush. Others immediately followed, and by the time the last went through, a new permanent trail had been gouged out.

They drove onto the Reef, roared and whined across the slopes, going all the way up to the crest. They gunned their engines on the Reef for a long time. I saw one doing wheelies along the ridgeline at sunset—he was in silhouette, and the image was like a science-fiction monster running. I was convinced that one of the machines would flip and slam 250 pounds of metal down toward me, so I climbed off the Reef and sat in the Jeep. When they were done capering they came down cautiously, a few at a time. They drove up onto a hill and talked with us, a couple sullen but most of them friendly. Six months later, motorcycle tracks were still fresh on the hill.

Why does the BLM tolerate this abuse? A clue comes from its response to Environmental Protection Agency criticism of the BLM wilderness studies. An important section of a slashing EPA review concerned off-road vehicles and wilderness study areas (WSAs). An EPA official thought the vehicles could be kept out by posting signs. The BLM Utah director, Roland Robison, replied by writing that the environmental agency "does not understand the topography of the area in question, the level of ORV use in the vicinity of WSAs, and has no expertise of its own in the practicality or cost of managing ORV use." In English, he was saying he could not easily control bikers.

Robison demanded that the Interior Department force the EPA to retract its comments, and the EPA's sharp criticisms were toned down. Meanwhile, the exchange had been revealing.

URANIUM CLAIMS

The biggest uranium producer in the Reef, Temple Mountain, was never in any of the BLM wilderness studies because it did not meet the roadless criteria. To give an idea of the past value of this mountain to the nuclear industry, consider that in 1951 alone, the Mountain King, Gateway, and Rex claims on Temple Mountain—originally located by Charlie Gibbons and Abe Glassman—paid more than $108,000 in royalties. That was just ten percent of the net mill returns on the ore. So ore from these Temple Mountain properties for one year was worth nearly eleven million dollars.

Between 1948 and 1956 the Temple Mountain District produced 261,000 tons of ore, which contained 643.5 tons of uranium oxide and 1,899.5 tons of vanadium oxide. In the same period, the Lucky Strike Mine, located near Link Flats in the Swell's west, produced more than 10,000 tons of ore containing more than 1.1 tons of uranium oxide and about 900 pounds of vanadium. Many smaller mines and prospects are found near the Chinle outcrops, and other uranium claims are scattered throughout the Swell.

Whether any of the region's mines pose a radiation hazard for recreationists, I don't know. For their sake some government agency ought to find out. Mines could be sealed or posted if necessary.

Hanksville people insist the formations still have a lot of valuable ore.

On August 18, 1983, the BLM announced that a uranium drilling program was proposed for Wild Horse Canyon. A uranium company with offices in Lexington, Kentucky, called Proto and Royce, proposed to drill one to three exploratory holes on each of eight uranium claims near the middle of the canyon. "Equipment would consist of truck-mounted drill, water truck, frontend loader, bulldozer and portable drill," said a BLM announcement.

Parts of the canyon are too narrow to pass trucks without blasting out the slickrock walls. In places, the wash is only three or four feet across. For access along the canyon bottom, explosives and a bulldozer would have to widen the route to twelve or fourteen feet across. Scars in the slickrock and smooth boulders would remain forever.

In addition to heavily damaging Wild Horse, uranium exploration would be a loud intrusion for all who love the canyon. Also, if uranium were discovered in valuable concentrations, Proto and Royce probably would have a legal right to mine it, once they got permission to explore in the first place. "There is a potential there," Royce said in a telephone interview. "There is ore there." The big question was the ore's quality.

Their claims were filed on March 2, 1980. For years afterwards, fading pink plastic streamers flapped from claim stakes planted deep in the canyon within the wilderness study area.

That date is important. If the claims had been filed before the Federal Land Policy and Management Act of 1976, development would have been almost impossible to stop, short of transferring the canyon to the National Park Service. The BLM ruled that since these claims were filed after the act was passed, they did not carry special privileges. But it still approved exploratory drilling, with tough stipulations to preserve the canyon's wilderness character.

The drilling was never carried out. If it had occurred and a large deposit was confirmed, what would have happened? We know the answer from the Death Hollow controversy near Escalante in southern Utah. When the Forest Service wilderness bill was debated in 1984, carbon dioxide gas deposits recently discovered there were the basis for knocking part of the area out of the measure. If people think uranium is there, that may be enough to prevent Congress from protecting the San Rafael Swell.

PETROLEUM

Certainly oil is present in the Reef too, sometimes as tarry as asphalt. It had to be pumped out of some mines during the uranium boom. Although the Reef has a low possibility of oil and gas development, claims have been filed on most of the land.

In the ten years after passage of the 1976 Federal Land Policy and Management Act, oil and gas leases were filed on: 13,955 acres of Crack Canyon Wilderness Study Area, covering more than half of the area; 37,330 acres of San Rafael Reef, or sixty-three percent; 35,192 acres of Mexican Mountain WSA, or fifty-nine percent of the study area, which also contains many square miles of mountains and benches within the Swell. In all three only one oil well is reported, and it was drilled and abandoned in the San Rafael Reef WSA in 1957.

Interest in tar sands was triggered by passage in 1981 of the Combined Hydrocarbon Leasing Act that was part of the energy panic caused by the 1973 Arab oil embargo. This act allows the BLM to convert standard oil and gas leases into a new kind of lease that allows extraction of exotic petroleum sources, such as tar sands and oil shale.

Tar sands are oil-impregnated sand or sandstone, rough and black. As a form of petroleum, tar sands can be refined into oil, although the process is more difficult and expensive than with conventional crude.

In the early 1980s the Interior Department set up eleven combined hydrocarbon leasing areas in eastern Utah. Among them was the San Rafael Special Tar Sands Area, made up of several strips that sprawl across 115,705 acres of the Swell.

The BLM estimates oil reserves locked within the tar sands of the San Rafael area at: Chute Canyon, 50 million barrels; Cottonwood Draw, 75 million barrels; Wickiup, 60 million barrels; Family Butte, 100 million barrels; Black Dragon, 100 million barrels. Most of these deposits could never be recovered with present technology.

The San Rafael Special Tar Sands Area is far from the richest in Utah. Other nearby areas are the Tar Sand Triangle south of Hanksville and the Circle Cliffs near the junction of Glen Canyon National Recreation Area and Capitol Reef National Park.

At none of the eleven special areas is commercial oil extraction taking place, although many leases have been issued. But some reserves may be recoverable, posing yet another threat to the natural environment. As an example of a low-tech, inexpensive use of tar sands, some of this material from a deposit in northeastern Utah has been used for paving roads.

South of I-70, at Taylor Flat in the center of Sinbad, three large, white, rusted metal sign arms mounted on a wooden post point the way to Temple Junction, Goblin Valley, Tan Seeps, Muddy Creek, Hidden Splendor, and Castle Dale. This three-way intersection is among rolling sagebrush-juniper hills at the center of the Swell. By the road that goes down Buckhorn Draw, under the freeway and across the Swell, this spot is about twelve miles northwest of our camping spot in South Temple Wash.

This is a critical spot, where a road takes off to the location of the resort-guest ranch that Utah State University researchers proposed for Hidden Splendor. It is just across the freeway from Buckhorn Draw and along the route that Royer and Dalton thought should take precedence over all scenic road proposals in Utah.

Beginning a mile and a half west of here, a Wyoming oil and gas interest holds leases on about three square miles of BLM land in the Swell in two tracts. The BLM approved converting the Kirkwood oil and gas leases into a combined hydrocarbon lease to allow extraction of tar sands, believed to underlie the entire lease. Based on core-hole samples, reserves were estimated at 100 million barrels of bitumen.

If five additional exploratory holes should show valuable tar sands deposits, a pilot plant would be built. Nine wells would be drilled on a five-acre plot. A center well would inject air, a fire would be ignited underground, water might be injected. The fire would force oil from the rocks and liquid bitumen would be pumped out at a production wellhead.

"An estimated 240,000 barrels of bitumen underlie the pilot site and, at 20 to 40 percent recovery, 48,000 to 96,000 barrels would be recovered. The pilot project would begin July 1, 1988, and be completed by July 1, 1991," says a final environmental assessment on the project.

For this pilot plant about twenty-six miles of road would be upgraded. About ten acres would be disturbed on site. Bitumen would be hauled out by truck, with two truck trips per day. It would be delivered to Green River, put in tanker cars, and shipped to a refinery.

Should the pilot plant succeed, the whole tract would be divided into twenty-acre production sites, with thirteen wells per site. Each site would be in production three to five years, with construction to begin on the production phase on January 1, 1993. The first commercial oil would be produced a year later. The operation is expected to last twenty-five to thirty years, with an extraction process similar to the pilot phase.

Air compressors would chug away continuously, electric generators would burn diesel; poisonous hydrogen sulfide gas would be burned, and this flaring would release sulfur dioxide pollution. Production tanks would be built on the site, and pipelines would be laid from each production well. Also at the center of the Swell would be fuel storage tanks, housing for workers, a warehouse, a repair shop, and sewage treatment facilities. At peak production, scheduled for the year 2002, the tenth year of production, 238 workers would be needed on site. They would commute from Green River and Hanksville.

At a maximum of 16,000 barrels per day, eighty truck trips a day would be required going to the refinery and eighty coming back, or more than six trips every hour through what is now the lonely, untouched heart of the San Rafael Swell. ("A pipeline could also be used instead of trucks," the assessment says.) About 6.5 acre-feet of water yearly would be trucked into the site from the Green River for use in the production process. Finally, workers commuting from Hanksville would have to drive through the Reef, probably at South Temple Wash. This traffic, plus the workers' off-duty play with ORVs, would wreck whatever solitude remained in the region.

The environmental assessment says,

> The increase in surface disturbance and onsite facilities would impact the visual quality of the area for sightseeing. Also increased traffic along the main routes in the affected area would raise safety problems for tourists having to negotiate between large trucks at frequent intervals.

These projections are for the highest possible production. Lower levels were analyzed, and the impacts would be smaller but important.

At Sid's Reservoir in the Swell—about six miles north of where the Buckhorn Draw road goes under the freeway—another tar sands lease conversion was approved. However, the actual conversion seemed hung up for a time as the paperwork was not completed.

This is the Valentine tract, covering 160 acres, a lease that could be host to a pilot plant and later a production plant. Eventually, a total of 67,000 to 134,000 barrels of bitumen could be pumped from the ground. "Facilities would include: air compressors, electric generators, production tanks, dehydration equipment, recovery system, fuel storage, housing, warehouse, repair shop, and sewage facilities," the final assessment says. Bitumen would be trucked to Green River. Because this would be a small operation, "Less than one truck trip per week would be required for a truck with a capacity of 200 barrels."

On September 30, 1985, BLM District Manager Nodine signed declarations that the Kirkwood and Valentine leases would not result in significant environmental impacts, and "Therefore, an Environmental Impact Statement is not required." Four days later, that finding was endorsed by State Director Robison.

In that year, however, the bottom dropped out of synthetic fuels. The U.S. Synthetic Fuels Corporation, set up to finance exotic energy production schemes, died in Congress. Then, in 1986, crude oil prices plummeted as OPEC lost its grip on events.

With the death of the Synfuels Corp. and tumbling oil prices, both tar sands projects seemed moribund. Under "diligent production" requirements of federal law, they must produce paying quantities of oil within ten years. So there is hope, provided Congress does not change the rules; but if the price of oil shoots back up, the San Rafael Swell may see rapid industrialization.

The Swell's desecration by off-road vehicles has begun. Scattered uranium mines gape, blowing out radioactive dust. The other projects are hanging fire for now. But even if those particular industrial calamities do not come to pass, without long-range protection the San Rafael country remains vulnerable.

16

San Rafael Swell National Park

I wanted to know the San Rafael Reef. I learned that it is only the steep eastern rim of the San Rafael Swell. Whatever happens to the Swell will affect the Reef's life and its naked rock.

Bureau of Land Management teams divided the Reef into three wilderness study areas. But that's only part of the Swell's edge. On the western flank, they designated three more wilderness study areas, all in natural regions that have passed muster as having outstanding opportunities for solitude and primitive or unconfined recreation. Yet even that's not half of it. Most of the Swell is just as interesting, and it's not even nominated for protection.

I've never hiked in the these three western flank areas. From north to south, they are:

—Sid's Mountain, a unit of 80,530 acres of federal property with badlands and mesas, deep chasms, grassy country, and odd rock formations. The BLM recommended protecting 78,408 acres as wilderness, deleting "traditional ORV routes" into Saddle Horse Canyon, North and South Forks of Coal Wash,

Bullocks Draw and Eagle Canyon. Altogether, twenty miles of routes would be cut from the unit, bisecting it.

—Devils Canyon, 9,610 acres of federal land. This is a rugged, twisting canyon a thousand feet deep and fourteen miles long, with several tributaries. It's surrounded by rolling ground and colorful mesas. "The southwestern portion . . . consists of sparsely vegetated pink, red, cream, and purple soil," says the BLM's wilderness statement. For seven miles, the unit runs parallel to Interstate 70. Although energy and mineral development potential is rated low at Devils Canyon, the BLM proposes that none of it become wilderness.

—Muddy Creek, from about eight miles south of I-70, stretching down ten miles south to near the Moroni Slopes. The tract is three to six miles across, on an east-west axis. "Deep-cut drainages, river-canyon bottoms, and stair-stepped mesas" make up its 31,400 acres. The BLM supports designating all of the unit as wilderness.

Then there are the wonderful places not even considered for wilderness. Stately Bottleneck Peak stands at the base of Buckhorn Draw, itself a beautiful but abused canyon. Window Blind Peak rises as a flat and mysterious monolith. The view from the Wedge Overlook provides an incomparable vista of cliffs enfolding a tiny San Rafael River.

Suppose the BLM wilderness recommendations are enacted into law. Then a gap in the wilderness ring would reach from the end of Muddy Creek WSA to I-70. The Swell's interior would be a playground for the dirt bikers. Those huge, unprotected regions could turn out to be fatal gaps in the armor of any wilderness eventually designated.

Also, the agency wants to drop a large chunk of the Mexican Mountain region—12,850 acres, or twenty square miles, of some of the most rugged landscape in Utah—for the benefit of the off-road vehicle drivers.

Nature has been shaping the canyons for at least the past thirty-five million years. Now the tawny, curving sandstone shelves are being broken. Skid burns remain where wheels buzzed over petrified sand dunes.

Something more important than the thrill of blasting across slickrock on a hot bike is at stake here. Wild nature is priceless and irreplaceable. Nature is our ultimate den. We lay claim to it by creating parks where it may be preserved forever: outside is freedom. A wilderness has no traps.

The San Rafael country may be the best remaining unprotected desert land. Yet it teeters on the verge of destruction. A new oil crisis, and a monstrous tar sands project begins pumping bitumen. A few more years of casual ORV abuse, and none of it remains undamaged.

Even if wilderness areas were established, the BLM would probably lack manpower and money to protect them. After all, the agency has only a few rangers to patrol the thousands of remote Anasazi Indian ruins throughout southeastern Utah, and it is chronically short of funding.

Even if the BLM were interested in protecting the Reef—instead of juggling competing interests in an attempt to please everybody a little—it couldn't. No agency could preserve the Reef without also saving the Swell. They are one system, in scenery, ecology, history, and geology. The chances they can be saved together at this late date are slim, but to save one without the other is impossible.

No, wilderness protection is just not strong enough.

A new national park, embracing the entire Swell, is the only solution. It should be a new type, an ecological park. Off-road vehicles would be banned. Mineral leases can be canceled or purchased—surely Congress has authority to do as it will with federal land. Stipulations must be inserted into any leases that remain to stand up for the national interest.

It's strange that preservation has to be justified, as if the radical act is to leave the land alone. Strange, when the land is untouched and so amazing. Stranger still, when the produce of this dusty region weighs lightly in the economic life of the country.

Why, this is destruction by happenstance. Will we miss it when it's gone?

Outside the Reef, many breathtaking vistas open up in the Swell. The view from the Wedge Overlook above Buckhorn

Draw thrills me more than the Grand Canyon. In fact, rafters float the San Rafael River through what is called the Little Grand Canyon.

Nobody lives in the Swell. Nearly all of it is federal land —property of every American citizen. It is as much mine as anyone's.

"But a park is just another kind of development," a Sierra Club member said. I agree. Some road-paving—development —is inevitable with parks. It's part of the American ideal of letting the people see what they have. That will harm the naturalness of the region, as will the thousands of people who can be counted upon to visit. But in a park, use can be regulated.

If a canyon is too popular for its own good, close it for a while. A region as large as the San Rafael Swell can afford to rotate crops. When the ephedra grows back, the cryptogamic soil recovers, or the coyotes return to Black Dragon Wash, then the canyon can be cautiously reopened.

Anyway, which is better, a park with a small visitor center and some hiking trails, or a giant tar sands development, a factory landscape tattooed with a network of motorcycle trails?

I've never witnessed any problems caused by grazing in the Swell or Reef. The cowboys I've seen, struggling to earn a living in a spartan countryside, are among its great attractions. I say, let them stay forever.

Representatives of the American people ought to take a look at the Swell and see whether they think it's worth preserving. A coalition of wilderness groups says the San Rafael country looks "like a composite of all of Utah's national parks." Would the congressmen and senators agree? Let them come and find out for themselves.

For myself, I can think of a hundred good reasons to preserve it and only a few reasons not to, and those are shortsighted and selfish.

If Congress were to create a San Rafael Swell National Park, I would not want to see developments in any of the regions that are important enough to be recommended for wilderness by the BLM. They could be set aside as wilderness areas within the park.

There is precedent for extra protection inside parks: the federal government has endorsed as suitable for wilderness some areas of Arches, Canyonlands, Capitol Reef, Bryce Canyon, and Zion national parks, as well as parts of Glen Canyon National Recreation Area and Cedar Breaks National Monument.

Better turnoffs would have to be built from I-70. A park headquarters near the Head of Sinbad could provide access to a few trailheads and show off the outstanding Rain God pictograph just north of the freeway. From the trailheads, hikers would head off to Crack Canyon, Wild Horse, Mexican Mountain—or such destinations as Eagle Canyon and San Rafael Knob on the other side of the Swell.

Why bother? Parts of the Swell aren't that good looking, although most of it is lovely. But I reject beauty as a prime reason for loving the San Rafael Swell. Judging it by conventions of beauty is like an angler hooking a rainbow trout so he can admire the play of tints on its gleaming scales. The desert should be appreciated as an untouched piece of Creation. Nature's value is intrinsic.

If you love the land, you have not done your duty when you've protected only the attractive regions. Wildness itself is precious. We must visit free wild places or our spirits will shrink. Often, in the Reef, my wounded heart was lifted.

We are territorial animals. So let's be territorial about this. Let us say, as simply as a lizard puffs himself up on top of a rock to show it's his, "We need this place to fulfill some deep longings. We mean to keep it. We'll defend it because it belongs to all of us, not the few who would profit by ruining it."

Let us tiptoe through the desert, so the land may continue its eternal dream.

17

Into the Rock

"Oh, wow!" Conrad called from ahead. "You've gotta see this!"

It was our first hike into Crack Canyon. We'd walked up to it beside the Swell, two miles across rugged terrain from Wild Horse Canyon, in the blast furnace heat of late summer. We were not yet deep inside, and already Crack was stunning: semicircular scars in sandstone where great pressure pops shot pieces away, dark brown turrets, potholes, a vertical sweep of tan rock against the brilliant, clear sky.

I hurried around the bend. Conrad sat on the slickrock bottom where the cliffs were only a few yards apart, staring, his striped cloth-covered canteen flat against his shirt. He was looking at a tunnel formed where shelves reached out from the opposite walls and nearly met. The roof was more than six feet up. For the next thirty feet on the wall, both sides looked more like Swiss cheese than rock. An eerie section of the right cliff looked like a cluster of huge half-melted skulls. The cliff's pink and buff ridges dripped columns and potholes, loops, stalactite clusters, flat planes. We had never seen anything like it.

Some parts of the cliff were stained red with iron oxide from the pour-off seeping over them through the millennia. One high band was yellow, and it curved into a sheer cliff that was purple, black, and streaked with white salts.

Walking through the dark tunnel, in the gravel and around boulders in the bottom, we could see through the crack at the top. It revealed distant walls, dark reddish brown in the shadows, dazzling white in the sunshine. Then the tunnel ended and the canyon opened up. A big cottonwood seemed to be bracing itself against the seasonal assaults of flood water. Low serpentine walls waltzed in and out through responding curves.

Only a mile into Crack Canyon we were stopped by a drop-off, a chute that went down about eight feet. Beyond it the canyon continued at a deeper level passing between high walls. Just past the drop-off, a log was wedged from side to side ten feet above the floor. Obviously, the flash floods in this narrow stretch were ferocious.

Any experienced rock climber could have hopped down the drop-off and scrambled back up. But we weren't experienced, and I could not depend on my bad shoulder. We were blocked. We hunched at the top for a long time studying the chute. First Conrad, then I, walked out on a ledge to the right of the drop-off. The bottom was still too far down and the wall too steep to climb.

Disappointed, we walked back to the car, which I'd left at a deep sandy spot near the mouth of Wild Horse. I made up my mind to get through Crack. As we drove back to Salt Lake City, we laid plans to return. I began thinking of the canyon as an adversary.

Through that fall and winter I bragged that Crack Canyon was not going to beat me. I would go back and finish the hike. A rope would simplify the task of getting up and down. We'd tie it to a strong branch and wedge the limb across the chute's top.

We returned in the spring, taking a twenty-two-foot line of scarlet nylon rope. Recent rain had packed the sand and I was able to drive the Datsun to the canyon's mouth. More tamarisk had sprouted, the feathery weeds slumping in front of red rock ledges. We pushed in quickly, glancing through the tunnel's ruddy roof at the tan cliff face beyond. The wall was draped with a big splotch of desert varnish. The tall cottonwood still hunched with its trunk bowed toward the Swell. Dead white branches at the lower trunk were lifted close to the cliff wall, which was bright pink sandstone streaked with white salts. Green, aspen-like leaves shook on the upper branches. Shimmering puddles reflected a shining sky, clouds, rock domes on the cliffs. We skirted patches of mud, but once I tracked through some, mistaking it for wet sand. Lizards would run a few feet, stop, watch, bob their heads to frighten us.

We found the nylon line would be worthless at the chute. A long pool stretched from the bottom of the drop-off, wall to wall, and we could not judge its depth. Next came a wide mud patch, then another pool. As far as we could see before the walls curved out of sight, the canyon was filled with brown water and mud. We could not climb down without slopping through the morass.

But we might be able to forge a way around the chute. If we could get above it on the wall, and climb far enough past it, the canyon might be dry ahead. A few rods back, the west cliff seemed to offer a way up, perhaps to the top of the Reef. A chimney formation in the wall was filled with boulders, making a vertical talus slope. At the rim, this chimney seemed to connect with a ledge running along the cliff. If we climbed the chimney and went along the ledge, the ridge might descend to the floor farther on. We'd bypass the chute and the water.

We climbed the chimney, Conrad leading. Near the top he discovered it did not connect with the ridge. But he could get across anyhow. He scaled a flat slab about twenty feet high that stood almost on end. It was a tilting, free-standing monolith, not touching the cliff. Then he pulled himself onto the side of the chimney and worked his way onto the ledge. The dangerous crossing spot was four or five feet wide.

Then I went. Atop the slab I leaned across, holding on with my right hand, and passed my tripod, camera bag, and big canteen up to Conrad. Beneath was a drop of eight feet, onto a steep, rough wall, then a possibly fatal plunge along the rubble.

As I was handing over the canteen, which was almost full, it slipped from my left hand and slammed onto the right. I managed to hang onto both its strap and the boulder. But the sharp blow unnerved me. If I had instinctively yanked back my right hand, I would have fallen.

It reminded me of the time I fell in Buckhorn Draw while climbing alone, dislocating my left shoulder. Memory of painful and terrifying hours—falling, praying, dancing across a cliff face, crawling down slopes—came back to me instantaneously.

Standing on the end of the slab, I felt around until I grasped two fairly good handholds on the opposite wall. Keeping my weight on my left leg, I gingerly reached my right foot across the gap and found a poor toehold. I could see a better one for my left foot, just a little above the right foothold. I lunged over, trying to pull myself up and swing my left foot into it. I wasn't strong enough. I could not get my foot in the hole. I clung to the cliff. My right boot was barely gripping the rock and my left swung in the air. My weight was almost entirely on my arms.

I knew that sickening tear in my shoulder, that sucking sound. "My shoulder's dislocating! I'm going to fall!" I screamed, an unearthly sound that seemed be to coming from someone else. It made my ears ring. Then I levitated my body and my legs back, and I stood again on top of the slab. I do not know how I did it.

Once the pressure was released, my arm bone settled into the socket. I sat at the top, shaken, staring around at the chimney, the chute, the muddy floor below it, the slim log wedged across the canyon. If I had fallen down the front of the slab when my shoulder went out, I would have been badly injured or killed. If I had slipped behind it, I'd have been jammed between it and the cliff.

Conrad handed my gear back across. I slid down the slab and picked my way to the canyon floor. He went on, exploring the ledge. I rested there.

The day was peaceful. I realized Crack Canyon was so beautiful that anywhere I aimed my camera I would get a lovely view. I took a shot almost at random, and it was fine, a picture of light green cottonwoods, flanks of big boulders, dark yellow shadows on the walls.

Conrad returned an hour later saying the canyon went on for a long way with high walls. Getting back to the floor anywhere ahead would be dangerous. I directed him in placing his feet when he climbed down the cliff and onto the slab.

How close I had come to falling! If I'd been severely injured Conrad could not have carried me out. Bitter defeat stung me. Crack Canyon beat us again.

We lay in the shade, unwinding. A spherical white cloud was dissolving in the hot sky. It revolved quickly. A vapor tendril reached out from it and extended into a circle as it spun. Three minutes later the cloud was gone.

On the way back I enjoyed a bright green spray of tall grass growing from brown sand, a hopeful color against the shadows of a ledge. There was a temporary pool in sand beneath the grasping branches of a cottonwood bush. Brush grew on ledges along the canyon sides.

During the next week I thought it over. Was I really defeated? No, impossible. Nature is never aware. Crack Canyon is as indifferent as a dead valley on Mars. Nature is a dumb rock.

From an unbiased standpoint, I thought, my accident was basic physics. Tendons holding the fulcrum of my arm together could not stand the strain I put on them. Weak cords had started to give way.

Next weekend, the stoic sculptor Tom Tessman and I drove to Crack Canyon. Tom is a man with a strong body, a fast and punning mind, a beard that bristles uncontrollably.

Close inside the entrance a dead juniper lifted its branches beside banded cliffs. We walked by the sheer walls and slopes, and then Tom stood in the tunnel admiring it. Yellow walls with their cavities rose beyond the turquoise lace of tamarisk and the branches of darker bushes.

Past the drop-off, the puddles had dried. Tom looked at the chute and said he thought we could climb back up without trouble. He'd boost me if I needed help. He hopped down the chute and climbed back easily. I jumped too. At last I was standing on the moist sand below the drop-off. For an instant that was a weird feeling—what if we couldn't get back? But I knew it would never block us again.

I sat on one side of the chute's smooth gullet and shoved with my feet on the wall. The rock was slick with Tom's wet tracks, yet it provided all the traction I needed to jimmy up, with a little grunting. I could use my legs and good right arm to work around a tawny boulder, then claw over the top by pulling myself onto a rock stuck between the wall and the boulder.

Tom and I looked at the log wedged across the canyon over our heads. Ahead, muddy pools reached from side to side. Tom climbed above the first, hands on both walls, which were only a few feet apart. The water lightly splashed his hiking boots. I was ready to take off boots and socks so I could wade through. But we worried about huge black clouds that were forming and moving swiftly back past the entrance. After all, we knew how that log got crammed across the canyon ten feet up.

We climbed out and walked back. At Crack's mouth, we stood in sunshine and watched a thunderstorm raging above the Swell. The eastern cliff face glowed, waxy yellow in the late afternoon light, towering above a purple talus slope. There were tamarisk, tumbleweeds, junipers, boulders, sand, dark cottonwoods. Dense blue, smoke-bottom clouds roiled. Lightning flickered onto the Swell. Gray lines of rain were lashing the distant tilted badlands of brown, white, and gray ledges.

I thought: we miss important facets of our world when we insist on concentrating on the places that are beautiful to us. Beauty is in man's mind. Thus, it's man-made and in a way irrelevant.

Usually we can't call the desert beautiful. For every slickrock canyon like Crack there are thousands of desolate arroyos nearby. If we could see beyond that cliff wall resplendent in the sunset, beyond the rolling blue clouds, we'd find swarms of biting blackflies. Dust sticks in the hair and itches inside the nostrils. That juniper dangles ragged shreds of bark because it died in strips so that the rest of the tree could live through some drought.

We should not preserve wildness simply to please human senses. It's valuable because it is unchanged. We can learn from it—not mere scientific knowledge. We must understand with our hearts the sagey hills, hard clay slopes, overcast skies; feel the way the root of a juniper in a desert gully can form a little dam holding back rock and soil.

I wanted to take tough desert pictures. I'd show the muscular, rough, dull landscape features, not simply beauty. A new landscape photography, deliberately neither pretty nor ugly, would be challenging to take and stimulating to study.

I went back with Conrad and Karen Bert a few days after a flash flood. Again, the day was threatening, with thunder growling over toward the Swell. We got down the drop-off and kept going. Shortly past the drop, I jumped across a long puddle and my boots went deep in quicksand. Miles beyond, we went through a crack where walls are hundreds of feet high and only a few feet apart.

The canyon soon became broader. Then we had to cross more water holes that stretched from wall to wall, take off boots, wade through calf-deep puddles over slippery rocks, put boots on, take them off, wade, put them on. After a mile of this we were wearing out. Thunder rumbled faintly.

Conrad was worried. Flash floods were always a possibility. He wanted to turn back. He stood exhausted on a knobby bulge of slickrock, surrounded by mud and water. The higher parts of the rocks were buff and gray while the lower levels were brown with mud. Barefooted, he carried his tennis shoes.

I was nervous about the weather, too, and discouraged by an ugly stretch of water immediately ahead. Past it was another drop. But Karen waded through and Conrad followed.

I started into the water. The bottom was slick. I had to walk on a slanted ledge that I could not see, as the water was solid brown. I was afraid of dropping my Hasselblad into it. A few inches to my right, it was so deep my probing foot could not find bottom. Both feet started to slide from under me. I threw my back and side against the cliff and swung out again, keeping my balance.

We should give up, I said. We had a long, tough hike back, sunset was coming, rain seemed certain to make climbing dangerous, and we might be facing a flash flood. I yelled that it was time to go back. I returned to shore. Conrad agreed and came back across. We called to Karen.

The most adventurous among us, she was climbing a ridge to the left to bypass a drop. Carrying her running shoes, camera and socks, she slipped but somehow managed to hang on and scramble to the top of the ledge. She called back, saying the rock had broken partly and thrown her off balance. If it had broken through completely, she would have fallen twenty or thirty feet. She said the canyon was opening up and seemed to be coming to an end.

I had to get through Crack, once and for all. Conrad said in that case, he'd would wait for us and meditate.

As I edged into the water again, I couldn't feel the bottom directly ahead and I was losing my footing by reaching for it. Then it was there again, to the right. I got through.

Thunder boomed more frequently and the lighting was gloomier. The cloud to the north was getting darker. We had to hurry. Karen and I trotted through the sandy canyon bed and leapt over boulders. Gravel sprayed from our feet.

. . . And I'm older than that gravel, older than the Reef. If my cells retain memories of past existence, they are shouting their antiquity. Nothing has ever broken my connection with the first living cell. It's not a chain. Life itself passes from one shape to another. I'm a middle man in billions of years of alive genetic stuff moving along, generations without number. I am part of an organism that never dies, and Sky is a continuation. Our first cell was knitting instructions long before these primordial sediments began to filter to the bottom of the inland sea, and that was ages before there was a Reef.

Life's record is an undimmed success. Each ancestor lived and reproduced, and the molecules continued to wind and unravel as they went from one body to another. We were born to thrive. Failure is unknown to our genes. Each time life passed on, whether through simple cells dividing or passionate matings, all parts were fully alive. Foreknowledge of my own death is just theoretical, as my ancestor cells had no feeling for it at that time. They remember nothing about it. History is a fragile veneer spread over animal nature. Intelligence is another survival tool, like sharp claws, but in the timeless dreaming of our planet, logic is worse than valueless.

So DNA is the highest creature. It shapes protective structures about itself—a single amoeba cell, or shells around soft arthropods, or man's bones. Mankind. We are life and we are vehicles for DNA. Some types of life are more successful than others, continuing in use a long time, like trilobites. Others are soon dropped. . . .

Now I am running without any thoughts. Karen runs beside me. Images register silently: cold wind, curling walls buzzing past, brush, a wide sand field. An automatic dodge around boulders. Water. Raindrops, the growl of thunder somewhere far away, gravel, walls lowering, canyon widening.

Effortless trotting. Breath comes easily. A blank mind—into the rock.

Finally we reached a stretch where the cliffs gave way to long dirt mounds. Crack Canyon did not stop abruptly. It was ending in zigzags. Ahead was a landscape of dark sandstone lumps. We could see what it must be like from here on. No need to go farther.

The thunder stopped before we reached Conrad. Then we had a long, steady pull, going fast, not doing much sightseeing. We paused to admire a rounded wall that was lined with light pink swirls, like sanded redwood.

BIBLIOGRAPHY

Suggested further reading in sources consulted:
—For more information about the San Rafael country's geology and minerals, see:

José Carlos Nellis, "Influence of Paleostructure on Paleochannels and Uranium Deposits in the Salt Wash Member of the Morrison Formation, San Rafael Swell, Utah," University of Utah thesis for a master of science degree in geology, Salt Lake City, 1979.

William Lee Stokes, "Stratigraphy and Primary Sedimentary Features of Uranium Occurrences of Southeastern Utah," in *Guidebook to the Geology of Utah*, Number 21, Utah Geological Society, Salt Lake City, 1967; also in same guidebook, Stokes, "A Survey of Southeastern Utah Uranium Districts."

R. E. Cohenour, "San Rafael District," summary in *Guidebook to the Geology of Utah*, Number 21, Utah Geological Society, Salt Lake City, 1967.

Norman J. King, "Physical Properties Contributing to the Relative Erosional Resistance of Sandstone and Shale-Derived Sediments," a master of science thesis, University of Utah Department of Geology, 1953.

Lehi F. Hintze, compiler, "Geologic Map of Utah," Utah Geological and Mineral Survey, Salt Lake City, 1980.

Kadir Uygur and M. Dane Picard, "Reservoir Characteristics of Jurassic Navajo Sandstone, Southern Utah," in *Henry Mountains Symposium*, M. Dane Picard, editor, Utah Geological Association, Salt Lake City, 1980.

Charles W. Chesterman, "The Audubon Society Field Guide to North American Rocks and Minerals," Alfred A. Knopf Inc., New York, 1978.

Eugene M. Shoemaker, "Structural Features of the Central Colorado Plateau and Their Relation to Uranium Deposits," a paper in Geological Survey Professional Paper 300, Government Printing Office, Washington, D.C., 1956. Compiled by Lincoln R. Page, Hobart E. Stocking, and Harriet B. Smith, this collection of articles is entitled *Contributions to the Geology of Uranium and Thorium by the United States Geological Survey and Atomic Energy Commission for the United Nations International Conference on Peaceful Uses of Atomic Energy, Geneva, Switzerland, 1955*.

C. C. Hawley, R. L. Robeck and H. B. Dyer, *Geology, Altered Rocks and Ore Deposits of the San Rafael Swell, Emery County, Utah*, prepared for the Atomic Energy Commission, Government Printing Office, Washington, D.C., 1968.

—For more about climate:
Dale J. Stevens, R. Clayton Brough, Rodney D. Griffin, E. Arlo
    Richardson, *Utah Weather Guide*, Society for Applied Clima-
    tology, West Jordan, Utah, and Department of Geography,
    Brigham Young University, Provo, Utah, 1983.

—For more on plants and animals:
Francis H. Elmore, *Shrubs and Trees of the Southwest Uplands*,
    Southwest Parks and Monuments Association, Globe, Ariz.,
    1976.
Lyman Benson and Robert A. Darrow, *Trees and Shrubs of the
    Southwestern Deserts*, The University of Arizona Press, Tucson,
    Third Edition, 1981.
Diane West Davidson, *Species Diversity and Community Organization
    in Desert Seed-Eating Ants*, a doctoral dissertation, 1976, Univer-
    sity of Utah Department of Biology, Salt Lake City.
Bobbie Vern Peterson, *The Black Flies (Diptera: Simulidae) in the Can-
    yons in the Vicinity of Salt Lake City with Notes of Their Biology*, a
    master of science thesis, 1952, University of Utah Department of
    Invertebrate Zoology and Entomology, Salt Lake City.

—For more about prehistory:
William J. Davis, director of Abajo Archaeology, Bluff, Utah,
    monograph on Green River finds, "The Montgomery Folsom
    Site," 1985.
C. W. Ceram, *The First American: A Story of North American Ar-
    chaeology*, Harcourt Brace Jovanovich, Inc., New York, 1971.
George C. Frison and Bruce A. Bradley, *Folsom Tools and Technology
    at the Hanson Site, Wyoming*, University of New Mexico Press,
    Albuquerque, 1980.
Roland Siegrist, editor, *Prehistoric Petroglyphs and Pictographs in
    Utah*, sponsored by the Utah State Historical Society, published
    by the Utah Museum of Fine Arts, Salt Lake City, 1972.
Fawn Brodie, "The Brimhall Saga: Some Remarkable Discoveries
    in the Cliffs of Utah," *American West Magazine*, Salt Lake City,
    September 1971.
Judith S. and Jesse E. Warner, "To Slay a Dragon," paper pre-
    sented to American Rock Art Research Association symposium,
    1985, Santa Barbara, Calif.
David Muench and Donald G. Pike, *Anasazi: Ancient People of the
    Rock*, Crown Publishers Inc., New York, 1974, fourth printing
    1977.
Robert H. Lister and Florence C. Lister, *Chaco Canyon: Archaeology
    and Archaeologists*, University of New Mexico Press, Albuquer-
    que, 1981.
Jesse D. Jennings, "Cowboy Cave," University of Utah Anthro-
    pological Papers #104, Salt Lake City, 1980.

—For more about the first explorers and early notions of geography: S. G. Goodrich, *Pictorial Geography of the World*, Otis, Broaders & Co., Boston, 1841.

George D. Brewerton, "A Ride with Kit Carson," *Harper's New Monthly Magazine*, August 1853, Harpers & Brothers, New York.

Philip L. Fradkin, *A River No More: The Colorado River and the West.*

Dominguez-Escalante Journal, J. Cecil Alter, editor, *Utah Historical Quarterly*, Vol. XI, 1943.

LeRoy R. Hafen and Ann W. Hafen, *Old Spanish Trail: Santa Fe to Los Angeles*, The Arthur H. Clark Co., Glendale, Calif., 1954.

C. Gregory Crampton, "Utah's Spanish Trail," *Utah Historical Quarterly*, Vol XLVII, No. 4, Fall 1979.

George R. Brooks, *The Southwest Expedition of Jedediah S. Smith*, The Arthur H. Clark Co., Glendale, Calif., 1977.

Dale L. Morgan, *Jedediah Smith and the Opening of the West*, University of Nebraska Press, Lincoln and London, 1964, reprinted from 1953 edition by arrangement with the Bobbs-Merrill Co.

Christopher Carson, *Kit Carson's Own Story of His Life*, dictated in 1856 or 1857 to Colonel and Mrs. D. C. Peters. Edited by Blanche C. Grant, published by Kit Carson Memorial Foundation, Taos, N.M., 1955.

Diary of Orville C. Pratt in the Western Americana Collection, The Bienecke Rare Book and Manuscript Collection, Yale University.

Gwinn Harris Heap, *Central Route to the Pacific, from the Valley of the Mississippi to California; Journal of the Expedition of E. F. Beale, Superintendent of Indian Affairs in California, and Gwinn Harris Heap, from Missouri to California, in 1853*, Lippincott, Grambo, & Co., Philadelphia, 1854.

Charles Wentworth Upham, *Life, Explorations and Public Services of John Charles Fremont*, Ticknor and Fields, Boston, 1856.

J. W. Gunnison, *The Mormons, or, Latter-Day Saints, in the Valley of the Great Salt Lake: A History of Their Rise and Progress, Peculiar Doctrines, Present Condition, Prospects, Derived from Personal Observation, During a Residence Among Them*, Lippincott, Grambo and Co., Philadelphia, 1852; republished in 1884 by John W. Lovell Co., New York.

Mary Lee Spence, "The Fremonts and Utah," *Utah Historical Quarterly*, Vol. XLIV, Summer 1976.

Mary L. Spence, *The Expeditions of John Charles Fremont*, Vol. III, University of Illinois Press, Urbana and Chicago, 1984.

Capt. Howard Stansbury, *Exploration and Survey of the Valley of the Great Salt Lake of Utah, Including a Reconnaissance of a New Route Through the Rocky Mountains*, Robert Armstrong, public printer, Washington, D.C., 1853.

National Archives, "Letters Received by the Topographical Bureau of the War Department 1824–1865," Roll 24, December 1851–

December 1853, ''G,'' National Archives Microfilm Publications, Microcopy Number 506. These letters have a wealth of detail about Gunnison's attitudes and his preparations for his last expedition.

Edward Griffin Beckwith, *Report of Exploration of a Route for the Pacific Railroad, Near the 38th and 39th Parallels of Latitude, from the Mouth of the Kansas to Sevier River, in the Great Basin,* Government Printing Office, Washington, D.C., 1854.

Frederick S. Dellenbaugh, *A Canyon Voyage: The Narrative of the Second Powell Expedition,* Putnam, New York, 1908.

Harold Francis Pfister, *Facing the Light: Historic American Portrait Daguerreotypes,* published for the National Portrait Gallery by the Smithsonian Institution Press, Washington, D.C., 1978.

Solomon Nunes Carvalho, *Incidents of Travel and Adventure in the Far West; With Col. Fremont's Last Expedition,* Derby and Jackson, New York, 1856.

Joan Sturhahn, *Carvalho: Artist — Photographer — Adventurer — Patriot: Portrait of a Forgotten American,* Richmond Publishing Co., Merrick, N.Y., 1976.

John C. Fremont, *Memoirs of My Life,* Bolford, Clarke and Co., Chicago and New York, 1887. Fremont, letter to Thomas Hart Benton, written in Parowan, Utah, Feb. 9, 1854; published by the *National Intelligencer* on April 12, 1854.

Jessie Benton Fremont and Lieutenant Francis Preston Fremont, *Great Events during the Life of Major General John C. Frémont, United States Army; F. R. G. S. and Chevalier de l'ordre pour le mérité, etc., and of Jessie Benton Frémont,* circa 1887; not published; original in the Bancroft Library, University of California, Berkeley.

Senate Miscellaneous Document 67, 33rd Congress, First Session, Government Printing Office, Washington, D.C., 1854, concerning Fremont's last expedition.

John Bigelow, *Memoir of the Life and Public Services of John Charles Fremont,* Derby and Jackson, New York, 1856.

J. W. Egloffstein, ''Map No. 1. From the Valley of Green River to the Great Salt Lake; from Explorations and Surveys made under the direction of the Hon. Jefferson Davis, Secretary of War,'' Selmar Siebert's Engraving and Printing Establishment, Washington, D.C., 1855.

— Later expeditions and settlement:

Ethan Pettit, diary, 1855, copy in Special Collections, Marriott Library, University of Utah, Salt Lake City.

Oliver Huntington, diary, original in Church of Jesus Christ of Latter-day Saints' Historians Office.

Charles Butler Hunt, editor, ''Geology of the Henry Mountains As Recorded in the Notebooks of G. K. Gilbert, 1875–76,'' Geological Society of America, in press.

Harold Schindler, *Orrin Porter Rockwell: Man of God, Son of Thunder,*
University of Utah Press, Salt Lake City, 1966.

Randolph B. Marcy, *The Prairie Traveler. A Hand-Book for Overland
Expeditions,* Harper & Brothers, New York, 1859.

C. Gregory Crampton, *Land of Living Rock,* paperback edition,
Peregrine-Smith Books, Layton, Utah, 1985.

David Lavender, *River Runners of the Grand Canyon,* Grand Canyon
Natural History Association and the University of Arizona
Press, 1985.

John Wesley Powell, *Exploration of the Colorado River of the West and
Its Tributaries Explored In 1869, 1870, 1871, and 1872, Under the
Direction of the Smithsonian Institution,* Government Printing
Office, Washington, D.C., 1875.

William Culp Darrah, *Powell of the Colorado,* Princeton University
Press, 1951.

Reports by Edwin E. Howell and Lt. R. L. Hoxie, in George M.
Wheeler's *Annual Report upon the Geographical Explorations and
Surveys West of the One Hundredth Meridian, in California, Nevada,
Utah, Arizona, Colorado, New Mexico, Wyoming and Montana,*
Government Printing Office, Washington, D.C., 1874.

Grove Karl Gilbert, Report on the *Geology of the Henry Mountains,*
Department of the Interior, U.S. Geographical and Geological
Survey of the Rocky Mountain Region, J. W. Powell in charge,
Government Printing Office, Washington, D.C., 1880.

"Map of the Utah Territory Representing the Extent of the Irrigible,
Timber and Pasture Lands," Government Printing Office,
Washington, D.C., 1878.

J. W. Powell, *Report on the Lands of the Arid Region of the United States,*
Government Printing Office, Washington, D.C., 1878; second
edition 1879.

Clarence E. Dutton, *Report on the Geology of the High Plateaus of Utah
with Atlas,* Department of the Interior, U.S. Geographical and
Geological Survey of the Rocky Mountain Region, J. W. Powell
in Charge. Government Printing Office, Washington, D.C.,
1880.

Especially important records of Powell's exploration are printed in
the 1947 and the combined 1948–49 volumes of the Utah Historical
Quarterly, published by the Utah State Historical Society, Salt Lake
City, in which all available diaries, notebooks, letters and articles by
members of both of Powell's river expeditions were printed. These
include:

J. W. Powell, journal, edited by William Culp Darrah, printed in
Vol. XV, 1947. Jack Sumner, journal, edited by William Culp
Darrah, Vol. XV, 1947. Stephen Vandiver Jones article by Dr.
Herbert E. Gregory, Vol. XVI–XVII, 1949. John F. Steward
journal, edited by William Culp Darrah, Vol. XVI–XVII, 1949.
Walter Clement Powell journal, edited by Charles Kelly, Vol.

XVI–XVII, 1949. Stephen Vandiver Jones journal, edited by Dr. Herbert E. Gregory, Vol. XVI–XVII, 1949.

— General history of the area:

Dee Anne Finken in *A History of the San Rafael Swell*, a study sponsored by the Bureau of Land Management, Moab District Office, San Rafael Resource Area, Price, Utah, 1977.

Leland Hargrave Creer, *Mormon Towns in the Region of the Colorado*, University of Utah Anthropological Papers, Number 32 of Glen Canyon Series Number 3, Salt Lake City, May 1958.

Ward J. Roylance, *Utah: A Guide to the State*, Utah: A Guide to the State Foundation, Salt Lake City, 1982.

O. Meredith Wilson, *The Denver and Rio Grande Project, 1870–1901*, Howe Brothers, Salt Lake City and Chicago, 1982.

War Department, *Grand and Green Rivers, Utah*, a letter from the Secretary of War, 1910, House Document No. 953, 61st Congress, 2nd Session, Government Printing Office, Washington, D.C.

Article by Ruben Brasher and Stella McElprang in *"Castle Valley"*: *A History of Emery County*, compiled by Mrs. Stella McElprang, Salt Lake City, 1949, produced by the Emery County Company, Daughters of Utah Pioneers.

John L. Jorgensen, "A History of Castle Valley to 1890," Master's thesis, University of Utah, 1955.

—Early twentieth-century geological reports:

J. M. Boutwell, "Vanadium and Uranium in Southeastern Utah," in USGS Bulletin No. 260, *Contributions To Economic Geology 1904*, Government Printing Office, Washington, D.C., 1905.

Joseph A. Taft, "Book Cliffs Coal Field, Utah, West of Green River," in U.S. Geological Survey Bulletin 285, *Contributions to Economic Geology*, Washington, D.C., 1905.

Frank L. Hess, "A Sulphur Deposit in the San Rafael Canyon, Utah," U.S. Geological Survey Bulletin 530, *Contributions to Economic Geology*, Government Printing Office, Washington, D.C., 1913.

Charles T. Lupton, "Notes on the Geology of the San Rafael Swell, Utah," Journal of the Washington Academy of Sciences, Vol. II, No. 7, Baltimore, Waverly Press, 1912. Lupton, U.S. Geological Survey Bulletin 628, *Geology and Coal Resources of Castle Valley in Carbon, Emery, and Sevier Counties, Utah*, Government Printing Office, Washington, D.C., 1916.

James Gilluly, "Geology and Oil and Gas Prospects of Part of the San Rafael Swell Utah," USGS Bulletin 806-C, *Contributions to Economic Geology, 1928, Part II*, Government Printing Office, Washington, D.C., 1929.

—Modern geologists' studies:

Charles B. Hunt, assisted by Paul Averitt and Ralph L. Miller, *Geology and Geography of the Henry Mountains Region Utah*, U.S. Geological Survey Professional Paper 228, U.S. Government Printing Office, Washington, D.C., 1953. Hunt's remembrance of Charlie Hanks, who was killed in an automobile crash in Salt Lake City, is in "Around the Henry Mountains with Charlie Hanks," printed in *Utah Geology*, Salt Lake City, 1977.

—About bandits:

W. H. Lever, *History of Sanpete and Emery Counties Utah*, printed by Tribune Job Printing Company, Salt Lake City, 1898; photographically reproduced, 1967, on microcards by Lost Cause Press, Louisville.

Charles Kelly, *The Outlaw Trail: A History of Butch Cassidy and His Wild Bunch*, The Devin-Adair Co., New York, second edition, 1959.

H. L. A. Culmer, journal, copy in possession of Utah Historical Society, Salt Lake City.

—Environmental issues:

U.S. Bureau of Land Mangement, *Statewide Draft Environmental Impact Statement, Vol. VI*, Salt Lake City, February 1986. BLM, draft site specific analyses of wilderness for Crack Canyon, San Rafael Reef and Mexican Mountain wilderness study areas, BLM Moab, Utah, District, 1983. *San Rafael Swell—I-70 Study Book II*, Appendix, Price, May 1, 1973. *Multiple Use Management Plan for Natural Resource Lands, San Rafael Swell*, Price District Office, 1973. *Utah Combined Hydrocarbon Leasing Regional Final EIS*, Vol. II, Richfield, Utah, 1984. Environmental Assessment, finding of no significant impact, Price District, 1983. File 1791/3802/8500 (028A), concerning uranium mining. *San Rafael Motorcycle Trail System, Final Environmental Assessment*, Price, 1985. BLM, Record of Decision, San Rafael Swell Combined Hydrocarbon Lease Conversion, Code 3140 (U-067), Moab and Salt Lake City, 1985. *San Rafael Swell Combined Hydrocarbon Lease Conversion*, draft environmental assessment, Price, 1985; final assessment, August 1985.

U.S. Bureau of Reclamation, bulletin, *Salinity Update*, issued in April 1985; *Finding of No Significant Impact for Dirty Devil River Salinity Control Unit, Utah, Colorado River Water Quality Improvement Program*, Salt Lake City, July 1986.

Lawrence Royer and Michael J. Dalton, *Land Use in the Utah Canyon Country: Tourism, Interstate 70, and the San Rafael Swell*, Institute for the Study of Outdoor Recreation and Tourism, and the College of Natural Resources, Utah State University, Logan, 1972.

San Rafael Coordinating Committee, *The San Rafael Region,* brochure, Salt Lake City, 1977.

Peter Hovingh, letter to Governor Scott M. Matheson, Salt Lake City, March 6, 1978.

Emery County Commission, letter signed by all three commissioners, Clyde E. Conover, chairman; Bevan K. Wilson, and Clyde W. Thompson, Castle Dale, Utah, Jan. 22, 1986.

National Parks and Conservation Association *ALERT,* April 1986, offices in Washington, D.C., and Salt Lake City, Utah.

U.S. Congress, The Wilderness Act, 1964; Federal Land Policy and Management Act, 1976.

In addition, many newspapers were consulted, including:

Deseret News, Salt Lake City, many issues from the early 1850s until the present, particularly November 1853, about the Gunnison massacre; May 1898; November 1970; December 1977; May 1982, an article by Barbara Ekker on Hanksville's history; October 1985.

Salt Lake Tribune, Salt Lake City, December 1909, May 1910, June 1986.

Salt Lake Herald, Salt Lake City, May 1909.

Manti Messenger, Manti, Utah, September and October 1894, March and April 1897, April 1898.

Eastern Utah Advocate, Price, Utah, April and May 1897, May 1898.

Sun-Advocate, Price, Utah, May 1980.

ACKNOWLEDGMENTS

I gratefully acknowledge permission to quote from published works or unpublished diaries, with thanks to: the Church of Jesus Christ of Latter-day Saints' Historians Office for letting me examine and take notes from the 1855 Oliver Huntington journal; the Utah State Historical Society for opening its collections to my use, particularly the H. L. A. Culmer diary, and for allowing me to quote also from the Stephen Vandiver Jones diary, as published in the Society's journal; the Western Americana Collection, The Bienecke Rare Book and Manuscript Collection, Yale University, for the passages from the diary of Orville C. Pratt; the Special Collections, Marriott Library, University of Utah, Salt Lake City, for allowing me to quote from the Ethan Pettit diary, 1855; the director of the Bancroft Library, University of California, Berkeley, for permission to quote from the unpublished Fremont Memoirs in the library's collection; the Arthur H. Clark Co., Glendale, California, for permission to quote from The Southwest Expedition of Jedediah S. Smith, edited by George R. Brooks; and to Mr. Brooks for his explanations about the Jedediah Smith field notes.

INDEX